The Big "R"

The Big "R"

An Internal Auditing Action Adventure

D. Larry Crumbley,
CPA, DABFA, CFSA
Louisiana State University

Douglas E. Ziegenfuss,
CIA, CPA, CFE, CMA, CGFM
Old Dominion University

John J. O'Shaughnessy,
CIA, CMA, CPA
San Francisco State University

Carolina Academic Press
Durham, North Carolina

ISBN 0-89089-728-X
LCCN 00-105408

Carolina Academic Press
700 Kent Street
Durham, North Carolina 27701
Telephone (919) 489-7486
Fax (919) 493-5668
E-mail: cap@cap-press.com
www.cap-press.com

Printed in the United States of America

Internal auditing is an independent, objective assurance and consulting activity designed to add value and improve an organization's operations. It helps an organization accomplish its objectives by bringing a systematic, disciplined approach to evaluate and improve the effectiveness of risk management, control and governance processes.

IIA Board of Directors

Dedicated to our families.

★ ★ ★ ★ ★

The songs "She's Wearing a Hole in My Sole," "Stubborn as a Stump," and "Two Tone Fender" are copyrighted by John D. Pehrson, Fort Worth, Texas.

The Big "R" is fiction, and except for historical characters and events, all other characters and adventures are imaginary. Any resemblance to actual persons, living or dead, is purely coincidental.

★ ★ ★ ★ ★

Thou shall not kill.

Deuteronomy 5:17

Contents

Appendices

Baseball, Apple Pie, and Internal Auditing

The Big "R" is a supplementary book to be used near the end of an internal auditing (IA) or an auditing course. The novel could be used in a graduate investment class, also. This IA novel would be ideal for a MBA course or a finance course that has a light coverage of accounting, or could be used in IA's in-house training programs. An external auditor interested in outsourcing or co-sourcing an internal auditing function should read this book.

This instructional novel mixes baseball, auditing, serial killers, fraud, risks, anthrax, and scuba diving to help students learn the principles of internal auditing. A certified internal auditor, a forensic accountant, and an FBI agent work together to find serial killers striking at baseball parks. As David Akst and Lee Berton have indicated, other accountants may look at charts, but forensic auditors actually dig into the body.

Andrew Carnegie advises to "aim for the highest." This highest in baseball is the elusive perfect game, which occurs only once in about every 20,000 pitching decisions. No other team sport has the equivalent of a perfect game, for nine players on a team must be flawless in order to achieve it.

Dodger Sandy Koufax's pitching philosophy should be the goal of all internal auditors. "When I start, I try to pitch a perfect game. If I walk a batter, then I try to pitch a no-hitter. If I allow a hit, I then try to at least pitch a shutout. Failing in that, I still try to win."

So put on your baseball cap and pull on your cleats. Enjoy the thrills, excitement, and humor of 16 unique events in baseball history as told to you in an exciting historical fiction. The plot is breathtaking as serial killers strike with impunity. The book will do to internal auditing what *Knight Moves* did to chess and *Silence of the Lambs* did to dressmaking.

Along with the auditing humor, a reader will follow the exciting life of an internal auditor for a professional baseball team, who is a part - time professor at Baruch College. For example, do you know that auditors come in after the battle and kill the wounded? Or just as pitchers try to outsmart batters, financial statement may be misleading or wrong. Fraud red flags, computer crimes, internal controls, deductive and inductive reasoning, spotting liars, risk assessment, and characteristics of fraudsters are covered. Learn about interviewing skills, expert witnessing, outsourcing, computer assisted audit tools and techniques, the finding form used in an audit, the Endorsed Internal Auditing Program, types of evidence, and analytical auditing. However, never assume in baseball and internal auditing.

D. Larry Crumbley
Baton Rouge, LA

Douglas E. Ziegenfuss
Norfolk, VA

John J. O'Shaughnessy
San Francisco, CA

Acknowledgments

Many people were of great assistance in sharing memories and perceptions. Pitchers, catchers, teammates, umpires, and managers have been gracious in providing invaluable history and insight about these unique pitching events.

We also wish to express our thanks to Cody Blair, Nick Brignola, Charley Clark, Kay Collier, Otis Elmore, Charles R. Enis, Thomas Galligan, Jim Greenspan, Steve Grossman, Ron Hassey, Dick Hise, Tom Horton, John Richmond Husman, Dennis Lassila, Franklin Milgrim, Milt Pappas, John Pehrson, Gary Previts, Will Simmen, Kevin Strawbridge, Murphy Smith, Jim Womack, and Barry Wilkerson for help with the early drafts. Judy Moore, Rachael McMahon, and Debbie Arledge made this book possible with their ability to decipher our notes and produce a readable manuscript.

The book is dedicated to baseball's most demanding craft — the catcher. The backstop is often the forgotten equation in the perfect game. Tim McCarver put it bluntly. "Willie Sutton chose to become a bank robber because that's where the money is. I became a catcher because that's where the ball game is."

Catfish Hunter was so humble that he said "catching is 50 percent of the pitching game." We would not go that far, but we like Waite Hoyt's comment: "A catcher is the wife of the battery couple. He must humor the pitcher and jolly him along to make him think he is the big cheese."

Pitcher Allie Reynolds says that "in baseball and other sports, and in business as well, a lot of things happen because of implied authority. You are the catcher; you call the game. You are the pitcher; you pitch. Every now and then you shake them off. Sometimes you do it just to get the hitter thinking, but most of the time the catcher calls the game. Most of the time the loan officer approves the loan, and the plumber fixes the sink. See what I mean? That was just the way it worked. We won a lot of games. I won 182 and lost 107 during the time I played for the Yankees."

Former Montreal manager, Buck Rodgers, was a catcher for nine seasons, and he understood the delicate balance between the pitcher and catcher. "I know pitching, and I've got a pretty good idea when a pitcher's starting to lose his stuff. But when I go out to the mound, I don't expect my catcher to say 'His pitches are not moving quite as much as last inning.' Or, 'He's having trouble with the spin on his curves.' I don't talk with the catcher where the pitcher can hear. I don't tell the pitcher that the catcher said he's through."

Much the same is true with the internal auditor. He or she must be objective and factual, avoiding words or phrases that are inflammatory to the auditee. An auditee can even become angry at descriptions in a *positive* audit report. Selling an auditee on the importance of making changes is a delicate art. An internal auditor should follow Daryl Zero's motto, the world's greatest detective in the 1997 movie *Zero Effect*: "Precise observation and careful intervention." Think of the pitcher as the auditee, the catcher as the internal auditor, and the manager as top management. The scorekeeper could be considered the controller, and the umpire could be the external auditor. The scoreboard could be the general ledger.

D. Larry Crumbley

Douglas E. Ziegenfuss

John J. O'Shaughnessy

The Big "R"

Chapter 1

Worcester

"Forget the stuffed white shirt, forensic accountants are more parts Philip Marlowe than Casper Milquetoast. They open the books and crack the code, transforming a dull science of numbers into a suspenseful mystery with a logical, even riveting resolution."

Cory Johnson

No one noticed the nondescript man wearing a baseball hat and sunglasses standing near the bathroom, watching people entering and exiting the bathroom. He was pretending to be reading the *Sporting News*. After observing the activities for about twenty minutes, he went inside the restroom to check out the killing site. He was careful not to touch the door or anything else. He noted the location of the stalls and the absence of a lock on the door.

He exited the bathroom and continued his observation. He saw a young boy wearing a little league uniform enter the empty restroom carrying a baseball bat, as his father walked to the concession area. The man hurriedly put on thin rubber gloves and followed the young boy into the restroom, placing an "Out of Order" sign on the outside of the door. He sees that the boy is still in a stall, so he quietly places a doorstop at the bottom of the door so it will not open.

As the boy starts to wash his hands, the man approaches the boy. "Nice bat; I'm Duke Snider. You want me to sign it?"

The boy responds, "No kidding. Sure!" The boy hands him the bat. "Why are you wearing gloves?"

★ ★ ★ ★ ★

As they had done in 1882, the teams arrived by horse drawn wagon. Two wagons, each with two benches with base ballists facing each other. The first to arrive at The College of the Holy Cross Fitton Field were the Troy, New York Haymakers. Only 12 players and their manager were aboard. The players were resplendent in their 19th-century green pinstriped flannel uniforms on a day perfect for baseball. Their wagon approached the foul line and stopped just before crossing into left field. As the players exited their vehicle and began to make their way toward the infield, the crowd of about 3,000 cranks (fans) stirred. The arrival of the Troy Haymakers signaled that the match was about to begin, but the fans were still anxious for a glimpse of the hometown Worcester team.

The event was baseball played where it was and as it was in 1882. Worcester, Massachusetts, about 40 miles west of Boston, was represented in baseball's first major league, the National, for three seasons, 1880 through 1882. Likewise, Troy, New York had an entry in the Senior Circuit from 1879 through 1882.

Because of low attendance these two cities lost their franchises to Philadelphia and New York following the 1882 season, after Troy and Worcester finished in next—to—last and last place, respectively, in the National League. Worcester was 37 games behind the winning Chicago White Stockings, losing 66 games and winning only 18. In their final game of the 1881 season, the Troy Haymakers drew the smallest major league crowd ever—12—in a driving rainstorm. In the 1882 season Worcester had less than 100 fans on three occasions when they played the Troy Haymakers.

This "Nostalgia Series" was the brainchild of civic leaders in both cities. Baseball would be played by the rules of 1882, using equipment and strategies of those days. The match in Worcester was the second of the series to turn back the clock. The first had been played at Knickerbocker Park in Troy two weeks earlier. The Troy Haymakers came out ahead 2 - 0 in the first game.

Then the wooden wagon carrying the Worcester contingent arrived, likewise stopping just short of the roped-off left field. The crowd in the $3 seats in the modern day bleachers cheered. Others rose from more traditional bales of straw and ground blankets to welcome their local heroes. The Worcester Brown Stockings had the look of a modern team with light brown uniforms, dark brown caps, and knee socks with knicker style pants as worn today. The uniforms had wide belts and brown drawstrings rather than buttons and snaps. Two narrow brown horizontal stripes encircled the convict—like hats.

The teams mingled briefly on the diamond and then set about preparing for the match. There was batting, infield practice, and fungoes for the outfielders. The bats and balls looked like today's, but noticeably, fielding gloves were not worn, except for the catchers' kid gloves. The bats were lighter and thinner, and some players even swung flat bats, which were not banned until 1893. The game about to be played represented another era, but was instantly recognizable as baseball.

Baseball in 1882 was similar to the game as it is played today. Basic rules defining the number of players per team, and the manner for scoring runs and recording outs had been codified long before professional teams formed. A fixed batting order, three strikes and you are out, and three outs per half inning were rules then, as now. The layout of the field had been a part of amateur rules, standardized by Alexander J. Cartwright in 1845, and it remains faithful to his specifications to this day. Even on-deck circles were a part of the original venue.

Basic tactics such as catcher's and coach's signs, pitchouts and brush backs, relays and cutoffs were coming into general use in 1882. Popups, passed balls, fungoes, grounders, assists, balks, walks and whitewashes were commonly-used terms in the baseball language. Base ball itself was two words, and remained so well into the twentieth century.

Bench jockeying was already considered standard behavior, as was berating the umpire. There was only one arbiter, and he couldn't see everything. Cheating on him was commonplace— often base runners took short cuts. Even the umpire's hand-held indicator of balls and strikes—a form of internal controls—was being used in the 1880s.

Usually, catchers stood far behind the batters because they had no padding or masks. The catcher's mask had been invented by F.W. Thayer, a member of the Harvard BaseBall Club, and was first worn by Jim Tyng in April 1877. The catcher had to get close to the batter only when there were two strikes because he had to catch the third—strike pitch on a fly to get a strike out. Today the catchers would wear thin cut—off fingertip gloves. Also, they had to catch any foul on the fly—a foul bounce was no longer an out for the catcher. Chest protectors were not worn until around 1885. The first shin guards were not invented and worn until 1908, by New York Giant catcher Roger Bresnahan. He also wore the first head protector after he was knocked unconscious by a pitch.

Pitching was the major difference. The pitcher was permitted to move around in a 4 by 7-foot sawdust-covered box 45 feet from home plate. He was required to deliver all pitches underhanded. Some pitchers' fastballs approached 80 miles per hour, and others were using curves regularly. A team had one regular pitcher, who pitched almost every game in the regular 84 game schedule. The pitching slab or rubber was not introduced until 1893, when the pitching distance was moved to 60 feet, six inches.

The horsehide balls were of similar size but a little softer and as only one was used during the course of the game, it became quite soft. Home runs were rare, not only because of the softer ball, but because fields were quite large. Most home runs were of the inside-the-park variety.

The old time rag band present at this re-creation began playing as game preparations continued. Pre-game ceremonies included comments by representatives of both cities and the teams, accompanied by predictions of the outcome. As always, it remained for the grudge match to be settled on the field. Though there had been little success connected with Worcester's short major league experience, one remarkable event had occurred. Baseball's first-ever perfect game happened in Worcester.

This historic game pitched by Worcester's J. Lee Richmond against Cleveland on June 12, 1880 was even worthy of a monument in the city. A perfect game is better than a no-hitter because no one from the opposing team reaches first base. There are no hits, no walks, and no errors. No other sport has the equivalent of a perfect game. As Reggie Jackson once said, "A perfect game is the standard. You grade them all from there."

During the opening ceremony today, the poem "Casey at the Bat" was read by a member of the Committee to Preserve Worcester's Baseball Heritage. The poem about Casey and the Mudville Nine had been written by Ernest Lawrence Thayer in his hometown of Worcester.

At the game to throw out the first pitch was John Richmond Husman, a great-grandson of J. Lee Richmond. To a reporter commenting on Lee Richmond's contributions to the national pastime, John said, "One of the first regular left-handed pitchers in the majors is not a member of the Hall of Fame, but he caused chaos by his arrival on the scene. It was specifically because of him, and 5'5" Bobby Mitchell of the Cincinnati Red Stockings, that the strategies of switch-hitting and platooning were developed."

John suggested that the cranks enjoy the game and concentrate on the similarities to the modern game, which far outnumber the differences. He told the reporter to get a photo of the monument at the actual site of the first game. The two-and-a-half-foot monument was on the Worcester Agricultural Fairgrounds or the Driving Park where the Worcesters played their games. Presently the site is occupied by Becker College, off Sever Street.

Today's game was not like the 1-0 pitching gem that Lee Richmond, the slender chap with a little brush of a mustache, tossed on a hot day in 1880. By the third inning Worcester had a 2-0 lead. There had been a number of hits, walks, and errors by both sides. Rain did not threaten to stop the game as it had during Richmond's one hour and twenty-seven minutes pitching exhibition on Saturday, June 12, 1880.

As the defenders changed at the top of the ninth inning a police car circled the field with its lights flashing and siren blaring. The car disappeared far down the right foul line under the stands of the adjacent football stadium. All attention from the field had focused on the car, but interest ceased as it drove out of view, and the game continued.

Underneath the football stadium about fifty people congregated in a long aisle that was open to the outside through bleachers. Several people frantically directed the two uniformed police officers to a restroom at the end of the aisle. The day was hot and sweltering, and this area was a refuge for those watching the game. It was still hot, but there was shelter from the sun, and also, here were restrooms and concessions. A single uniformed Holy Cross security officer had cordoned off one of the men's restrooms and was directing people to another. The two Worcester policemen entered the restroom. Most people went about their business of consuming food, cold drinks, and cigarettes.

On the field, the ninth inning began. Worcester held a slim 3-1 lead. Attention focused on the game once again as the Worcesters were close to a win. After the first two Trojans were retired, sirens once again broke the spell of the game. This time there were two vehicles: another police car and an emergency medical van. They followed the same course as the first car and likewise disappeared under the football stadium. Again all action on the field stopped as the vehicles progressed. And, again, after they disappeared, action resumed.

The last out was quickly made, and the victory was fittingly secure for the hometown team. The field was immediately covered with people; both teams and cranks and more cranks, all seeming to want to keep the event alive and not let it end. They succeeded for a long time. Players congratulated each other, and cranks spoke with each other and players. Clusters of people formed; the largest cluster was around the television reporters and the press people present.

Fleet Walker, an internal auditor for the New York Yankees, and Fred Campbell, a local CPA specializing in forensic accounting services, were in the crowd. Both were members of the Society for American Baseball Research (SABR) and members of its 19th Century Committee that Fred chaired. However, they had not seen each other for several months and during this time Fleet had changed jobs.

Fred had come to Worcester from his home in Providence, Rhode Island. He also had been to the Troy game at Knickerbocker Park. He and Fleet were long time correspondents and research sharers, and they reveled in their rare meeting.

"Hello Fred. How's life treating you?"

"Fine, and you Fleet? How's the job and family?"

"The family is fine, but I have a new job. I don't think I told you. I switched jobs shortly after our last committee meeting. I decided to hang up my spikes with the public accounting firm and go with the internal auditing department for the New York Yankees," said Fleet.

Fred said, "I thought I heard rumors that you joined the Yankee organization. I am glad to hear the news. I know how much you are devoted to baseball and to the New York Yankees in particular. However, isn't this move a step down for you, like being sent to the minor leagues?"

Fleet explained. "Many people share that misconception. In fact, I have never enjoyed auditing as much as I do now. You see Fred, during the standard public accounting engagement, I was too preoccupied with the financial statements. Everything we did was focused toward preventing material misstatements from occurring in the financial statements. Sure we tried to look at and understand our client's business, but our work was always in relation to the financial statements. On the other hand, as an internal auditor I get into other issues which will have a greater impact. For instance, I have focused our internal audit effort away from the financial statements to operational and compliance issues."

"What do you mean, operational and compliance issues?" asked Fred.

Fleet explained. "When I performed financial audits my biggest fear was that the financial statements would be wrong, and I wouldn't detect the error and would issue a clean opinion rather than a qualified or adverse opinion. Now the financial statements are a scorecard or a box score of how well a company did or what they owned. Financial auditing always dealt with past events or transactions. Operational audits ensure that the organization or parts of an organization are run efficiently and effectively, or in other words, are well managed. Operational audits identify areas in which the company can improve its performance. They are future driven, and managers and boards of directors value them more than a financial audit."

"Okay, calm down, Fleet, I didn't know internal auditors could get so worked up. Tell me about compliance auditing."

"Compliance auditing is when we ensure that the organization or part of an organization is complying with company procedures, laws and regulations or terms of contracts. We must also ensure that our contractors are complying with the terms of contracts they have with us," Fleet replied.

Fleet went on, "We don't spend too much time ensuring compliance with company policies. That is as popular as being an umpire. However, our management does not want the negative publicity or fines that result from violating laws regulating business today, such as the employment, safety, environmental, and tax laws. In addition, a professional sports team has many league rules to abide by, and my job is to ensure our organization complies with them."

"Well I would not forget about financial statements altogether. There are a lot of class-action lawsuits against companies—about 500 cases pending or resolved against them each year. Any time a company's earnings do not meet the consensus earnings estimates and the stock drops rapidly, a group of lawyers will sue the company and the external auditors. I would think internal auditors are often in harm's way."

"Of course you are correct," Fleet replied. "The SEC is apparently on a campaign to increase its attacks on companies' weak internal controls and employees at companies responsible for doctoring their books. That clearly includes the internal auditor."

Fred smiled, "Don't let the SEC catch you doctoring the books like some pitchers try to doctor the baseball. What is your status within the Yankee organization?"

"George Steinbrenner personally hired me. He said he needed someone like me who loved the game of baseball and the New York Yankees. Someone who would take a fan's perspective to the role of the internal auditor. He has been great. He gave me a high profile. I report directly to him, but I have access to the audit committee of the Board of Directors. In addition, he approved the wording of the charter establishing the internal auditing department and fully supports my professional activities with the Institute of Internal Auditors. I work very closely with the external auditors, and they recognize that we have separate but valuable services to render to the Yankee organization. We have a coordinated audit plan to ensure a minimum of duplication and a maximum degree of audit coverage for our organization."

"Wow, sounds like you have had a great time since I last saw you." Fred smiled.

"I have," replied Fleet, "However, I'll keep in closer touch with you from now on."

The field was covered with people. Fans and reporters took pictures and players signed autographs. An ambulance quietly made its way around the field to the now common entrance under the football stadium. The concession stand had closed, and there were only three or four people making their way from the restrooms. One person was sweeping the long aisle, and two workers were closing the snack shop. The driver of the ambulance parked where directed by a Worcester cop.

"You got a cadaver to haul, bud?"

"Yep, we do. But you can't do anything or move it before the detectives clear it."

"How long?"

"Don't know, but they're on the way."

"If it's gonna be all day, we'll go over there and see those old time baseball guys."

"No way," replied the cop. "Wait here with us; we're trying to keep this quiet with all these people around. We don't need you out there with them. Besides, the game is over."

"Who's gonna get excited about some guy dying of a heart attack in the bathroom?"

"That's not exactly the case; just wait with us," was the policeman's order.

The field began to clear. The heat and length of the afternoon's happenings had taken their toll. The media people had their deadlines and seemed to lead the exit. Another vehicle entered the area and began the circle of the field that would lead to the football stadium. This time an unassuming dark sedan with only a driver, passed over the path of those exiting. The driver was recognized by Dave Pope, one of the television crew.

"Hey, Captain Stryker, what brings you to a ballgame?"

Obviously annoyed, Sterling Stryker snapped. "I'm not here for a ballgame while I'm working, Dave; just step back, and I'll be on my way."

"Not here for the game, huh? Anything going on that might be of interest to me?"

Even more annoyed now, Stryker shot back, "Just forget you saw me. I'm outta here."

With that, the Captain drove his car around the several people gathered with the TV crew and quickly made his way toward the football stadium.

Sportscaster Dave Pope pondered for a moment and called his cameraperson. "Bernie, the Captain seems a bit on edge; let's follow him and see what's going on." Dave and Bernie headed across the diamond on foot. Their angle enabled them to get to the football stadium just after the captain's car disappeared into it. They followed the car and were greeted by one of the uniformed Worcester cop.

"That's as far as you go, folks."

Pope knew immediately that something was happening. Both policemen treated him more curtly than what he thought was "normal" even with his limited news experience. There were four emergency vehicles under the stands. He could see the roped off men's room at the far end of the aisle and uniformed policemen guarding the scene.

"Where's everyone?" he asked the officer. Getting only a shrug, he pointed towards the men's room, "In there?"

"Look," replied the officer, "I can't tell you a thing; why don't ya just go about your business?"

"I am about my business. I'm in the news business, and I think there's news here."

The cop stiffened, "Well, I'm in the police business, and I'm telling you to move along."

"Not until..."

With that the restroom door opened. The ambulance crew wheeled out an empty gurney followed by Captain Stryker who had a consoling arm on the shoulder of another man.

Pope passed by the uniformed policeman, moving toward Stryker. "Captain, a word please. What's going on?"

Captain Stryker wanted out. He continued to guide the man by the elbow toward his car. "Listen, Pope, we've got a mess here, and there's an awfully lot more that I don't know than I do. You'll get nothing from me until we've got some more answers. I'll be in touch with the Chief about a statement for you guys."

In his car, Captain Stryker addressed the man he had escorted from the restroom, his head buried in his hands. "I'm going to send you home in a squad car. You're to talk to no one other than your wife about what has happened. I'll stay here. The Chief and some crime lab people are on the way. We want to find everything we can before we move your son's body, Mr. Ketchum. The squad will stay with you. I'll be there as soon as we've finished here."

As Stryker dispatched Fred Ketchum, Worcester Chief of Police Henry Kessler arrived in a plain car. Stryker moved with him toward the restroom, but stopped short so they could talk privately. Before Stryker could start, Kessler blurted, "This better be good to ruin my Saturday afternoon. What's the big deal?"

Seemingly pleased that he had a big deal for his boss, Stryker recounted what he had learned. "Seems this man Fred Ketchum and his 14-year-old son, also Fred, were here to watch this old time ballgame today."

"They come over to use the restroom and to get a drink. They go into the restroom, and the kid has to take a crap. Dad leaves him and goes to buy refreshments. Father returns and finds his son lying with his back on the toilet. His head was on the floor behind it and against the wall. He moves over to him and looks down at his face. He says he couldn't recognize him. It was such a bloody mess. Chief, it is a bloody mess. Somebody really smashed him. Smashed the life out of him. Used the kid's own baseball bat and then stood it up in the corner of the stall."

Kessler had lost all concern for his interrupted Saturday afternoon. "Do you have anybody who saw this? How could this happen in such a busy place? Send someone to look over the crowd. The assailant should have blood all over him."

"I've already sent Hank looking for any suspicious people. He's not back yet." Stryker relayed that the father told him that he thought there were other people in the restroom when he left. "But he didn't see anyone when he exited the stall after finding his son. He went back to the concession stand and asked them to call 911. Then the father went back and waited with his son. Apparently the campus police closed the area off then."

Once photographing and sketching were completed, the crime people went about their work putting the weapon and other evidence into paper bags. Paper bags were better because moisture inside plastic bags could affect the evidence. Next the body was placed onto a gurney for removal. Kessler and Stryker checked for the obvious, careful not to touch anything. Wallet intact in the rear pocket, watch on the arm, and a gold chain around the neck. There were several other items in the pockets including a scorecard for the day's game.

Somewhat curiously, a badge or nametag holder was clipped to the front of the young man's shirt. It contained a single baseball trading card, that of Nate Colbert. "What do you make of this?" the Chief queried Stryker. "Not unusual for a person here to have a baseball card, but that's an odd way to carry one. We need to ask the father about the significance of the card. I've never heard of Nate Colbert."

The Chief ordered Stryker to have the body held at the morgue. "Don't overlook anything. I want to see all detail notes." Then he silently asked the question. "Why would anyone kill a small boy with a baseball bat in a bathroom in Worcester? Why not use a knife? Probably not premeditated."

Both Fleet and Fred were watching nearby.

No mention was made of the murder in the write-up about the game in the local paper. Instead the reporter, Dave Rosenbaum, talked about the catching:

> During the recreation game played in Troy on Saturday, Mike Hetman caught barehanded 1882-style 80-mile-per-hour pitches from Troy's pitchers. By the end of the third inning, Hetman's hands were nothing more than five-fingered objects dangling at the end of his arms, good for nothing except the reflex act of catching a baseball. Gripping a bat became almost impossible.

> Hetman, once a catcher in the Boston Red Sox organization, said on Wednesday after the Saturday game, "My hand is still tender. The ball was as hard as a baseball in the beginning, but once it was hit around a little, it got a little softer. Still, it hurt like hell."

Chapter 2

Providence

Auditors will continue to miss fraud because much of their work is predicted on the assumption that separation of duties prevents fraud (i.e., one person hold the money and another person keeps track of it). The Equity Funding case shakes the foundation of auditing in that so much is based on the assumption that people don't collude very long. These people worked together as an efficient team for a very long time [9 years].

Lee Seidler

From the recreation game Fleet Walker returned to New York City to prepare for a talk he had agreed to give to a chapter of the American Association of Individual Investors.

The next day Walker was standing before a group of about 45 investors. He donated his time often to give speeches to investor groups. Maybe they came to hear about investing, or maybe they just wanted to hear someone who had not been fired by George Steinbrenner. After George fired Yogi Berra as manager of the Yankees 16 games into the 1985 season, Yogi did not make up with George until Yogi Berra day on July 18, 1999. That was the date David Cone pitched his perfect game. Somehow Walker always worked this story into his discussions.

"Financial statement users must appreciate the fact that financial statements may be wrong. Some companies use creative accounting techniques to disguise damaging information, to provide a distorted picture of the financial health of the business, to smooth out erratic earnings, or to boost anemic earnings or no earnings at all. Investors and auditors should have a healthy skepticism when reading and evaluating financial reports. Businesses are often clever in hiding these accounting tricks and gimmicks, so users must be ever alert to the signs of outright financial shenanigans. Investors must attack financial statement and company information the way the fictional Sherlock Holmes approached murder cases."

Using overheads Walker began an extended discussion of certain clues and red flags that suggest a company is engaging in financial shenanigans.

- **Earnings problem**. One of the most significant red flags is a downward trend in earnings. Companies are required to disclose earnings for the last three years in the income statement, so don't look just at the "bottom line." The trend in operating income is just as important as the actual earnings.

- **Reduced cash flow**. To a certain extent, management can exploit GAAP to produce the appearance of increased earnings. Some popular shenanigans include booking sales on long-term contracts before the customer has paid up, delaying the recording of expenses, failing to recognize the obsolescence of inventory as an expense, and reducing advertising and research and development expenditures. You can use the cash flow statement to check the reliability of earnings. If net income is moving up while cash flow from operations is drifting downward, something may be wrong. Cash flow and net income should track together.

- **Excessive debt**. Crucial to determining whether a company can weather difficult times is its debt factor. Companies burdened by too much debt lack the financial flexibility to respond to crises and to take advantage of opportunities. Small companies with heavy debt are particularly vulnerable in economic downturns. Investment professionals pay special attention to a company's debt-to equity ratio, the total debt to stockholders' or owners' equity. While the optimum ratio varies from industry to industry, the amount of stockholders' or owners' equity should significantly exceed the amount of debt by a significant amount. This information is available on the balance sheet.

- **Overstated inventories and receivables**. Look at the ratio of accounts receivable to sales and the ratio of inventory to cost of goods sold. If accounts receivable exceed 15 percent of annual sales and inventory exceeds 25 percent of cost of goods sold, be careful. If customers aren't paying their bills and/or the company is saddled with aging merchandise, problems will eventually arise. Overstated inventories and receivables are often at the heart of corporate fraud, resulting in future declines in profits. As significant as the ratios are, trends over time are also important. Although there may be good reasons for a company to have bloated or increasing inventory or receivables, it's important to determine if the condition is a symptom of financial difficulty.

- **Inventory plugging**. Inventory fraud is an easy way to produce instant earnings and improve the balance sheet. Crazy Eddie, an electronic equipment retailer, allegedly recorded sales to other chains as if they were retail sales (rather than wholesale sales).

- **Balancing Act**. Inventory, sales, and receivables usually move in tandem because customers do not pay up front if they can avoid it. Neither inventory nor accounts receivable should grow faster than sales. Furthermore, inventory normally moves in tandem with accounts payable since a healthy company does not often pay cash at the delivery dock as purchases are received.

- **CPA Switching**. Auditor switching and the financial condition of a company are dependent to a limited extent. Firms in the midst of financial distress switch auditors more frequently than healthy companies.

- **Hyped Sales**. According to court documents, CEO Emanuel Pinez at Centennial used a form of trickery rarely seen: He hyped sales by using his ample personal fortune to fund purchases. "Any auditor would have had a hard time catching that," says William Coyne, an accounting professor at Babson College. Centennial Director John J. Shields, a former CEO of Computervision Corp., says in an affidavit that Pinez admitted to him that he altered inventory tags and recorded sales on products that were never shipped. Pinez's lawyer says he is innocent.

★ ★ ★ ★ ★

That evening darkness was settling in as the people from the neighborhood gathered at an old burning building. The faces were Asian and Hispanic as well as some black and some white. The Willow Street School had stood at the corner of Messer and Willow Streets in Providence for well over one hundred years. Its steeple had long since been removed and all the openings were covered with wood. But still it stood. No doubt it was a kind of home for the homeless, especially in winter. But this was June 17; not the time of year that a fire built for warmth in an abandoned building would set it ablaze. Perhaps one or more of the multitude of young people from the surrounding residences was responsible. Whatever the cause, the old school that had seen and survived so much, was burning.

The pump and ladder truck made its way swiftly northward on Messer Street from the station house at Union Avenue. Battalion Chief Pete Castiglione was a savvy veteran fire fighter. His first orders were to move the crowd away from danger and to establish barricades. He studied the building as this preliminary work was being done. The fire appeared to be localized on the first floor, at the center of the building. The big brick and stone structure had three stories with an irregular roof. Smoke billowed from chinks in the boarded up front entrance. The Chief thought the fire might be burning on the backside and was probably impassable. No need to risk it anyway.

He dispatched a party to the rear to break and enter with instructions to find access on the front of the building for hoses to be put through. The rear entry party found the double doors at the back of the old school standing partially open. Smoke was pouring from the opening, but not as heavily as from the front. Chief Castiglione was summoned. The door was fully opened to a larger and continuous rush of smoke. Castiglione then ordered the ground level windows, which were covered with plywood to be opened. Each window, when vented, emitted thick black smoke. But each window in turn emitted less smoke. Again with axes the other half of the rear double door was opened. No rush of smoke this time. Although the building was full of smoke, little smoke was now leaking through the openings. Sensing that the fire may be out, Castiglione pulled all his fire fighters back. They brought two large exhaust fans to two of the rear windows to pull smoke from the old school. The monster fans quickly accomplished their task. In a flash the building appeared to be void of smoke.

Chief Castiglione, flanked by fire fighters climbed the steps to the now open rear entrance and peered into the building. They immediately saw the body.

Two firemen, fully protected, and equipped with breathing apparatus quickly entered. The body was about ten feet inside the door, on the floor, face down as if the person might have been kneeling and collapsed. The buttocks were extended into the air and pointed toward the door. There was no movement. Each fireman took an arm of the body. They lifted it upright and then over backwards and pulled it from the building. One of the firemen stepped on something that caused him to stumble. He kicked at it, and something rolled away. They continued out and down the stairs and laid the limp body on its back on a stretcher that had been quickly provided. There was little need to rush the removal. There was no helping this person.

The man, probably young, had no recognizable face. The front of the head was only a bloody mass of pulp.

The Chief barked orders in rapid succession.

"Cover that poor guy."

"Have one of our traffic control cops call this in. Tell them what we've found."

"Get these people back from here—way back."

"Don't let anyone in the building, even near it."

"Let's get around the front and knock those doors down. We've got to get in and check on this fire without tramping over the area where the body was. We've probably screwed up enough already. Cops are gonna have our behinds."

The front had double doors, too, bigger than those in back. After a great deal of work with the axes, they were loosened. As they were swung open a huge hallway was revealed, high and wide and extending all the way through the building. Lights shown through the opened rear doors, directly in line with those in front.

Just inside the front doors, on the floor was the source of the smoke. A smoldering smudge pot. "A goddamn smoke bomb! I don't understand what the hell's going on here. Let's back off," screamed Castiglione. "There's no fire at all; let's save this for the cops."

With the front of the building open, the two fans quickly drew out all of the remaining smoke. Then they were shut down. The fire crew helped the already reinforced uniformed police contain the ever-growing crowd. The time was now just after 10:00 p.m. and completely dark. The neighborhood people talked and speculated incessantly. The uniforms, all anxious to be out of here, awaited the arrival of the homicide people. They didn't have to wait long.

While they waited, Castiglione looked at the blend of humanity at the scene. Every race and age seemed to be represented. This crowd of course, represented the neighborhood, one of Providence's oldest; one in transition and now home to all of these. By now, all of the fire fighting equipment had been retrieved, and the bulk of the units had returned to the station at Union Street. Remaining behind were the Chief and an assistant with his medical unit. The emergency medical technicians were standing by the unmoved stretcher with its covered body. Castiglione was anxious to pass command to the police. He knew that he had discovered a murder and was concerned that his people may have made the police work more difficult by damaging evidence at the scene.

Detective Frank Houseman was obviously perturbed as he quizzed Castiglione. The men knew each other; although not well. Both had had long careers of public service in Providence, and their paths had crossed many times.

"Damn, damn, damn; what timing you've got Pete. I'm off at eleven and only Friday afternoon to work before vacation, and you guys dump a murder on me."

"Us guys didn't do anything, and neither did I. Take it easy, will you."

"OK, OK. Sorry, I'm a little anxious to get away. What have you got here?"

"Come over here, Frank." The two sat alone in the Chief's car to talk.

"We responded to a fire call for the old school. Seemed routine enough; arson for some reason. Maybe fun for kids. I thought we caught it early, but apparently there was no fire at all. Just a smoke bomb behind the front door. But we found a body inside the back doors. We pulled it out and saw a kid with the most godawful face you've ever seen. Beaten to a pulp and looks like hamburger meat. We've got him on a stretcher out back. We didn't move anything once we found out what we had found. I'm sure we really messed up the scene, sorry."

Castiglione looked at Houseman for some sign of forgiveness. He saw only anger. "This is just great; a case like this when I'm wanting to be outta here. And to top it off, you people trample all over the scene. Let's go see what we got."

As they exited the car, an Hispanic couple ran at them. They were coming from around the rear of the old school. The woman, about 35, was frantic. The man had a hard time keeping up with her.

"My son, that may be my son back there. Is he dead? I want to see him." She absolutely screamed.

Houseman tried to talk to her, but she was frantic and mostly incoherent. He asked a uniformed policeman to take the couple to his car and sit with them. "Come on Pete; show me what we've got."

Houseman lifted the blanket and saw the bloodied face, not even recognizable as a face. He immediately covered it again. "Let's get those people back here to see if this body is their son," Houseman barked to a policeman. "Wait, maybe you'd better only bring the man. Leave the woman in the car."

The man was trembling as he approached the gurney with his police escort. Houseman pulled away the blanket, but this time, from the lower two thirds of the torso.

"That is my son. That is Chico. What has happened?"

"We don't know yet. Are you sure this is your son?"

"Oh, yes, it's him all right. See that tattoo," pointing to the right arm. "That's him all right."

Detective Houseman again covered the body and asked the man his name.

"Rodriguez, Marcie, Uh Marcelino. This is Chico. Is he really dead?"

"He is, Mr. Rodriguez. We're sure," replied the detective. "We're going to try to find out what happened here, and we'll be needing your help. Is that your wife in my car?"

"Si, that's Helen."

Houseman asked Rodriguez to return to her, promising to join them in a minute. He instructed the emergency medical technicians to remove the body to the morgue. He then asked Castiglione to show him inside. The place was now very dark. Armed only with flashlights, they peered inside.

The big room just inside the rear entrance was empty. Litter, mostly paper, was strewn everywhere. There were some beer cans and a whiskey bottle. What looked like a makeshift cardboard bed was in a corner. There was a trail of blood from the door toward the center of the room. Castiglione pointed to where the trail ended. "That's where he was," he told the detective.

Just past that spot, Houseman spotted a wooden baseball bat. From the doorway it appeared to be smudged with blood. Castiglione saw it too. "When we were in here, one of my guys almost broke his leg on that thing. Let's get it."

"No. Let's stay out of the building. I don't want to disturb anything else. It's too dark to see what we're doing. I'll have the place secured and watched until in the morning. Ride back to the station with me, and we'll try to piece this disaster together." Houseman was firmly in charge now. His earlier anger had been replaced by the demeanor of the seasoned professional detective. He knew he had a murder case on his hands.

As they turned from the door and descended the steps, the glare of the television camera lights stunned them both. There were two cameras and four or five people shouting questions. Houseman had been through this type of questioning many times before. He knew these people had a job to do, and that they were zealous about it. There would be no putting them off, especially since they were probably near their deadline for the 11 o'clock news. He knew he had to give them their story. "And we do have a story," he thought to himself.

"OK people, we don't have much, but I'll give you something," Houseman shouted.

"Tell us what you do have, Frank," was a reply from among the group.

As several microphones were thrust into his face he said, "We've got an apparent homicide here. The fire department found the victim, apparently a young man, Chico Rodriguez, in the old Willow Street School, just behind me. They were called because of a smoke bomb that had been set off within the building. My guess is that the smoke was done to call attention to the scene. Rodriguez appears to have been bludgeoned. There's a baseball bat inside that could have been used, but we don't know. We don't really know anything more than that. We're not doing anything more here until it's light in the morning. But we'll be talking with the boy's parents tonight. No one can go inside."

"Why? What's the motive?" came the question.

"That's it," Houseman snapped back. "You've got all I've got; you've got your story. Let's all get outta here."

Houseman had done a masterful job. The television crew had what they wanted. They got it quickly and just in time for the late news. Houseman thought it good to get the word out on this one quickly. Maybe someone out there could help. Frank knew he needed help. This might be a tough case.

The detective made sure that the building was secured and that a watchman was in place for the night. He returned to the car, asking the few remaining onlookers to be about their business. He drove with Castiglione sitting beside him. The Rodriguezes rode in the back, but they were worlds away. She still sobbed, and he appeared to have been doing the same. Houseman hoped they could talk on the way to the station, but it wouldn't work. They had to be face to face and really concentrate.

Detective Frank Houseman sat at a large table in the station conference room. With him, in addition to the parents, were a stenographer and two other detectives. They were drinking coffee and talking about Chico.

"Seventeen years old," volunteered his father. "Good kid; no trouble. Good student too; was gonna graduate in a year. Liked sports, too. In fact, he played baseball tonight."

"Go on," prodded Houseman.

"He went after dinner," this reply from Helen. She went on. "Most nights, when the weather is fine, he plays at the park next to the fire station at Union and Messer in the evening. There's always a big game on Thursday. Good high school players from all over Providence come there. Tonight was no different. He left about 5:30."

"When did he normally come home?" asked another detective.

Marcie replied that it was usually just after dark. "They played until they could see no more; then he'd always come home. Sometimes he'd bring people home with him to talk baseball and listen to the Red Sox if they were on the radio. He loved baseball and loved to talk about it. He reads about the old teams. I mean real old. He knows about the old park across the street from the school where you found him. Major league ball used to be played there. He'd like to take people there and show them where the big leaguers played—almost in his back yard."

The same detective asked, "Was he there today?"

"Every evening," said Marcie.

"Did he have someone with him?" was the next question. Marcie shook his head, "I dunno; we never would."

Mrs. Rodriguez was having a difficult time with all of this questioning and again began to quietly sob. Houseman offered her food, which was immediately refused.

"One more question, please folks," Houseman quietly asked. "Any ideas as to a motive, or who might have done this thing." "No. No," gasped Helen Rodriguez. "He was liked by everyone; no one would want to hurt him." Marcie nodded in agreement.

Houseman thanked the parents for their help. He explained that Chico's body was at the morgue, and that there would be an autopsy before it could be released to them. He told them that they would be driven home in a squad car, and he would be in touch the next day.

Back in his own office and alone for the first time in a while, Frank Houseman thought of how to proceed and about his own schedule. The time was now after 1:00 a.m. Friday. He had planned on packing for his family's summer vacation after his shift ended at the normal 11:00 p.m. That was shot. He hadn't even called his wife. He thought he might have to get ready Friday night. At any rate, he was determined that nothing was going to interfere with the long awaited vacation.

He called Sara. He awakened her and started to explain his tardiness.

"I know," she said sleepily. "When you were late, I called the station. The desk sergeant told me what you were doing. I knew as much because I saw you on the news. Will you be able to wrap this mess up so that we can leave on time?"

"I won't wrap it up, but we'll leave on time," was her husband's reply. "This murder will be a tough one, so someone else will have to handle it. I'll come back in the morning and get it straightened out with the Chief. Be home soon, hon."

At the instant the handset was placed in its cradle, Houseman's phone rang. He picked up the phone and said, "Detective Houseman."

"Detective Houseman, my name is Fred Campbell, and I thought I should call about the Rodriguez murder."

"Why?"

"I think it's more than a coincidence," said Campbell.

"What is?" asked Houseman.

"Let me explain, I'm a member of SABR."

Houseman cut him off, "What's a saber?"

"Sir, S-A-B-R is the acronym for the Society for American Baseball Research. We do just what the name says. My specialty is the nineteenth century games. I've been pondering calling you since I saw the news. I don't want to be a bother, but..."

"OK, what's the coincidence?"

"I was in Worcester last Saturday for a re-creation of a 1882 baseball game between Worcester and Troy New York."

"Sooo," was Houseman's impatient reply.

"Well, there was a murder at the park. A young lad was killed with a baseball bat in one of the restrooms there. Struck in the face repeatedly as Rodriguez was here."

"Look Mr. SABR, murder is not the world's most unusual event. I recall reading about that one, too. But I don't get the connection. Both were probably done with baseball bats. So what?"

"There's more. More of a coincidence than that. Part of the festivities at Worcester concerned the first perfect game in baseball."

"Yeah." Houseman wanted to go home and go to bed.

Campbell went on. "That first game was pitched in Worcester on June 12, 1880."

"Sooo," again was the reply.

"The second perfect game was pitched in Providence by John Montgomery Ward just five days later on June 17, 1880. That was last night's date."

"Ummm, I'll admit they're similar, but I think you may be reaching a bit. You're matching dates of today with events of, uh, 120 years ago. That and the similar method of killing doesn't make a firm connection at all."

"But there's more," Campbell continued. "Locations match. The Rodriguez boy was found in a school that overlooked the park, Messer Street Grounds, where the Providence perfect game was played."

"Saay, the kid's parent's told me there was an old park nearby."

"That's it; *was* nearby. The park's long gone. In fact, few people know where it was. I've just recently located it myself. But that site was the first major league park to have a screen behind home plate to protect spectators from foul balls. There's not even a historical marker telling about Ward's perfect game."

"Well, it's still too much of a coincidence."

"But there's more. I remember reading in *Baseball Weekly*, that there have been several other murders in baseball stadiums this year. One person was killed in the Detroit stadium on April 30, and another one killed on May 5 at the Boston Baseball Park. Now on both of those dates perfect games were pitched *in those stadiums*. There might be more."

"You've given me something to ponder. Can you give me a why?"

"No. I cannot," apologized the caller. "That's why I hesitated to call. I can't possibly imagine the connection, but something seems to tie these murders together. I thought you should know."

"Didn't Nolan Ryan pitch a bunch of these perfect games?"

"Oh, no. Nolan Ryan pitched seven no-hitters, but never a perfect game. Only five Hall of Famers have pitched perfect games. Actually some mediocre and forgettable hurlers have pitched perfect games. Catfish Hunter said it best. 'You've got to have good stuff to throw a perfect game. God has got to be looking down on you that night. It's not only the pitcher that does it, but the whole team.'"

"Mr. Campbell, were you in Providence yesterday?"

"Why no. I was at work. I'm an accountant. Why do you ask?"

"No reason. Look, Mr. Campbell, I appreciate your interest and your call, but I don't think you've got more than a coincidence here. Just a coincidence. Give me your phone number and address, and I will call you if I need you. Could you send me copies of the *Baseball Today* reports about the other murders?"

"*Baseball Weekly*. No problem."

★ ★ ★ ★ ★

At half past one o'clock in the morning Frank called Sara, woke her a second time, and told her he was on the way home.

Driving home at nearly 2:00 a.m. on Friday morning is a quiet time. Time to think. "I'll go in with the first shift, wrap up what I know in my report, and ask the Chief to cover my afternoon shift. I'll be out early. There does seem to be a lot of baseball connections with this Rodriguez case. He plays, studies the game's history, lives within sight of the old park, and I'll bet we find that the bat on the floor of the old school is what killed him."

Detective Frank Houseman slumped into bed, and Sara was awakened for yet another time. But not for long. She was fast asleep again in seconds. Frank stared at the ceiling, anxious for morning. So much to do. He mentally went through his "to do" list. Return to the scene, go to the morgue, see the Rodriguez couple, write my report, see the Chief, and get away for two glorious weeks. Sleep came in batches for him that night.

Houseman was in his office at 7 a.m. He had asked for the crime lab crew for 7 a.m. "Where are they? Oh, give 'em a few minutes Frank," he said to himself. Two cups of coffee later he was driving to the Willow Street School. Alongside him was Dr. George Flynn, head of the Providence Police Department's Crime Laboratory. Houseman was briefing him.

"We've had a manned police line up all night, so things will be as we left them in the dark. But probably too late. The fire guys simply pulled the corpse out and trampled over everything. We know the victim's face was smashed, and I saw a baseball bat on the floor. Looked like blood was on it. We left it there. Two bits says he was killed with it. Trail of blood on the floor, too."

"OK," said Flynn, "that's enough. Let me take a look and assess what's there for myself."

The two greeted the lone uniformed officer at the back door. He opened the double doors wide. Light streamed into the room. Flynn peered into the room from outside. There was not much to see. An empty room. But he was standing in dried blood. He went no further. Looking back he saw a trail of blood transcending all of the stairs. He could not see the trail in the tall grass below. The trail went into the room about ten feet and terminated in a pool. To one side was the baseball bat, the business end smeared with what appeared to be dried blood. Two technicians wearing surgical gloves had followed. He had them sample the blood. They took photographs and videos of the whole room. They picked up the bat and put it in a plastic garbage bag. They did the same with the smudge pot.

Flynn spoke, "Simple. The victim was beaten with the ash Louisville slugger. The fire guys find him and drag him out leaving a trail of blood. We can match the blood on the bat. That ought to do it. Maybe you will get some prints from the bat."

"Not so simple," Houseman snapped back. "Fire Chief Castiglione told me that they found Rodriguez where that pool of dried blood is now." He pointed. "He was face down and on his knees with his bottom in the air. His men straightened him up and pulled him over backwards, dragging him out of the building face up."

"So, I don't get it," replied Flynn.

"Our teenager was killed outside, pulled in here face down, dripping blood from his face, and placed where the pool is located. The bat, if it was the murder weapon, was brought in and placed next to the body. One of the firemen stepped on it."

"It fits."

They retreated to the outside. The ground at the base of the steps had been trampled until some of the grass was flat. They could not see from where the trail of blood came. Immediately the technicians were on their knees looking for bloodstained grass. They found another pool about three feet from the bottom step.

"Ah ha," surmised Houseman. "Rodriguez was struck down here, the fresh facial wounds spewed blood onto the ground while the killer opened the door and maybe took the bat inside. He returned and pulled Rodriguez inside. Then don't forget, he lit that smudge pot at the front door."

"Why did he do that?" asked Flynn.

"Only one reason, to draw attention to what he had done. But I don't know why he would want to do that. In fact, there are a lot of whys about this case that I don't understand. Let's go to the morgue and see what the coroner has found."

Around 10:30 Flynn and Houseman arrived at the morgue. Nothing had yet been done that day. The previous night Rodriguez's body had been stripped and placed in storage. The detective asked for the clothing and personal effects. He emptied the bag onto a table. An envelope and clothing were all there was. The envelope contained a gold chain, crucifix, and an earring, nothing else.

Flynn immediately thought robbery. "No wallet, no money, and no watch," he noted.

"Yes, but they left the jewelry, and remember he was playing baseball in these clothes. He wouldn't be carrying those other things anyway."

Houseman fumbled through the clothing, sweatshirt and pants, shorts, and jock. There was a cardholder, a nametag, or business card holder pinned to the seat of the pants. Inside was a baseball trading card. The card was that of Cito Gaston. "Odd," said Houseman. "Why would a guy wear a card on his tail while he was playing ball? Why would a kid wear a card on his tail anytime? Plus, another reference to baseball. This card was put on his pants. This behavior is crazy. Maybe some type of signature."

Houseman was now in his Chief's office reviewing what he had found. The Chief wondered out loud about the Cito Gaston baseball card. "A clue? I know it's a long shot, Frank, but call up to Worcester and compare notes. Baseball pops up at every turn here. See what they think. Get right back, OK?"

Houseman's counterpart on the Worcester force, the detective assigned to the murder, was on vacation. "Like I'm gonna be soon," he said to himself. He asked for the property room and then for a list of the victim's effects. He had it faxed to him.

Ordinary enough items were on the list, except there was a cardholder with a single baseball card. The card had been pinned to the victim's shirt.

"He may be right. That baseball SABR guy may be right. These killings may be related. The killer leaves a signature, and it's a baseball card. He sticks it on his victim. Chief, we've got a serial killer on our hands. We need to check out this Campbell fellow. He knows too much. Our killer is killing people where there was some kind of special game. He might be involved. Otherwise, he may be able to help us. Let's get him in here and find out where the next game will be."

"Not for us, Frank. I'd say you're right, and this mess is the work of a serial killer. And besides Rhode Island, he hit in Massachusetts. You're welcome to get your Campbell man in here, because he may be involved. But I'll have the FBI on this pronto. This one's bigger than us, Frank."

★ ★ ★ ★ ★

Fred Campbell had other problems to handle. He was in the courtroom to testify against a computer programmer. Fred had been called in by bank management to perform a fraud audit. While tracing computer entries back to the source documents, Campbell found that accrued interest for a savings account did not match the detailed total printed on a report. Campbell suspected either an accounting clerk or a computer programmer.

Eventually, Campbell found that the programmer had used a salami technique to steal more than $100,000 from bank customers without their knowledge. Using a modified accrued interest computer program, the programmer took twenty cents in interest for each account above $300. The doctored program was switched with the proper computer program and left for the night operator to run. Each morning the programmer switched the programs.

The programmer did not add the stolen interest to a valid savings account. The culprit added the purloined interest to her mother-in-law's checking account. Since the programmer was an authorized signer, she was able to withdraw the funds. Because most customers do not check their savings interest precisely, this fraud had gone undetected for a number of years.

The Computer Security Institute conservatively estimates that computer crime in 1999 costs corporations and government agencies more than $100 million. Campbell always told his clients to be proactive and spend time and money on security products and services. Why wait and incur heavy financial losses and public relations disasters later?

Campbell's claim to fame was forensic accounting or litigation support services. The American Institute of Certified Public Accountants defines a forensic accountant as a fraud auditor or investigative accountant who searches for evidence of criminal conduct or assists in the determination of, or rebuttal of, claimed damages. Much of Campbell's outside income was from plaintiffs and their lawyers. They hired him to provide investigative accounting services, to prepare financial analyses in support of their case, and to serve as an expert witness in the courtroom. He was a formidable opponent for the other attorney to cross-examine. The job paid well, but it took a pretty thick hide. The job was not a sideline for the faint-hearted.

Now he did more than just disputed divorce-settlement work. His areas included antitrust analysis, general consulting, and cost allocation. Anytime someone had to dig into the books and records, he was available. Super Accountant Campbell! Maybe he should get a special cape to wear like Superman. Or was that Batman? He packed a HP 12-C pocket calculator and a notebook computer.

Today's testimony would be delicate. Computer records had to be admissible in the courtroom. Since the incriminating evidence was discovered in computerized accounting files, lack of diligent preparation could result in the evidence not being admissible. A hearsay rule prevents the introduction of unreliable second-hand testimony in the courtroom. There are about twenty exceptions to this hearsay rule, including business records. The computer records must be prepared regularly, and management must rely on its relevance and accuracy in making business decisions.

But Campbell liked the grueling task of preparing beforehand and participating in a courtroom battle over auditing principles. There was the challenge to react and respond to the many innuendoes and leading questions asked by the opposing attorney. The stress probably was not worth the daily fees he received, but he enjoyed it. He sometimes imagined the opposing attorney to be a black-clad medieval knight racing toward him on horseback with a long, sharp lance. He always toppled the vicious knight in his daydreams, though not always in court.

The culprit in this fraud was female, which was somewhat unusual. Most fraud perpetrators are college educated white males, according to a study by the Association of Certified Fraud Examiners (ACFE). Almost three-fourths of the offenses are committed by men. Losses caused by managers are four times higher than those caused by employees, and media losses caused by executives are 16 times those of their employees. The most costly abuses occur in organizations with fewer than 100 employees, and the average organization loses more than $9 a day per employee to fraud and abuse. According to ACFE, fraud and abuse cost U.S. organizations more than $400 billion annually. Such huge losses create jobs for forensic accountants, internal auditors, and external auditors.

Chapter 3

Providence

The distinction between pilferage and outright theft is a small one. But the dollars involved are not necessarily small. According to a 1992 GAO report, the Department of Defense alone maintains an inventory of at least $100 billion in spare parts, clothing, medical supplies, and fuel. And even though the defense department doesn't classify pilferage as a major problem, its annual inventory shrinkage alone runs a billion or two a year—enough money to fund the annual budgets of a few smaller nations.

Joseph T. Wells

Providence Police Chief George Crawford insisted that Frank Houseman call in SABR's Fred Campbell. Crawford knew this matter was a FBI case, but he would have liked nothing better than to be one-up on the Feds. He thought he really might have the gem of his career in this case, especially as he thought about Campbell's chance discovery of the "Worcester/Providence Coincidence." Or was it chance? He smiled at the possibility of *him* solving an FBI murder case and handing the perpetrator over to his Federal counterparts. That would be a crowning achievement to an otherwise lackluster career.

As requested, Houseman quickly arranged for a meeting with Campbell. Fred came over to the station around 11:30 a.m. and assembled with the detective and the chief in the latter's office. With them was a stenographer and another detective. After the introductions, the chief harshly asked the first question.

"Why are you such an expert on all of those perfect games pitched in 1880?"

"Sir, I'm not an expert, but I do know how rare and special perfect games are. There have only been a handful in the entire history of the game. After his perfect game, David Cone said you have a better chance at winning the lottery than pitching a perfect game."

"Whaddya, mean a handful?" scowled the chief.

"Only about 16," was Fred's reply. He went on, "I do know about the first two. The second was right here in Providence by Monte Ward. The game was pitched only five days after the perfect game tossed by Lee Richmond. Just five days apart."

"What about the rest of the perfect games in 1880?" asked the Chief.

Again the polite reply. "Sir, there were no others in 1880. In fact, there were no others in that century. They are *extremely* rare."

"Oh, really?" was all Chief Crawford could muster. He immediately realized the ignorance he had exhibited.

"Well, yes. And I do know a bit more about the first two. They happened right here in our area, and the murders seem to coincide. Look at these dates and places."

Fred pulled a well-worn copy of *The Complete Baseball Record Book* from his briefcase, apologizing that it was the 1999 edition. "Here's the list." He pointed to the list of all of the perfect games.

Perfect Games—Nine or More Innings

Sixteen perfect games have been pitched in major championship play including one in the 1956 World Series by Don Larsen of the New York Yankees, but not including Harvey Haddix's 12-inning effort for Pittsburgh in 1959, Pedro Martinez's 9-inning game in 1995, and Ernest

Shore in 1917. The perfect games follow, with the letter in parentheses after the date indicating home or away:

1880—J. Lee Richmond, Wor. vs. Clev., N.L., June 12 (H)

1880—John Ward, Prov. vs. Buff., N.L., June 17 (H)

1904—Denton Young, Bos. vs. Phil., A.L., May 5 (H)

1908—Adrian Joss, Clev. vs. Chi., A.L., Oct. 2 (H)

1917—Ernest Shore, Bos. vs. Wash., A.L., June 23 (H)*

1922—Charles Robertson, Chi. vs. Det., A.L., Apr. 30 (A)

1956—Don Larsen, N.Y., A.L., vs. Bkn., N.L. (World Series), Oct. 8 (H)

1959—Harvey Haddix, Pit. vs. Mil., N.L., May 26 (A)*

1964—James Bunning, Phil. vs. N.Y., N.L., June 21 (A)

1965—Sanford Koufax, L.A. vs. Chi., N.L., Sept. 9 (H)

1968—James A. Hunter, Oak. vs. Min., A.L., May 8 (H)

1981—Leonard H. Barker, Clev. vs. Tor., A.L., May 15 (H)

1984—Michael A. Witt, Cal. vs. Tex., A.L., Sept. 30 (A)

1988—Thomas L. Browning, Cin. vs. L.A., N.L., Sept. 16 (H)

1991—Dennis Martinez, Mont. vs. L.A., N.L., July 28 (A)

1994—Kenny Rogers, Texas vs. Calif., A.L., July 28 (H)

1995—Pedro Martinez, Mont. vs. San Diego, N.L., June 3 (A)*

1998—David Wells, N.Y. vs. Minn., A.L., May 17 (H)

1999—David Cone, N.Y. vs. Mont., A.L., July 18 (H)

[*The Shore, Martinez, and Haddix entries were penciled into the book.]

"That's all the perfect games," Fred said. "The Shore, Haddix, and Martinez games are only unofficial perfect games. Basically, you have to pitch the entire game *and* win to be official."

"Why are you so interested in perfect games?" asked the Chief.

"I guess I'm not really all that interested in perfect games, but I do know a lot about these first two."

"Why?"

"As I said, they're the only nineteenth century ones, which is my main baseball interest. Sometimes they are forgotten. Newspapers often list only the modern ones. And they were local, so to speak, for me. I've studied and written a great deal about the Providence team that represented us in the major league."

"I've heard about that," replied Crawford.

"Yes, the Grays played in the National League from 1878 until 1885. They won the pennant in 1879 and 1884 and also won what might be called the first World Series. And Lee Richmond played in Providence, too."

"I thought he was at Worcester?" questioned the Chief.

"Well yes," replied Fred. "But he played college ball here at Brown. He pitched against Ward and the Grays many times while a collegian."

"Colleges and professional teams played each other in those days?" asked Crawford.

"Sure, in exhibitions, mostly pre-season. That still happens some today. Back then, the colleges could hold their own, too. But what has always fascinated me about the first two perfect games is the relationship between the pitchers, Richmond and Ward."

"What do you mean?" asked Detective Houseman.

"As I said, the two knew each other and played against each other a lot. Two of the top pitchers in the country right here in Providence—one a pro and one an amateur. They competed in more than one way."

"How so?"

"Directly against each other in games," explained Fred, "and, I think, for the notoriety or top billing, so to speak. I think they were always trying to outdo one another. From all that I've read, they were always at odds. Their rivalry was intense. Maybe that's why Ward's perfect game happened."

"How do you figure that?" Crawford asked again.

"Two perfect games in five days defies all odds. Look at the list. Lee Richmond pitches a perfect game something probably not thought possible before he did it. Games were typically high scoring, and errors were much more common. Fielders played barehanded, you know."

"No kidding?" mused the Chief.

"No kidding," smiled Fred.

Police Chief George Crawford did not care about the game himself and had little use for any sport. But he was quickly coming to appreciate Fred's vast knowledge of the game and its history.

Fred wondered how a person could know so little about our national pastime.

Campbell went on, "Anyway, just five days after Richmond's gem, Ward gets his perfect game. There's not another one for twenty-four years until Cy Young tosses one in 1904, and not another one in the National League until 1964! I think that, just maybe, Ward wanted to prevent Richmond from being one up on him."

"Interesting concept," mused Crawford. "If you'll excuse us a minute, please." Crawford motioned for Houseman, and the two left the room.

Standing in the hallway but away from the Chief's office, the puzzled Chief spoke. "Ok, there are two murders done in the same manner and on dates on which perfect games were pitched in 1880. They're tied together by baseball cards pinned to the victims."

"Not to mention the crime sites; both were near where the 1880 games happened," inserted Houseman.

"And what's the motive? What's the motive, Frank? I don't have a clue at this point. Do you?"

"Not even a guess."

Crawford continued, "We've got definite connections here; too many ties to be a coincidence. But what obscure ties they are. And we've got a man in there that knows every detail. He knows more than anyone should about such remote stuff. He's even telling us about the psychology of Ward's pitching over 100 years ago. I think our Mr. Campbell might even know more about these murders."

"But if he did them, why would he step forward?" queried Houseman.

"I don't know the answer to that either, but let's try to find out."

They walked back into the room.

"I know you've been here a long time already Mr. Campbell, but if you told us something about this ballgame of Ward's, maybe we could piece something together."

"I can do that easily, sir. I've brought material on both of them. Here's a story on Ward's perfect game written by Fleet

Walker. He's the authority on perfect games. He's studied and written about them all. He's an internal auditor for the New York Yankees."

"Really?" asked the Chief.

"Oh yes. In fact, he was with me at Worcester for the recreation game there June 12."

Campbell paused, and then said, "Actually little is written about the second perfect game because of modest reporting. The opposing pitcher for the weak-hitting Buffalo team was James 'Pud' Galvin. Although he died at the age of 47, he was the father of eleven children. Pud, as in pudding, Galvin pitched 5,959 innings, winning 361 games in 14 seasons.

"Shortstop Mike Moynahan, Buffalo's best hitting player at .330 was not even in the line-up. A large crowd of 2,000 watched Ward toss his perfect game, striking out only two players.

"Ward was traded to the New York Giants after the 1882 season, and he only pitched for a total of seven seasons. He became a manager of the Giants, and then managed the Brooklyn team. He became a union organizer, a club owner, and after retirement, a lawyer."

"A union organizer?" the Chief asked.

"Right," answered Campbell. "Many of baseball's strikes can be traced to John Ward. The reserve clause came into baseball in 1879, when the owners agreed to reserve five players on each team. In October 1885, nine players on the New York Giants revolted by forming the Brotherhood of Professional Base Ball Players and electing Ward their first president. Although unionism spread to the other teams, the owners eventually placed the reserve clause into the players' contract. The owners and players still argue and strike over the reserve clause. There was a strike in 1994, as you may recall."

"What is the reserve clause?"

"That's a clause that was once included in all baseball contracts to keep players tied to a team. But in 1974 an arbitrator, Peter M. Seitz, ruled that Oakland owner, Charles Finley, reneged on Catfish Hunter's contract, and Hunter had the right to terminate the playing agreement. Hunter declared himself a free agent and signed with the Yankees for $2.5 million. Catfish Hunter, another perfect game pitcher, was baseball's first free agent.

"Seitz ruled in favor of two other pitchers, Andy Messersmith and Dave McNally, and eventually a federal court struck down the reserve clause. However, even today for the first six years players must work for the one club, without the right to move from one team to another one. After six years a player becomes a free agent and may move from one team to another team.

"Of course, the minimum salary is $200,000 and the average salary was $1.72 million in 1999; still there's been nine strikes in twenty-two years."

"Mr. Campbell," the Chief said, "you said you were an accountant. What firm do you work for?"

"Oh, I have my own accounting firm." Fred handed the Chief a business card.

Crawford read the card. Fred Campbell, CPA, DABFA, CFE, Forensic Accounting.

"What is forensic accounting?" Crawford asked. "Are you like Quincy, the television pathologist who used autopsies and pathology to find murder clues?

"Somewhat like Quincy. DABFA is a fancy term for forensic accountant. CFE means Certified Fraud Examiner. I look behind the facade and do not accept accounting records at their face value. Paul Regan, a forensic accountant in San Francisco, says that 'we work in a quiet, isolated world. It's a tough environment, but it can be pretty exciting.' Basically, forensic accounting covers two broad areas: investigative accounting and litigation support."

"So you help lawyers," Crawford interrupted.

"That's part of my services. I examine and interpret evidence and facts in legal cases and offer expert opinions regarding my findings in the courtroom. But I do more. I'm like a detective who hunts for cooked books. You know—fraud, manipulated figures, false invoices, divorce conflicts, phony computer programs...."

Crawford raised his hand. "Stop. No more lectures. I have a murderer to capture."

Chapter 4

Boston

Internal auditors must help their organizations to make informed decisions and to take intelligent actions on every aspect of business contingency planning, especially testing. While nothing can completely mitigate the devastation of some disasters and emergencies, the comfort level of most managements will be decidedly elevated when internal auditors can help to provide assurance that appropriate safeguards are in place and working.

Kevin Mead, CIA

Providence Police Chief George Crawford didn't want to make the call. He knew this was a blockbuster case, and he did not want to give it away. He had really thought that Fred Campbell was a legitimate suspect, but he had given up on that theory when he discovered that Campbell had worked for the FBI for several years. Campbell knew more about baseball than anyone the Chief had ever known. Maybe Campbell's forensic background would be helpful with the case.

And Fred Campbell had helped. He had convinced Crawford and Detective Houseman that there was a definite connection between the Rodriguez murder and that of Fred Ketchum in Worcester. This Fleet Walker had been on location at one of the deaths. Could he be the murderer? They were almost certainly killed by the same person, who used a baseball bat and attached a baseball card to each person. Apparently, the killer wanted his crimes to be recognized—he killed one person in a public place and set a smoke bomb to draw attention to the other.

The chief sent copies of the police reports, photographic evidence, pathologist's report, and other forensic data to the National Center for the Analysis of Violent Crime in Quantico, Virginia and requested a profile. His 10-section questionnaire was directed to the Violent Criminal Apprehension Program. VICAP is the FBI's multi-million dollar computer system which has a serial crime databank, housed in the Washington, D.C. headquarters of the FBI. The purpose of VICAP is to store, collate, and analyze all unsolved homicide crimes reported to NCAVC by law enforcement agencies.

Established by President Reagan on June 21, 1984 to identify and track repeat killers, NCAVC is located 60 feet underground in a former nuclear bunker below the FBI Academy on the U.S. Marine Corps base at Quantico, Virginia. The FBI Academy covers a 600-acre guarded enclave in the Virginia countryside.

Quantico automatically submits any new case to the VICAP computer, which matches it with other cases in the appropriate modus operandi category. Overnight, the computer checks the new case and sends the top ten matching cases back to Quantico. This template is received by the Behavioral Science Investigative Support wing at Quantico, and a VICAP analyst determines if any of the top ten matches are linked with the new murder. In other words, is there a likelihood that a serial killer is involved? BSIS found four possible matches with the recent case sent by Chief Crawford and sent a profile of the suspect to Providence. BSIS also informed the other four law enforcement agencies, giving them details of the Providence homicide.

Serial killers fit certain profiles, and systematic profiling techniques are used by the FBI analysts at Quantico. For example, Jack the Ripper had a modus operandi of slitting prostitute's throats in post-mortem mutilations. Pedro Alonzo Lopez, the

Monster of the Andes, targeted pre-pubescent girls. This Ecuadorian peasant holds the numerical record of about 350 kills. His closest known competitors in modern history were possibly Henry Lee Lucas and Ottis Toole with 200 plus kills as a tag team. Between 1979 and 1983, FBI agents conducted a detail behavioral study of 36 serial killers and spree killers in order to develop behavioral characteristics and habits of these monsters. This interviewing of notorious killers is an on-going process to develop behavioral traits. Interviewing techniques also are important for internal auditors, since the people they interview may not always be honest.

How do you spot a liar? Dr. Paul Ekman, a professor of psychology at the University of California at San Francisco says you have to focus on more than one clue. The following are signals that someone is not telling the truth:

Lack of eye contact.

Throat clearing.

Signs of guilt, despair, anger, fear, or distress.

Vocal pitch changes.

Unusual pauses in speech.

Nonverbal signs, such as hand shaking or fist-clenching.

Of course, an experienced liar may not show any of these signs, and a person may show some of these signs and not be lying.

Each of the ten Quantico senior analysts, called Supervisory Special Agents, is responsible for a given area nationwide, and they have a force of more than 100 specially trained FBI agents throughout the U.S. known as Field Profile Coordinators. Special Agent John Quincy at Quantico was assigned the task to profile the type of person responsible for the baseball killings. VICAP Analyst John Quincy worked from his office in Quantico near the BSIS computer center. His function was to analyze, but not investigate, serial crimes in Eastern U.S. He pulled up robot PROFILER on his computer screen and began to compare the automatic profile and his human profile of the possible baseball killer.

The baseball murders appeared to be motiveless homicides. Motiveless murders began to emerge in the U.S. in the 1940s and '50s. Ruth Steinhagen had a crush from afar for two years on Eddie Waitkus, the unmarried first baseman of the Philadelphia Phillies. In June 1949, the pretty nineteen-year-old brunette asked the ball player to see her briefly in The Edgewater Beach Hotel in Chicago. In her room she shot Eddie in the head with a rifle. Her reason: "she wanted the thrill of killing him." Green fly is the name given to a baseball groupie, especially a woman, who with the pestering persistence of a fly follows a player away from the ballpark.

Quincy felt that the offender was a disorganized *asocial* killer based upon the crime scene evidence. There was no way to know if the killer had carried the baseball bat to the scene. If he had, such a characteristic would indicate an organized *nonsocial* type of killer. The more frenzied and less methodical manner of killing with the bat indicated an asocial type of offender. Killing quickly, leaving the bat and the body at the scene indicated a disorganized asocial person. A disorganized type is more of an opportunist.

The killer apparently was not a sex offender, probably a white male, high school dropout. The crimes appeared unlikely to be robbery, drug, or alcohol-related. The absence of sex, torture, or mutilation pointed away from an organized killer, but the kills in different cities meant that the offender cruised away from his home or place of employment. Probabilities indicated to Quincy that the killer was a loner. He was probably a nice, quiet male with few interpersonal skills, possibly unemployed. Yet if he was killing only on the dates of perfect games, he was an organized nonsocial type, who had an interest in or connection to baseball. Apparently he chose his victims completely at random, so without a relationship between the killer and victim, authorities were missing one of the most important clues in solving a murder case. Since the murders took place quickly and without ritual, the killer was probably young—in his twenties. Older killers take a longer time with their victims.

Quincy assigned William Douglass, a Field Profile Coordinator, to visit and meet with the Providence officials. Douglass was a member of the elite A team in Quantico.

★ ★ ★ ★ ★

Police Chief Crawford did not know Federal Bureau of Investigation Special Agent William Douglass. Douglass had been transferred to the National Center for the Analysis of Violent Crime at the FBI Academy in Quantico, Virginia in 1989. The chief had related only a few details about the murders to Douglass over the phone. Douglass had been an FBI Agent 17 years, and he instantly recognized that this situation was a matter for the FBI. However, he first had to decide if the murders had been done by a serial killer, and second, he had to develop a profile of the offender. Such a psychological packet would focus any investigation in order to speed-up a successful resolution of the matter.

They met the next morning at the FBI offices: Douglass, Crawford, Houseman, and FBI Providence Agency Director Frank Fennelly. Douglass was approaching forty with no grey hair on his short reddish-brown hair. He was dark complexed with bright, hazel eyes. His six-foot frame carried about 175 pounds.

Houseman, at Crawford's request, had invited Fred Campbell, but Fred was left cooling his heels as the law enforcement officers met initially. After a few minutes however, Campbell was asked to join the meeting.

Frank Fennelly was a no-nonsense type of person, interested in the facts and nothing else. He immediately saw the factual connection between the murders, but wanted to know the basis for the facts. That, of course, was the reason for the invitation for Fred Campbell to join the group.

Fred entered with his trusty *Sporting News* record book under his arm. Fennelly asked about Fred's baseball interest and apparent perfect game expertise. Fred related matter of factly, his Society for American Baseball Research work. He again declined to declare himself a perfect game "expert" and said, "If you want a perfect game expert, better get Fleet Walker. He knows everything about perfect games."

Frank Fennelly listened intently, and agreed with Fred's suggestion to consult Fleet Walker. "But, in this case, I understand you have the basics—the record of all the perfect games ever pitched."

"Well, not exactly as you say," replied Fred, "but I do have a reference that lists all of the perfect games pitched in the major leagues."

"Oh, yes, in the major leagues. I see," Fennelly went on. "May I see the list?"

Fred handed him the book. Frank opened it to the marked page. No one spoke as Frank pondered the list. He asked the group's impression, but realized that he had the book in his hand and the others could not see it. He awkwardly attempted to share the volume. He then called his secretary, Shannon Hajduk, and asked her to copy the page on to a transparency. As she left, Frank asked Agent Douglass to set up a screen and overhead projector. Both were in the room and quickly made ready. Nearly as quickly, the transparency was ready and flashed onto the large screen. Shannon had placed it upside down at first. She corrected the mistake and left the room.

The whole group stared at the list.

Fennelly finally broke the silence. "What does all of this mean? We know we've had murders in the cities where the first two games were, and they occurred on the dates of the games themselves. We suspect that the same person did them both because of the similar methods of killing and, most importantly, both had a baseball card pinned to them."

"Fred, what about the cards?" asked Fennelly. "Any connection between them, uh the players on them and these games?"

"I don't know. I mean, I don't know who the players were," replied Fred.

"Nate Colbert and Cito Gaston," interjected Crawford.

"I remember them both. They were National League sluggers, mostly at San Diego, I think."

"Any connection to the games?" Fennelly again asked.

"What games?" Fred asked back. "The Worcester and Providence games, or all of them?"

"Good question. I meant Worcester and Providence, but maybe I should have meant all of them. We've been looking at 1880, but maybe this problem is bigger than that. Just maybe we've got a killer that's going down the list."

Fred immediately agreed. "There have been at least two other deaths in stadiums this year on perfect game dates."

"That would mean we could expect the killer to strike again in Boston. That's the next perfect game, in 1904," Agent Douglass almost shouted as he looked at the transparency. He went on, "But we'll have to wait nearly a year to find out." They were all once again staring at the illuminated screen of perfect game data. "That's when this Cy Young pitched the third perfect game."

"Not so sure," replied Fennelly. Now everyone shifted their stares to Fennelly.

Crawford said, "Whaddya mean?"

"Perhaps he has already done it," proposed Fennelly.

"What do you mean?" asked Douglass.

"I mean that perhaps on April 30 or May 5 or May 8 or May 15 or on May 17 there was a murder in Detroit or Boston or Oakland or in Cleveland that fits the Worcester and Providence murders. How about Boston? That's close to us. Was there a murder in Boston on May 5?"

"I don't know if there was or not," was all that Douglass could say.

"Of course you don't. Why would you?" said Fennelly. "But why don't we find out, pronto?"

Agent Douglass left the room to call the Boston police. Fennelly huddled with Campbell. "If I'm right, we have a serial killer who hasn't been recognized as such. Do you have any idea, from a baseball point of view, why anyone would do this?"

"None whatsoever," replied Fred.

"Help me look at the list for clues. We have listed year, pitcher, teams, league, date, home or away, and score. So far we have year and league in common. And...date and city of the game. And also a connection to the game site. At a similar game in Worcester there was a monument designated for the actual game site. In Providence the murder happened within sight of the actual game location. If we have a killer working from your list, for whatever reason, he could be doing it in cities where the games happened in the order they occurred. Or if Douglass finds that there was a murder in Boston on May 5, he would be doing them all within this year. But in date order. Follow?"

Fennelly had just completed his sentence when Douglass returned to the room. "There was a murder in Boston on May 5," he reported. "I spoke with the desk Sergeant who didn't have a lot of details. Detective Lieutenant Charlie Krehmeyer who's heading the investigation will be calling back. At any rate, there was a brutal beating death of a college student. It's a big story there."

"Did you get the location?" asked Fennelly. "Was it near Fenway Park?"

"I don't know, but the body was found at the kid's campus."

Fred Campbell broke in, "Sir, Fenway Park would not be the place where Cy Young's perfect game was pitched. Fenway Park wasn't built until 1912."

"Well where, then?" asked Fennelly.

"Don't know, offhand," replied Fred. "There have been a number of parks in Boston, including some early ones in the south end. I can find that out though. I could call Alma at home."

"Alma?" questioned Fennelly.

"My wife. She does this type of research too. She can check a reference on parks. As former Yankee manager Casey Stengel once said, 'You can look it up.'"

"Please do," suggested Fennelly.

"How about the game itself? What do you know about it?"

"Nothing really, but, again, I can find out details. As I told the police, Fleet Walker of the Yankees is the authority on perfect games. I'm sure he will help. Should I ask?"

"Yes, please do that too, Fred. We really appreciate all you are doing to help us."

"And Bill, hurry up that reply from Boston. Get the initial report or something. And also Bill, send Shannon in, please."

The office's only secretary, Shannon returned as requested.

"Shannon, would you take this list and arrange it in chronological order by date; not as it is now by year, but by date. OK?"

"Got it."

"Never mind all the asterisks and footnotes. I'm surprised all that stuff is necessary for perfect games. You'd think the list would be perfectly orderly, no exceptions. Anyway, just date, year, pitcher, teams, and score. And put it on a transparency as you did this one."

"Right away," was Shannon's snappy response. Fennelly had set everything he could think of in motion. He went back to his own office, picking up a cup of coffee on the way. He took a cigarette from his desk. He'd been "quitting" for several months and didn't smoke in front of anyone else. He sat alone, but he didn't smoke. He just held the cigarette captive. He sat and thought.

A quiet knock at his door let Fennelly know that Shannon had completed her task. She told him that she had added a couple of items for each game, but that all entries were consistent. He returned to the conference room where the projector still cast a bright light on the screen. He substituted the new transparency. He pondered Shannon's work.

Perfect Games — Nine or More Innings

April 30 1922   Charles Robertson, Chi. vs. Det., A.L. (A)

May 5 1904   Denton Young, Bos. vs. Phil., A.L. (H)

May 8 1968   James A. Hunter, Oak. vs. Min., A.L. (H)

May 15 1981   Leonard H. Barker, Clev. vs. Tor., A.L. (H)

May 17 1998   David Wells, N.Y. vs. Minn., A.L. (H)

★May 26 1959   Harvey Haddix, Pit. vs. Mil., N.L. (A)

★June 3 1995   Pedro Martinez, Mont. vs. S.D., N.L. (A)

June 12 1880   J. Lee Richmond, Wor. vs. Clev., N.L. (H)

June 17 1880   John Ward, Prov., vs. Buff., N.L. (H)

June 21 1964	James Bunning, Phil. vs. N.Y., N.L. (A)
*June 23 1917	Ernest Shore, Bos. vs. Wash., A.L. (H)
July 18 1999	David Cone, N.Y. vs. Mont., A.L. (H)
July 28 1991	Dennis Martinez, Mont. vs. L.A., N.L. (A)
July 28 1994	Kenny Rogers, Tex. vs. Calif., A.L. (H)
Sept. 9 1965	Sanford Koufax, L.A. vs. Chi., N.L. (H)
Sept. 16 1988	Thomas L. Browning, Cin. vs. L.A., N.L. (H)
Sept. 30 1984	Michael A. Witt, Cal. vs. Tex., A.L. (A)
Oct. 2 1908	Adrian Joss, Clev. vs. Chi., A.L. (H)
Oct. 8 1956	Don Larsen, N.Y. vs. Bkn., World Series (H)

* Unofficial perfect games.

Fennelly was interrupted by Bill Douglass. "I've got more details, and I think they fit."

"Well, go ahead," pressed Fennelly.

"I spoke with Krehmeyer in Boston, and he's sending his complete file. They're stumped. No leads at all."

"Never mind all that," Fennelly waved his hand. "We may know more about the killer than he does. How about the basics?"

"OK. The victim was a student at Northeastern University, in Boston. Name of Edward Hill Rothermil. Called Bobby. He was from Barre, Vermont. He was found on campus the afternoon of May 5, behind one of the main buildings, in a fairly well traveled area. The body was found right after the killing. Krehmeyer thinks the killer wanted the body found immediately for some reason. And the most important point, he was beaten to death with a baseball bat that was left at the scene. Salt was sprinkled around the head of the student. I asked

Krehmeyer about a baseball card. There was one. He remembered because everyone he talked to said Bobby had no interest in baseball at all."

"Wow, it all fits," said Fennelly. How about the card. Who's was it?"

"Gerry Jestadt."

"Never heard of him, but that's no surprise," frowned Fennelly. "Maybe Fred knows. No matter now; all the rest ties together perfectly."

As if queued, Fred re-entered the room.

"Who's Gerry Jestadt, Fred?"

"I don't know the name. Why? Should I?"

"Baseball player. His card was found on a body in Boston on May 5."

"Oh no! These killings are tied together, but I don't know of Jestadt. Rather an obscure name, but I can check," Fred said.

"You seem to be able to check everything."

"Baseball is superbly documented. The game lends itself to that, you know. Lot of analytics in baseball, like accounting and auditing. Debits on the left; credits on the right. Ratio analysis."

"How about the park in Boston?" asked Fennelly shaking his head.

"Got it from Alma. There were two parks close together in Boston in use in 1904. The National League park, where the Braves played, was the South End Grounds. The American League Park was just a few blocks away, called the Huntington Avenue Baseball Grounds. It was home to the Red Sox before Fenway Park, and that's where Cy Young's perfect game happened."

"And the park is no longer there?" asked Fennelly.

"Don't know for sure" replied Fred, "but I'll bet it's long gone. It was on Huntington Avenue at Rogers Avenue which is now Forsyth Street...maybe that will help you find out. The infield grass was transferred from the Huntington stadium to Fenway Park."

"I'll bet I know what's there," said Fennelly. "Bill, call Northeastern University and put them on the speaker phone."

As instructed, William Douglass first called information for the number and then dialed Northeastern University. Frank Fennelly determined from the operator who answered that Northeastern bordered on both Huntington Avenue and Forsyth Street. Frank then knew, but the operator could not confirm, that the campus was on the former ball park site. She knew who could however, and connected Fennelly with Edward W. Seward, the Facilities Manager at Northeastern. Seward was the man to talk with because he was familiar with the police investigation of the Rothermil murder. He also knew the campus and its history.

Fennelly asked about the Huntington Avenue Baseball Grounds.

Seward had the answers. "Oh, yes. That's where the old American League park was located. Our indoor athletic building, the Godfrey Lowell Cabot Physical Education Center is precisely where the old field was located. A room in the building is called the World Series Room and is devoted to mementos of the 1901 to 1911 era. And a plaque commemorating the location of where the original right field foul pole used to stand was unveiled in May 1956. The pole stood just outside this building where the Rothermil lad was found. There's a statue of Cy Young near Huntington Avenue on the Northeastern campus. That's not too far from the indoor Athletic building."

"Pay dirt," Fennelly exclaimed. "We've got it! We've got the pattern! So much is falling into place, I can scarcely keep it straight in my head."

"Fred, you've done great on the park. Were you able to get us anything on the game itself? There's still the signature of the baseball card."

"Sure, I called Walker, and he faxed us one of his articles about the game." Fred handed the fax pages to Fennelly, who began reading.

Denton True "Cy" Young

May 5, 1904

by M. Fleet Walker

Twenty-four years passed before the third perfect game was pitched—the first in the American League. This flawless performance was pitched under what were close to modern baseball rules. The pitching distance was 60 feet, six inches, and four balls resulted in a walk. The pitcher's box was eliminated and replaced by a slab 24 inches by 6 inches. Beginning in 1901 in the National League and 1903 in the American League, a foul ball was considered to be a strike. The baseball, however, did not have a cork-center (not until 1910 in the National League), and the era from about 1900 through 1919 became known as the dead ball period. It was legal for the pitcher to add substances to the ball, and the spitball, mud ball, and scuffed balls were commonly thrown.

On Friday, May 5, 1904, the Boston Pilgrims were hosting the Philadelphia Athletics at their ballpark on Huntington Avenue. This ballpark, used before the construction of Fenway Park, is the current site of Northeastern University. A portly 37-year-old control pitcher, Cy Young, took a minimum number of warm-up pitches for the Red Sox in order to "save" his arm. Apparently his magic number was 12 warm-up pitches.

The Athletics' pitcher on that day was left-hander Rube Waddell, who was a notorious flake and spitball artist. During the next season on July 4, 1905, Rube would pitch 20 innings against Young and win, 4-2. During those 20 innings Young would *not* walk a batter. After the win, the future Hall of Famer Rube turned cartwheels off the mound. Cy was so tired that he could not lift his arm.

Manager and third baseman Jim Collins gave Young the pitching assignment on May 5, 1904. The six foot, two inch Young would win and make baseball history. He would pitch an awesome game. The plow boy from Gilmore, Ohio would face some strong hitters: Harry Davis, one of the league's top home-run threats, at first base; Lave Cross, shortstop; Socks Seybold, right field; Danny Hoffman, left field; and Danny Murphy, second base. The Athletics had been the champions of the American League in 1902.

No Philadelphia players had reached first base when Monte Cross came up to bat in the third inning. He hit what appeared to be a sure Texas Leaguer to right, but Buck Freeman snagged it on the run.

On his first time at bat in the game in the fourth, Danny Hoffman hit a long foul, which was caught by left fielder Patsy Dougherty. Later in the fourth, catcher Lou Criger made a difficult foul catch on a ball hit by first baseman Harry Davis. By the end of the seventh, Boston was ahead 3-0.

During the eighth, Danny Murphy's long fly ball to right field was foul by inches. In the ninth the spectators became silent as Monte Cross stepped to home plate. Cross watched a third strike go by, and the crowd roared. Cy struck out five batters during the last four innings.

Silence again when weak hitting Ossee Schreckengost dug in at home plate. Ossee smashed a grounder to shortstop Freddy Parent who gracefully made the long toss to first base for the second out. The crowd roared again.

Parent would bat 2-for-4 during the Young perfect games, but in 1908 he would go 0-for-3 on the losing Chicago team during the Addie Joss perfect game.

Poor Ossee Schreckengost would catch two *losing* perfect games—Philadelphia today and Chicago in 1908 against Addie Joss. He would go 0-for-5 in both games.

Manager Connie Mack let Rube Waddell—with an average of only .122—hit for himself. Connie Mack had been a catcher in the late 1800s, and he could simulate the sound of a foul tip to try to confuse umpires.

The first pitch to Waddell was a wide ball one. Rube swung and missed the second pitch. One and one. Two outs. Bottom of the ninth. The spectators were silent.

Waddell hit the third pitch toward center field. Young watched center fielder Chick Stahl run back and catch the ball. The crowd rushed on to the field and carried Young on their shoulders off the diamond.

The future Hall of Famer, did not realize that he had pitched a perfect game until center fielder Chick Stahl presented him with the last ball of the game. The *Boston Post* mistakenly reported this to be the first perfect game, and not the first perfect game under modern rules.

After Fennelly finished reading, he was exasperated. Nothing he read connected the now three murders. At least now he knew for whom they named the Cy Young awards after each baseball season. He decided to chart what he knew. He again called Shannon and asked her to again redo the list of perfect games. This time he asked her to include only the date and city in which the game was played. He made sure she understood the home and away notation on the list. He also asked her to include a third column to list the player found on the baseball card at each murder site. Finally, almost as an afterthought, he asked her to add a column for the murder victims. After she left to comply, the group re-examined Walker's work for clues to the murder in Boston, or to all of them. They found none. The group was silent.

Shannon returned with her latest revised transparency and placed it on the projector. All heads turned in unison to observe the new table.

Perfect Games—Nine or More Innings

Date	City	Player / Victim
April 30, 1992	Detroit	
May 5, 1904	Boston	Gerry Jestad / Edward Hill Rothermil
May 8, 1968	Oakland	
May 15, 1981	Cleveland	
May 17, 1998	New York	
*May 26, 1959	Milwaukee	
*June 3, 1995	San Diego	
June 12, 1880	Worcester	Nate Colbert / Fred Ketchum
June 17, 1880	Providence	Cito Gaston / Chico Rodriguez
June 21, 1964	New York	
*June 23, 1917	Boston	
July 18, 1999	New York	
July 28, 1991	Los Angeles	
July 28, 1994	Arlington	
Sept. 9, 1965	Los Angeles	
Sept. 16, 1988	Cincinnati	
Sept. 30, 1984	Arlington	
Oct. 2, 1908	Cleveland	
Oct. 8, 1956	New York	

* Unofficial games.

"That's it," said Fennelly. "We can see that our serial killer is going down the list and is killing someone at the perfect game site on the date of the game."

"We've more to do to confirm that," inserted Douglass. "We've got to check and see if there were any murders earlier in Detroit, Oakland, Cleveland, New York, Milwaukee, and San Diego."

"Fred," Fennelly stated, "These unofficial games that you penciled into the list; those guys don't get credit for the games. Right?"

"That is correct," Fred replied.

"OK, I see San Diego on June 3, 1995. The pitcher is this Martinez fellow. The perp is dropping San Diego baseball cards at the scenes of the crime. Martinez is mad, and he's taking revenge on baseball."

"I doubt it," replied Fred smiling. "Pedro is laughing all the way to the bank. Pedro Martinez now pitches for Boston, making $11 million each year. During the 1999 season I calculated for an article that he got $4,000 per pitch, whether he threw a ball, fired a strike, hurled a wild pitch, or hit a batter."

"We'll still check him out, but that's not the important thing," Fennelly continued.

"What is then?" asked the long silent George Crawford.

"Simple," answered Fennelly. "We must stop the murder planned for June 21 in New York. That's only two days from now. Who pitched the perfect game on June 21?"

"Jim Bunning," Fred responded quietly.

"Any more pertinent information about Cy Young?" Fennelly asked.

"He has one baseball record that will never be broken: winning 511 games. Of course, he holds the record for the most losses, 316, and the most complete games, 749. He once told a reporter that he had won more games than the reporter had ever seen." Fred answered. "He did have to stop playing baseball because he got so fat that he couldn't field bunts."

"Gee, that's helpful." Fennelly smiled as he thought about his small beer belly, or love handles as his wife called them.

Fred continued, "To appreciate how great Cy Young was during his career, let me compare him with Nolan Ryan. Ryan pitched for 27 years and Young 22. Ryan won 324 games and lost 292, versus Young's 511-315 win-loss record. Young had a 2.63 ERA, and Ryan had a 3.19 ERA." Young pitched 7,377 innings; Ryan only 5,387. Of course, Ryan is the strikeout king. Ryan had 5,714 strikeouts and Young only 2,796."

"What's ERA?" Douglass asked. "Equal Rights Amendment?"

"A very important statistic for a pitcher: earned run average. This term measures the number of earned runs that a pitcher allows every nine innings. Walter Johnson's 2.37 career ERA is the best. The smaller the better, like golf. Similar to the ratio of sales and returns allowance to total sales."

"How many perfect games for Johnson?"

"Zip," answered Fred.

"Any more ideas about this killer?" Fennelly interrupted.

Douglass spoke up. "Maybe it has to do with the word perfect. Perfect games. Perfect murders. Suppose someone is killing people randomly in order to prove they can commit perfect murders."

"I believe we have to consider a group of terrorists," Chief Crawford remarked. "You know, mom, apple pie, and baseball. How better to attack America. Stop people from going to baseball games. What a plot."

"Since we are speculating," Fred said, "let me mention an economic aspect of the Chief's theory. Suppose there's someone who does not like baseball. The baseball strike in 1994 was very bruising. Many people were injured. Arbitration battles. Contract squabbles. Soaring salaries. Declining skills."

"More recently twenty-two umpires lost their jobs in 1999 when Commissioner Bud Selig accepted the resignation of some umpires. The umpires' union and the replaced umpires were trying to force Major League Baseball to the bargaining table with the resignation strategy. However, some umpires did not resign, and many of the ones that at first resigned, withdrew their resignations. Bud Selig called their bluff, and one-third of the union ended up in early retirement. You have at least twenty-two unhappy former umpires.

"Or suppose one of the other professional sports," Fred continued, "for example football, basketball, or hockey would like to decrease attendance at baseball games, hoping to increase attendance in their sport area."

"Of course," Chief Crawford said, "we may soon receive a extortion note from someone demanding several million dollars. I recall seeing an old movie, Roller Coaster, in which the bad guy was systematically destroying roller coasters in various theme parks."

After the meeting Douglass asked Fred Campbell to talk to him about the labor problems. "I understand why the twenty-two umpires are suspect, but could there be a connection between the killings and the players' strike?"

"Well, there were many victims due to the strike—players, managers, owners, shareholders, employees, advertisers, and fans. But that's been some time ago. Only umpires benefited," Campbell replied with a wink.

"Why did the umpires benefit?" Douglass asked in bewilderment.

"They were contractually paid for the balance of the season. The men in blue didn't have to travel and call games. They received a long paid vacation. Your best suspects are the 22 unhappy umpires."

"We'll get a list of the 22 umpires. Easy to check their whereabouts. So what players were affected by the strike?" Douglass asked.

"The higher the salary, the more the player lost. But the players had a $200 million strike fund. However, there was $300 to $400 million in lost salaries to the players. The owners lost $750 million in revenues from the stadium and $300 million from lost ad revenue." Walker paused. "In 1995, the 28 major league teams supposedly lost $326 million, and in 1996, $185 million."

"The strike also stopped a number of potential records. Tony Gwynn might have hit .400. Gwynn finished with a .394 average, the highest since Ted Williams hit .406 in 1941. Ken Griffey, Jr. and Matt Williams might have beat Roger Maris' mark of 61 home runs before Mark McGwire and Sammy Sosa did. Atlanta pitching ace Greg Maddux had a 1.56 ERA, while the rest of the National League had a 4.21 ERA."

"So there was a labor-management conflict in 1994. What were the issues?"

"I need to give you some history. Players for the first two years are tied to one team by a reserve clause. From 3 to 6 years players are tied to the same team by the reserve clause, but they are eligible to have their salaries determined by final-offer arbitration. The arbitrator must select either the player's demand or the team's offer—not anything in between. After 6 years of major league service a player is eligible for free agency. The owner's long for a return to a longer reserve clause, or at least a salary cap.

"Owners maintain that player salaries are out-of-control. Baltimore outfielder Albert Belle earned $11.49 million in the 1999 season, hitting only 37 home runs. Boston pitcher Pedro

Martinez got $11 million, and the L.A. pitcher Kevin Brown, $10.7 million. In 1999, there were 348 baseball player million-aires. Keep in mind that the lowest paid team's payroll was Montreal, at $17 million."

Campbell continued. "Players also get promotional income, individual bonuses, team bonuses, licensing income, perquisites, and employee benefits. Aside from hitting 66 homers in 1998 and 63 in 1999, Sammy Sosa received about $11 million of en-dorsement income in 1999 along with his $9 million salary. A high school player out of Spring, Texas in 1999 received a $7 million signing bonus from the Florida Marlins. Josh Beckett is the kid's name."

"They make more than I do. What is licensing income?"

"From baseball card companies," Campbell said. "A player may make as much as $70,000 a year. Players get free tickets, cash incentives from athletic equipment companies, travel money, buffet-style meals, first-class travel and hotels, concerts, and vacations. They get superb pension payments. Unlike most employee pension plans that provide benefit payments geared to an employee's pay, baseball's plan is based solely on service. If a player plays for 10 years, the player gets the maximum of about $130,000. Doesn't matter if you are a superstar, a bullpen coach, or a utility outfielder. I'm talking about at least $10,000 per month for today's ten-year player. I would look for a player who had nine years of service, *but was not hired after the strike.* But they would have had to hold a grudge for a long time— since 1994."

"That's a good suggestion," Douglass said. "So the owners were right that the players were greedy."

"Well, the players say they have a right to market value. They point to the $500 million the owners make. No one puts a salary cap on Wayne Huizenga, the former owner of the Florida Marlins. Look at the amount of money that Bill Cosby, Oprah Winfrey, or Garth Brooks makes. Jerry Seinfeld got $1 million per episode. Don Fehr, the Director of the Players' Association, stated that if one goes through *The Sporting News* for the last 100 years, two things are always true. There are never enough pitchers, and nobody ever makes money."

"Did any players stick out as a result of the 1994 strike?" Douglass asked.

"Well the baseball owners filed unfair labor charges against three New York players: Bobby Bonilla, John Franco, and Scott Kamieniecki. Mets outfielder Bonilla said any player who crossed a picket line would end up in the East River. Franco, a Mets reliever, said he would go after with his fists anyone who broke ranks and attempted to play while the union was on strike. Yankee pitcher Kamieniecki said that after the strike he would throw at any players who broke rank."

"With the players' salaries so high today, how can the owners make any money?" Douglass asked incredulously.

"Taxation loopholes. When a person or group buys a team, up to one-half of the purchase price is allocated to the value of the players. There's a tax law, which allows the owners to amortize the sports contract over 5 to 10 years. So if a group pays $300 million for a team, the owners can write-off $150 million over say 5 years. Assuming the owners are in the 40% tax bracket, the government has paid about 20% of the purchase price," Campbell explained.

"Do the teams appreciate in value?" Douglass inquired.

"Some baseball teams are closely-held businesses and adequate financial information is difficult to find. In 1998, a media conglomerate bought the L.A. Dodgers from the O'Malley family for $311 million. The Cleveland Indians went for about $320 million in 1999.

"Not bad," Douglass said in a serious tone.

★ ★ ★ ★ ★

"What is 1960 and the Ohio River!"

"Fleet, why do you have to scream at the TV like that?" shouted a voice from the next room. Florita knew the pattern: Each weekday around 6:30 p.m., her husband would sit in front of the television with a glass of tea before dinner and shout questions at Alex Trebek. It was just her luck that this time there was a sports category in the Double Jeopardy round.

"That's the year Muhammad Ali won the Olympic gold medal, and that was the river he threw the medal into," Fleet shouted back at her "He should be ashamed! A black guy answered, and he answered wrong!" He shook his head. Fleet thought everyone should know history—especially sports history. He also thought that African-Americans drew more attention to themselves when they messed up on Jeopardy, which translated into him being scrutinized as well.

Fleet Walker was a sports' historian first, internal auditor, second. He wasn't "the" Fleet Walker, though, and made it immediately clear whenever introduced. The "real" Fleet Walker was his father's favorite baseball player, which played an important factor in getting him the name. Fleet's father went to Korea in 1950 and was not present at his birth. To make sure that her husband approved of the name, Mrs. Walker named her child after her husband's favorite baseball player—Fleet. Coincidence had it that "Walker" was their last names anyway.

Of course, his father had never seen Moses Fleetwood Walker play. An honor student at Oberlin College, Fleetwood Walker caught 42 games for the Toledo Blue Stockings in the old American Association in 1884, being the first black major leaguer. Cap Anson, one of the founding fathers of professional baseball, would not allow his Chicago White Stockings to take the field against Toledo in 1884 because Walker was in the lineup. By 1889, there was an unwritten rule to bar blacks from the major leagues. Not until opening day in 1947 did another black player, Jackie Robinson, start his 10-year career with the Brooklyn Dodgers. Moses Fleetwood Walker died in

Cleveland, Ohio, on May 11, 1924, before Fleet's father was born.

"Hey Flo, did you know that he didn't go to Vietnam?"

"Who? Alex Trebeck?" She used a normal tone now that she was coming into the room.

"NO! Muhammad Ali!—What is 1942!" He was at it again.

Florita and Fleet had met when they were children living next door in Louisiana, and she still had the same spunk. Her hair was sandy, and her skin the color of coffee with extra cream. People had to look real hard at them both to notice that they were African-Americans. Since they had come to New York from Louisiana, she had cut her hair short, and wore it natural, like a mini-Afro. Though Fleet really didn't like it, she didn't care. She always responded to his criticism by saying. "It keeps my head cool and my heart proud." Then she'd say, "You don't have any, so why should I?" He would chuckle every time. Fleet was balding on top, and most of his hair was on the sides. He considered himself lucky because his hair hadn't started turning grey yet.

Fleet was the type of guy who would give his last dime if it was for a worthy cause, and considered himself a "humanitarian," as he would put it. Each year he donated 10% of his salary to a worthy cause. Last year the recipient was the National Negro College Fund. Just last week he had taken a pair of his old shoes to the homeless person who hung out at McDonald's. He was an only child and spent most of his childhood years reading books his father had around the house about sports and sports heroes. He had been barred from playing sports trivia on the local Cooperstown radio station; listeners complained that he had an unfair advantage.

He wasn't excellent at playing sports though, and decided during his college years that the next best thing to playing sports would be studying it. So he majored in Sports' History at

North Carolina A&T and minored in accounting. He worked in public accounting for a few years before recently becoming the Director of the Internal Auditing Department with the New York Yankees. He was always irritated when people thought he was a former professional player. It irritated him more because he thought that people drew the conclusion just because he was black and could afford expensive things. Otherwise, he was carefree about most things.

He did look the part though. He was 6'2" and had dimples the size of dimes. He made sure he spent several hours in the gym each week and would run many mornings at 5:30 a.m. Flo thought that because he was approaching mid-age, he exercised too hard. He assured her that the exercise only improved his golf game. He didn't play golf.

"I'm going out for a couple of things before dinner. Do you want to add anything to the list?" Flo asked while looking around the room for her purse.

"No! They're made from leather, not pigskin." He shouted at the TV and not paying attention to his wife's question.

"Fleet, I'm going to take that as an 'I don't need anything, thank you.'" she said patiently. "I'll be back in about an hour." She leaned over and kissed him on his shiny forehead. "Maybe that'll make your hair grow," she said and smiled.

"It hasn't yet!" Flo and Fleet had a great sense of humor. Surely that was why they had been married for fifteen years.

Walker picked up the latest copy of the *Internal Auditor*, the professional publication of the Institute of Internal Auditors, but the phone interrupted his reading. He reached over and picked up the phone.

"Hello, Walker's residence..."

"...This is Fleet."

"...Yes, I am familiar with the baseball killings, but I'm not specifically sure how I can help though."

"...That would be fine. I'll be at the Hall of Fame in Cooperstown for the next week. Exactly. Goodbye."

Fleet went back to reading the article on "Regulating Disaster Recovery" by William Dimartini and Pat McAnally. He agreed with their summary statement: "Contingency planning may once have been optional—but no longer. New regulations and mandates have pushed the costs for non-compliance to a high-risk level."

Fleet thought about his own organization the New York Yankees and whether they had a proper disaster recovery plan in place. Fleet began to wonder if the baseball killings that the person on the phone spoke about might have a negative impact on his organization. According to Standard 330 from the Institute of Internal Auditors' *Standards for The Professional Practice of Internal Auditing*, as the internal auditor of the Yankees, he was responsible for safeguarding the organization's assets. This safeguarding responsibility rested squarely on his shoulders.

In 1999, the Institute of Internal Auditors adopted a new definition of internal auditing that recognizes the importance of risk management in the internal auditing function. With risk management or risk assessment, auditors must examine the large exposures or risks that may create serious problems for any organization and then plan their audits to ensure that management has policies and procedures (controls) in place to address those risks.

Fleet had heard one speaker call it the "Big R." The speaker said that each organization has many small risks, some moderate risks, and one or two huge risks. The "Big R" can destroy the organization. Risks can also be classified as operational, financial reporting, and compliance risks. Some auditors because they have an accounting background focus on the financial reporting risks and ignore the potentially more severe operational and compliance risks. None of the risks can be ignored.

Fleet realized the importance of risk assessment. Resources are scarce in any organization and especially in internal auditing departments. They must be spent wisely where they will do the most good. Risk assessment allows the internal auditor to identify the parts of the organization that are the most risky and to then allocate precious audit resources to ensure the risk associated with those areas is addressed. Fleet annually broke down the Yankee organization into "Auditable Units" and then ranked each auditable unit in terms of riskiness. Fleet measured risk using several "risk factors" such as "impact on operations and customer satisfaction," "legal impact," "degree of computerization," "recent organizational or technological change," and "time since last audit." Audits were placed on the audit schedule based on their total ranking. Fleet was proud of this system because he had purposely designed the risk factors to measure operational and compliance risks.

Fleet was currently reviewing the Yankees' disaster plans and assessing how well prepared his organization was for a crisis. What impact would potential killings in Yankee Stadium have on the Yankee organization? Would killings in other ballparks affect the Yankee organization? These were tough questions to answer.

After the Centennial Olympic Games' bombing in Atlanta, Fleet had to add a separate risk management audit. The Centennial Games' auditors had approached disaster recovery like fraud and had ensured that policies and procedures were in place to address this risk. This planning resulted in the park where the bomb exploded being reopened two days after the bombing with a grand opening ceremony and increased security. The risk management audit had been helpful in 1998 when the 500-pound steel joint had pulverized a second deck seat in left field during practice. The Yankees had to play some of their home games in Shea Stadium (the New York Mets' stadium), but long term disruption of operations was averted.

The morning after a death on May 17 in his stadium, Fleet had one of his auditors check on any deaths that had occurred at the 28 professional baseball parks. Over the past several years, there had been only one or two deaths in the parks each season. Yankee Stadium had none last year, but one this year. And there had already been more than three at other parks early in this season. Fleet instructed the employee to monitor the deaths at the major league baseball parks over the next months. Fleet did not like the trend line.

When thinking about disaster recovery, Fleet had to think outside the box. When dealing with crime and murder, he had to think like a criminal's mind. Criminals can change an entire industry. For example, in 1982 a company selling painkillers was confronted with seven deaths attributed to poison contaminated containers of their products. The company reacted swiftly by recalling all of the old containers and issuing new products in tamper-resistant sealed containers. The company not only avoided long-term harm, but was actually praised for its swift action.

One of the costs of terrorism or fraud is the disruption and inconvenience caused by the controls, which are implemented to prevent reoccurrance from happening. These can range from the innocuous child resistant tops on pill containers to the metal detectors in airports. Internal auditors must constantly weigh the cost of a control (inconvenience and disruption of operations) against its benefit (prevention of loss) and recommend only those controls whose benefits exceed their costs. This concept is known as reasonable assurance, and it means that there will always be some risks that are too costly to control.

Recently, some internal auditing organizations have begun to form partnerships with managers in performing risk assessment. This technique is called Control Self-Assessment or CSA for short. Under CSA, the auditor becomes a trainer or coordinator educating members of management in conducting risk assessment and designing controls to address those risks. The internal auditors guide the managers through the risk assessment process offering suggestions as the process is performed. CSA is a big improvement because it leverages internal audit resources, which leads to excellent exposure for the internal auditing department. Fleet was familiar with CSA, but he felt that the Yankee organization was not quite ready for it.

Fleet picked up his latest copy of the *Preventing Business Fraud* newsletter published by the Institute of Management and Administration. He started reading a piece on how Chevron is using digital signatures and encryption to protect its business data.

Chapter 5

New York

I knew that becoming a Certified Internal Auditor would improve my credibility with my colleagues and managers, and with our clients. It proves I know what I am doing and that my recommendations are important.

Mark S. Rendely, CIA
World Bank

After talking to Fleet Walker, Douglass called the authorities in New York City and warned them of the potential risk of a murder at Shea Stadium on the twenty-first. The next day he flew to Utica, with a stop in Syracuse. At Utica he rented a car and drove to Cooperstown.

Fleet Walker was also a part-time consultant with the research department at the National Baseball Hall of Fame. Fleet informed Douglass that he was *not* the Fleetwood Walker who had been the first professional baseball player. "Many people confuse me with him. I'm from North Carolina and Louisiana and coached a minor league team with the Detroit Tigers' organization. *He* was from Ohio."

While they were still discussing a few preliminary items, Douglass received a fax indicating that there had been the following deaths in baseball stadiums during the year. He showed the list to Walker:

April 30	—	Detroit	baseball card found
May 5	—	Boston	baseball card found
May 8	—	Oakland	?

79

May 15	—	Cleveland	baseball card found
May 17	—	New York	?
June 12	—	Worcester	baseball card found
June 17	—	Providence	baseball card found

"The May eighth death has been ruled a heart attack, but an autopsy is to be performed," Douglass said. "What do you know about this May 17 death in your stadium?"

"Well I believe everyone thought it was a heart attack, but you have me curious now. In fact, you have me nervous. I'll check to see if there was a baseball card near the body. Do you think we need an autopsy?"

"Probably," Douglass replied.

"Well, he's certainly up-to-date on perfect games," Walker said as he handed the list back to Douglass. "He skipped the Haddix game at Milwaukee."

"Okay, I read your piece on Cy Young and the May 5th game. I know a little about the Worcester and Providence perfect games, but why did the killer skip the Milwaukee ballpark?"

"Have you checked Atlanta-Fulton County Stadium on May 26? The Braves now play in Atlanta. The American League Milwaukee Brewers now play in County Stadium in Milwaukee."

"I'll check on that," Douglass replied politely. "These ball teams move around a great deal."

"We're talking about a long time period—from 1880 to 1999."

"Yes, you're right; there have been very few perfect games."

"Probably the killer is a purist." Walker suggested. "He is following the new definition of a perfect game. Poor Haddix had his greatest perfect loss, and then his perfect game was taken away from him by a statistical committee in 1991."

Douglass thought for a moment. "So it could be Haddix doing this to get even."

Walker smiled. "Don't believe so, unless you believe in reincarnation. Harvey Haddix died several years ago—1993 I believe."

"Talk to me about the game anyway," Douglass said.

"Tell me to stop when you get bored," Walker said in his booming voice.

"A 33-year-old slim southpaw, nicknamed, 'The Kitten,' was nursing a head cold on Tuesday, May 26, 1959. Harvey Haddix was called 'The Kitten' because he resembled Harry Brecheen, another southpaw, who was called The Cat. Kitten's 5'8" catcher also had a nickname. Smoky Burgess, a native of Caroleen, N.C., was calling the signals. Vinnie Smith, who had played for Pittsburgh in 1941 and 1946, was the plate umpire."

Walker opened a manila folder labeled "Haddix," and glanced at a piece of paper. "Haddix, a native of Medway, Ohio, was pitching in an away game for the National League Pittsburgh Pirates, looking for his fourth victory of this season. Most perfect games are pitched on the home field—fewer errors I guess. He had won eight and lost seven games in the past season pitching for the Cincinnati Reds. Rain was threatening, lightning was flashing, and a strong breeze was blowing.

"During the team meeting before the game, Haddix was going over the Braves' line-up, telling how he would pitch to them. Apparently third baseman Don Hoak, an aggressive ex-Marine, spoke up and said, 'Hey, if you pitch that way, you'll pitch a no-hitter.'

"Harvey's opposing pitcher was right-hander Lew Burdette of the league-leading Milwaukee Braves. Lew's flirt with baseball immortality in 1960 ended when he hit a batter—snapping a perfect game. Lew was a notorious spitball pitcher. Gaylord Perry said that Lew could spit between his teeth. Tommy

Holmes said that 'three-fourths of his pitches were wet. Lew washed his pants with a lot of soap. He would wipe his hands on his pants to get the soap. If the umpire asked for the ball, he would roll the ball to the umpire.' One way to sidestep internal controls."

Walker smiled at Douglass and continued. "Since Harvey was a southpaw, the league-leading Braves had stacked their line-up with seven right-handed batters. The small (5'9") boy-ish-looking curve-ball specialist would face future Hall of Famers Eddie Mathews batting .306 and Henry Aaron (.355), as well as sluggers Joe Adcock (.292), Wes Covington (.279), Del Crandall (.257), and Johnny Logan (.290) on this cloudy Tuesday. Mathews would hit 46 home runs and Aaron would hit 39 during the 1959 season. In his book, *The Story of Hank Aaron*, Hank indicates that 1959 was his best hitting year."

"In the third inning, Braves' Johnny Logan drilled a line drive toward shortstop which was caught by a leaping Dick Schofield. Again in the sixth, Logan hit a pitch in the hole between short and third, but Schofield speared the grounder and made a long throw to first for the put-out.

"There was some rain in the seventh, but Harvey's sliders, curves, and fastballs retired the Braves one after the other. The problem: the Pirates got hits, but they could not score a run. A base-running blunder in the third by Roman Mejias kept the Pirates from scoring, even though they had three hits during the inning.

"The Pirates had two hits in the top of the ninth, but no runs. So the score was 0-0 by the middle of the ninth in the warm, muggy air.

"A crowd of 19,194 watched veteran Harvey strike out Handy Andy Pafko in the bottom of the ninth. One out. This would be Pafko's seventeenth and last season in the major league. Johnny Logan then flied to Skinner in left field. Two outs. Lew Burdette struck out too. Twenty-seven batters up, twenty-seven batters down."

Walker looked at Douglass for permission to continue. "Harvey Haddix had pitched a perfect game—for nine innings. He received a standing ovation from the Milwaukee crowd, and Manager Danny Murtaugh and his Pirate teammates mobbed him when he got to the dugout. But the score was still 0-0, so the game went into extra innings.

"During the top of the tenth, Pittsburgh's Dick Stuart, with one on and one out, hit a long drive toward the center field fence. At the last moment Andy Pafko caught it."

Walker referred to his notes. "In the tenth, Joe Christopher replaced Mejias in right field and would have one time at bat. This was Christopher's first major league game.

"Through the tenth, eleventh, and twelfth, Harvey silenced the Milwaukee sluggers one by one. He was tired and was munching cold pills to relieve a heavy cough. But his slider was still sharp. No one had ever pitched a no-hitter past the eleventh inning—much less a flawless game."

"In the unlucky thirteenth inning, Pittsburgh again did not score. Lew Burdette had given up 12 hits, but not a single run." Walker emphasized the word unlucky.

"The first Milwaukee batter, Felix Mantilla, in the bottom of the thirteenth inning hit a routine grounder to temperamental Don Hoak at third base. Hoak often complained to his teammates if they were not playing well. Hoak's throw hit the ground near the feet of first baseman, Rocky Nelson. The Puerto Rican second baseman, who had entered the game in the tenth inning, was safe on an error.

"Catcher Smoky Burgess argued briefly that Mantilla had turned toward second base after running out the ground ball and, therefore, was out when Burgess tagged him. The base umpire would not buy the argument, however.

"Harvey had hurled 12 perfect innings, extinguishing 36 Braves in a row. Harvey's perfect string had been snapped, but his no-hitter was intact," Walker stated with obvious disappointment.

"Afterward Haddix said, 'I thought I had Mantilla struck out on the previous pitch. If the plate umpire had called it a strike, Mantilla would have been out of there. I'll never forget that play. Hoak had all night after picking up the ball. He looked at the seams, and then threw it away.'

"If. 'If' is a big word in the quest for a perfect game.

"Ed Mathews sacrificed Mantilla to second. One out in the thirteenth.

"The major league's leading batter, Hank Aaron, was up next. First baseman Joe Adcock once described Aaron as follows: 'Trying to sneak a pitch past Aaron is like trying to sneak the sunrise past a rooster.' Aaron was given an intentional base on balls. Still one out.

"Joe Adcock, the next batter, had struck out twice and hit two ground ball outs. On a 1-0 pitch, Adcock stroked a high slider over the right-center field fence at the 394-foot marker. The ball barely cleared the wire fence over a leaping Bill Virdon's outstretched glove. The home run fence is similar to a measuring control.

"Adcock hesitated for a moment, but started running around the bases. Aaron running from first to second, touched second base. Thinking the ball was not a home run, Aaron made a mental error and headed towards the Braves' dugout crossing the pitcher's mound, not touching third base." Walker took a sheet of paper and began drawing stick figures on a diamond.

"Mantilla scored. Adcock reached third base; thereby passing Aaron.

"Initially Adcock was credited with a home run and 3 RBIs and the score was announced as 3-0. RBIs are somewhat like the rate of return on assets." RBI indicates how productive a batter is in driving in runs, whereas the rate of return on assets indicates how productive management uses corporate resources.

"After some confusion, Manager Fred Haney had Aaron and Adcock retrace their steps and touch home plate. Umpire Frank Dascoli agreed that only Mantilla and Aaron scored, making the score 2-0. Adcock was declared out for passing the runner. However, the next day National League President Warren Giles eliminated Aaron's run and made the official score 1-0," Walker explained. "Somewhat like a corrective internal control.

"Suppose there had been two outs when Aaron's mental error occurred. Bob Wolf, of the *Milwaukee Journal*, hypothesizes that the first run by Mantilla would not have counted unless Mantilla crossed the plate *before* Adcock passed Aaron. No one seemed to know if Mantilla crossed the plate first. Internal controls were lacking.

"Harvey had lost the deadly struggle with his mound rival. He pitched twelve perfect innings and lost on a home run that wasn't a home run. He pitched twelve no-hit innings and lost. This battle was a bizarre and disappointing perfect game." Walker shook his head.

Douglass raised his hand. "Wait a minute. Haddix pitches 12 perfect innings and doesn't get credit for a perfect game. Other pitchers pitch nine innings and get credit for a perfect game."

"You got it," Walker said loudly.

"There are some stupid baseball people," Douglass grunted.

"Wait, there's more. Harvey had retired the last two Cardinal batters in his prior start, so he retired 38 consecutive batters. The only other pitcher to come close was Boston's Waite Hoyt, who retired 34 Yankees in order from the second through the thirteenth inning in a game in 1919. Hoyt pitched eleven perfect innings sandwiched between hits in a thirteen-inning marathon."

"I believe you like Haddix," Douglass said.

"You bet. I saw him pitch once," Walker said with a genuine smile.

Douglass looked at the fax again. "Please tell me about this Detroit game on April 30."

"Rookie Robertson was the hurler. On Sunday afternoon, April 30, 1922, 25 year-old Charles Robertson started his *second* major-league game. Chicago's manager, Kid Gleason, nick-named the Youngster, had managed the infamous 1919 Black Sox team."

"Robby's opponent was the powerful American League Detroit Tigers. He had to face the dangerous Ty Cobb, batting .401, Lu Blue (.300), Bobby Veach (.327), Harry Heilmann (.356), and Toppy Rigney (.300). Ty Cobb became a member of the Hall of Fame in 1936; Harry Heilmann was elected in 1952. These Tigers bats would be silent that day, however.

"There's an Aggie Marketing Professor at Texas A&M University who has ranked all of the hitters based upon a number of variables. Professor Dick Hise ranks Ty Cobb 11th, Harry Heilmann 14th, Bobby Veach 62nd, and LuBlue 157th. Robertson probably pitched a perfect games against the best hitting team."

"Who are the best hitters?" Douglass inquired.

"The top five, in order, were Lou Gehrig, Ted Williams, Stan Musial, Roger Hornsby, and Joe DiMaggio. A player's batting average would be similar to the net income of a company, or maybe earnings per share."

"I've heard of some of them," Douglass said. "Tell me about Robertson's perfect game. Please."

"There were 25,000 fans in the Detroit stadium—called Navin Field—as the six-foot right-hander threw the first ball to the squatting Ray Schalk. The 5'7" veteran catcher would call all of the pitches for the rookie during the thrilling game. Schalk, nicknamed Cracker, would be elected to the Hall of Fame in 1955, even though he has one of the lowest batting average—.253—of any Hall of Fame member. He played on the infamous 1919 Chicago White Sox team, but was not tainted by the fix of the World Series. Cracker was the first catcher to run down to first base behind a hitter to catch any overthrows, and he would catch *four* no-hitters." Walker held up four fingers.

After a short pause, Walker said, "There's an interesting fact about the forerunner of Navin Field, called Bennett Park from 1900 until 1911. The field located between Michigan Avenue, Kaline Drive, and Trumbull Avenue was named after Charlie Bennett, a catcher who played for the Detroit Wolverines in the 1880s. In 1880, Bennett caught the first perfect game, tossed by Lee Richmond. Charlie Bennett lost both of his legs in an 1884 train accident. According to your fax someone was killed with a poison baseball card at Tiger Stadium, which was built on the site of Navin Field, on the date of Robertson's perfect game.

"But let me get back to Robertson's perfect game," Walker apologized. "In the prior season, 1921, umpires began to introduce new balls throughout the game. The new balls were slick, but the rosin bag was not introduced until the 1925 season.

"This battle would be right fielder Harry Hooper's second time on the winning side of a perfect game. He played right field during Ernie Shore's pitching gem, batting 1-for-4. During this game, Hooper would go 0-for-3, but he did score a run and had three putouts. In two perfect games, the left-hander went 1-for-7, but his lifetime batting average was .281. There was one deep fly to left field by Bobby Veach, a great hitter, in the bottom of the second which was caught by Johnny Mostil at the fence. Later in the inning Harry Hooper caught Bobby Jones' line drive on the run.

"Starting in the fifth inning, the Detroit players began to harass rookie Robertson about throwing a spit ball, which had been outlawed two years earlier," Walker related in a serious tone.

"Harry Heilmann, a former bookkeeper and future Detroit broadcaster, complained to umpire Dick Nallin that the ball was soiled by a foreign substance. Nicknamed Slug, Heilmann had batted .394 in the prior season, would win four American League batting titles, and had a lifetime batting average of .342. He liked his liquor. Arthritis ended his playing career after 17 seasons, and he later became a Detroit sportscaster," Walker added.

"Nallin checked the ball and found nothing. 'Let's get along with the game,'" Nallin told Heilmann.

"The Tigers continued to 'cry wolf,' especially Heilmann. Ty Cobb even went over to see whether the first baseman's glove contained some coloring material.

"Writing in the *Chicago Daily Tribune* on May 1, Irving Vaughn wrote: 'To a non-partisan spectator it sounded like the squawk of a trimmed sucker.'

"In the bottom of the ninth manager Ty Cobb used two pinch hitters to try to stop Charlie Robertson's spell on the clawless Tigers.

"Pinch-hitter Danny Clark swung and missed the first pitch and watched a second strike sail by him. Cobb ran out of the dugout and demanded that the umpire look at the ball.

"Umpire Nallin again inspected the ball. He walked out to the mound and carefully inspected all parts of Robertson's uniform. Finding nothing, he said, 'He's just throwing sinkers. Get along with the game.'

"Clark watched a fastball cross the plate.

"'Strike three,' Nallin exclaimed. One down.

"Catcher Clyde Manion (.275) popped up to Eddie Collins at second base. Two outs. Collins would play for 25 years, manage, and become a member of the Hall of Fame in 1939," Walker added.

"Ty Cobb sent in pinch-hitter Johnny Bassler (.323) to try to sabotage the perfect game. Bassler, a catcher, was a slow runner.

"Robinson later said in *Literary Digest*, 'You know, it never occurred to me that I was nearing the big thing until after two men were out in the ninth inning. Then, when Cobb sent up a pinch-hitter, it suddenly dawned on me that I was standing right on the brink of the thing.'

"The Texan continued, 'It made me feel a bit funny, and I wondered if the rest of the fellows realized the fact. I turned and walked over to Mulligan, who was playing shortstop. "Do you realize that the funny little fat guy is the only thing between me and a perfect game?" I asked him. He didn't say anything, just turned me around and gave me a little shove toward the pitcher's box.'" Walker paused and smiled at Douglass.

"He went back to the box and served one up; the fat guy swung and the ball sailed into Mostil's hands in the outfield. That's all there was to it," Walker explained.

"As left fielder Mostil was running off the field, a fan grabbed the ball from his glove. Later in the clubhouse someone asked him where was the ball he caught. Unnoticed Mostil picked up another ball from the ball bag, and all of the Chicago teammates signed the wrong ball. Apparently Robertson never knew the real history of his 'prized' last ball. I wonder where the real last ball is now.

"Because of the powerful hitters that Robertson faced, he probably pitched the best of the perfect games. It was perfect in every way. This game was during the era of the lively ball. The lean Dexter, Texas native struck out six Tigers, including the immortal Ty Cobb. Only six balls were hit into the outfield.

"The perfect game was the end of it for Robby," Walker said in a serious tone, "because he was a flash in the pan, enjoying the baseball limelight only briefly. This season would be his best year with 14 wins and 15 losses. He had his one day in the sun and shortly disappeared from the professional baseball scene — from the top of the heap to sayonara. The White Sox traded Robertson to the St. Louis Browns in 1926, and he played for the Boston Braves during 1927-28. Pitching a total of 166 games, he won only 49 and lost 80. After his perfect game, there would be 34 years before another one was pitched."

Douglass said, "You mentioned Ty Cobb several times. How good was he?"

Shaking his head Walker stated, "Cobb may have been the greatest player of all times, but when he faced Robertson, he did not have a chance to practice his spikes-high slide. During the first Hall of Fame voting, the egotistical Georgia native received 222 of the 226 votes. By investing his earnings in Coca-Cola and General Motors stocks, the Georgia Peach probably became baseball's first millionaire," Walker acknowledged.

"I know about Cy Young's game in Boston on May 5th. Talk about the game in Oakland on May 8," Douglass asked.

"Catfish Hunter." Walker showed Douglass a photograph of Catfish Hunter.

"I remember Catfish. Oakland A's. Funny Moustache. Right?" inquired Douglass.

"I think that was Rollie Fingers, a relief pitcher. Fingers won the Rolaids Relief Award three times. After Oakland, Catfish signed a $3.75 million five-year contract with the Yankees. He was elected to the Hall of Fame in 1987."

"Have all of the perfect game pitchers been elected to this Hall of Fame?" Douglass asked.

"No. Only Catfish, Jim Bunning recently, Cy Young, Sandy Koufax, Adrian Joss, and John Ward."

"Look Fleet, I need your help." Douglass pleaded. "Can you go with me to New York for the Mets game on the twenty-first? I have a rental car, and you can tell me about Catfish, Barker, and Bunning as we drive to New York. The FBI will reimburse you. We could leave as soon as possible."

"I believe I can. My wife wants me back in New York. I want to help you. My philosophy is to do today what most people would postpone until tomorrow. This maniac could destroy baseball. I'm not finished here at the Hall, but I can postpone the research. Please let me call Flo and let her know that I'm now working for the FBI. She'll never believe it." Fleet smiled. "Can you get me a FBI commission?"

"I doubt it, but I'll get you a free seat at the Mets' game. The Giants are playing."

"Fair enough," Walker said cheerfully. "I want to see Bobby Bonilla." After Walker made a few personal calls, he and Douglass started the long drive from Cooperstown to New York City. Cooperstown, itself, is surrounded by rolling hills covered with stands of evergreen and hardwood trees. Walker told Douglass that Otsego Lake was christened "Glimmerglass" by James Fenimore Cooper, after whose family the town is named. "The lake is a sheet of limpid water extending about nine miles and varying in width from about three-quarters of a mile to a mile and a half. It has many bays and points for swimming, fishing, or skiing."

Douglass' first question was how did Catfish get his nickname.

Walker pulled out a book from his briefcase and turned to a page. "In his book titled *Catfish: My Life in Baseball*, Catfish indicates that Charlie Finley gave him the nickname when he signed a $75,000 bonus with the A's. Funny. He lost a toe in a hunting accident. He could have been called '9-toes.' "

Walker laughed slightly and put the book down and continued. "James Augustus Hunter, a 22-year-old American League hurler in his fourth major league season, was on the mound in the Oakland Stadium facing the hard-hitting Minnesota Twins on Wednesday, May 8, 1968. His catcher was 6'4" Jim Pagliaroni, nicknamed Pag. Dave Boswell was the Twins' pitcher, who would hurl six scoreless innings that day."

"The Athletics had moved to Oakland-Alameda County Coliseum from Kansas City that year. Yet there were only 6,298 fans in the stadium, the second smallest turnout for the young season. That was the smallest turnout for any perfect game except for the two in 1880." Walker slowly shook his head.

"The round concrete stadium itself with eight feet tall circular outfield fences is a pitcher's park with a lot of foul ground to catch a pop fly. Green ivy slopes surround the complex that is run by Levi-Strauss. In the late 1970s with the many bad years the park was called the Oakland Mausoleum. Aside from the Athletics, the Golden State Warriors and the Oakland Raiders use the complex," Walker added.

"Anyway, Catfish's fastballs and sliders shut down the normally slugging Twins. There were only three almost-hits on the natural-grass field during the night game. In the fourth, lead off-hitter Cesar Tovar smashed a sinking liner to left field. Outfielder Joe Rudi made the catch on the run at his knees on the tall outfield grass for the first out.

"In the fifth, Bob Allison's hard-hit grounder toward third base was grabbed by Sal Bando for a fine defensive play. Bando played every inning in every game during the 1969 season.

"In the sixth inning, Catfish became aware that he was pitching a no-hitter. He noticed some of his teammates whispering, but he thought he had walked someone in a prior inning," Walker continued.

"Hunter and Boswell had a scoreless duel in the clear, cool 65 degree air until the seventh, when Catfish himself beat out a run-scoring squeeze bunt. Catfish had doubled to right-center in the third." Walker continued to explain.

"During the seventh, Catfish said to his catcher, Pag, 'Hey, Dago, I think I've got a no-no. Let's don't out dumb each other.' " Walker turned and hurriedly said, "Pag told me that in an interview.

"Again in the eighth, Catfish was productive with his bat. With the bases loaded, Hunter hit a single into right-center for two more RBIs. Hunter went 3-for-4 and drove in three of the four A's runs.

"At the top of the ninth, umpire Jerry Neudecker told Pagliaroni that Hunter was working on a perfect game. Pag did *not* tell Hunter, however.

"The round-faced hurler faced pinch-hitter John Roseboro, who grounded out. In 1965, Gabby Roseboro, who was then with the Dodgers, had been resting, and therefore Jeff Torborg caught Sandy Koudax's perfect game. Essentially, unlucky Gabby *watched* two perfect games from the bench." Walker emphasized the word.

"Catcher Bruce Look, in his only season in the major leagues, then struck out. Two outs. Only one out away from a perfect game. Manager Cal Ermer put in another pinch-hitter—big, strong Rich Reese.

"Left-hander Rich Reese, would not go down easily. He fouled off the first fast ball. Strike one.

"Ball one, on a low, inside fast ball.

"Ball two on a similar fast ball.

"Six-foot, three inch Reese then swung and missed. Strike two.

"Pagliaroni signaled for another fast ball, but Catfish shook him off. According to Pag, Catfish hardly ever shook off a signal. Pag knew that Reese was a dead fast ball hitter, so he signaled for a slider.

"According to Catfish the slider 'knifed through the strike zone, cutting the plate in two.' Pagliaroni jumped into the air in celebration.

"But umpire Jerry Neudecker shouted, 'Ball three!'

"Oakland manager Bob Kennedy rushed out and complained to Neudecker to no avail. Kennedy said, 'The pitch was letter high, and I hit the roof when Neudecker called it a ball. That pitch was perfect.'

"Catcher Pagliaroni signaled for a fast ball. He was nervous, because he did not wish to drop a third strike. He had previously caught the Bill Monbouquette's no-hitter against the Chicago White Sox on August 1, 1962. A second inning walk had torpedoed the perfecto for the 26-year old right-hander, pitching for the eighth place Red Sox.

"The count was three-and-two on Reese.

"Fouled off.

"Another fast ball. Fouled off again.

"Fast ball. Foul. There had been 3 fouls.

"Pagliaroni flashed for another fast ball. He was worried. He didn't want a walk. Another foul.

"Fast ball. Reese liked fast balls. Foul ball number five.

"The one hundred and seventh ball came toward home plate, a fast ball.

"Reese swung and missed." Walker slammed his right fist into his left hand. Douglass jumped. "Control pitcher Catfish Hunter had tossed a jolly good game. At age 22, Catfish became the youngest modern pitcher to hurl a perfect game. John Ward was 20 when he pitched his perfect game.

"Third baseman and captain Sal Bando came running toward Catfish shouting, 'Perfect game! Perfect game!' His teammates mobbed Hunter.

"Until that moment, Catfish thought he was merely pitching a no-hitter. 'I just thought it was a no-hitter. I thought I'd walked a batter earlier.' He even wrote no-hitter on the last ball thrown past Reese."

Both Douglass and Walker were silent for some time. Douglass looked at his watch. It always seemed that in conversations in real life that there was silence around 20 after the hour. It was 1:18.

Douglass glanced into the rear view mirror and saw the difference between his white skin and rather long brown hair and Walker's short black hair and black skin.

Both men watched the New York scenery for some time. Finally when Douglass stopped the rental car at a stoplight in Stamford, he asked Walker why he knew so much about perfect games.

"Actually I'm working on a book about these perfect games. I'm almost finished," Walker answered with a broad smile.

"So tell me about this Len Barker," Douglass replied warmly.

Walker looked into his briefcase again and pulled out a folder labeled "Barker." He read for a few minutes and then began his discussion of Barker's game.

"On Friday night, May 15, 1981, a 25-year old Fort Knox, Kentucky native was warming up in the bullpen. He had been a castoff from the Texas Rangers in 1978. Today Cleveland was in first place, one game ahead of Baltimore and the Yankees. The right-hander had a 2-1 record and a 1.67 ERA early in the season.

"The temperature was 49 degrees at game time, and there was a fine mist blowing off Lake Erie onto the grass in Cleveland's old Municipal Stadium. The opposing pitcher was Toronto's Luis Leal, a right hander.

"No one could guess that history would repeat itself. Another Cleveland ace right-hander had pitched a perfect game for this same American League team on a Friday also. Addie Joss, a 6'3" Hall of Famer, in the heat of the pennant race mowed down 27 consecutive Chicago White Sox players on Friday, October 2, 1908."

Douglass repeated the date, October 2. "We have to catch this killer before October"

"I agree," Walker said quietly and then continued. "There were some differences between these two Cleveland games. The Toronto Blue Jays in 1981 were currently in last place in the American League East with a team batting average of .218. The Cleveland Indians in 1908 were in second place, ½ game back, and Chicago was in third place 2 ½ games back. Barker was in his sixth season, following a 19-12 record in 1980. Joss was in his seventh season, after a 27-11 record in 1907."

"Joss would die at an early age in Toledo, Ohio, after only 9 seasons," Walker said with disappointment. "Barker would retire after 11 seasons.

"Barker had an unusual pitching style. He brought his right leg up very high, which would hide his glove, his right arm, and most of his head.

"Number 39 dug a hole in front of the rubber before the first inning. His long light-brown hair was sticking outside of his black hat with a red bill. Many colorful umbrellas were out in the stands because of the foggy dew and swirling mist," Walker paused. "I saw a video of this game.

"Catcher Ron Hassey was wearing his black mask and a red chest protector—a preventive control. The first pitch to Alfredo Griffin, the Jay's first batter, was a called strike. Possibly because of the swirling mist, Hassey did not catch the second high pitch, which went all the way to the blue padding on the backstop. Of course, the dangling contraption from his mask which most catchers wear to protect their throats, didn't help his reflexes.

"Barker almost gave up a hit to switch-hitting Alfredo Griffin, batting left-handed. He grounded a slow roller up the middle, and shortstop Tom Veryzer went far to his left behind the mound to catch the ball. His throw to first almost pulled Mike Hargrove off the bag and barely beat the speedster Griffin. This game would be the first of three perfect games Griffin would suffer through *on the losing team*.

"The Tribe jumped into an early lead in the bottom of the first. There was one run in, two outs, with Mike Hargrove on second base when Ron Hassey came up to bat.

"The first pitch from Luis Leal was a ball, and plate umpire Dave Garcia called time and motioned the field crew to come on to the field. Three ground crew members—two in yellow raincoats and one in red—came on to the field with a wheelbarrow and put a white chemical material, which looked like sand, on the mound and around the batting boxes. Barker had complained that the pitching area was soggy. Management's preventive controls at work," Walker laughed. "Similar to the screen behind home plate to stop foul balls from hitting spectators.

"The second pitch was a strike, and then Leal threw Hassey a change of pace. Hassey drove a double into right field, and Hargrove scored the second run, both being unearned. Toby Harrah was unable to bring Hassey in, but the Tribe had provided Barker with a two-run lead.

"In the top of the second, Damaso Garcia hit two screaming liners outside the first base line. First base umpire Gregory Kosc recalled in 1992 that the second shot down the first base line barely went foul. Then Garcia hit a liner to left-center, which was caught by center fielder Rich Manning after a long run.

"In the fourth, Barker almost hit Alfredo Griffin with a high pitch. Griffin then hit a long fly ball to left field, and center fielder Rick Manning almost ran into left fielder Joe Charbonneau on the play. Charbonneau caught the ball." Walker wiped his left hand across his forehead.

"The next Jays' batter, Lloyd Moseby, smashed a liner down the right field line which went foul at the last moment. Moseby then struck out to end the fourth inning.

"Upshaw was the designated hitter, batting fifth. The designated hitter rule was introduced into the American League in 1975. Thus, this day would be the first perfect game where there would be no cheap outs from the opposing pitcher," Walker said in a soft Louisiana drawl.

"The next batter, Damaso Garcia, argued briefly with umpire Garcia about a low called strike. Probably not in retaliation, Damaso Garcia fouled a pitch off Hassey's left leg, the unprotected part."

"Is catching that bad?" Douglass asked.

"Catching is tough. The catcher is constantly squatting down, and he must throw almost as many balls as the pitcher— back to the pitcher or to a base on a pick-off or an attempted steal. The catcher must be prepared to throw the runner out in the case of a steal, and yet he can not interfere with the batter's swing," Walker explained.

"Another danger point is on a hit-and-run. A catcher sees a runner stealing a base and the batter swings a deadly weapon at the ball as the catcher attempts to catch it. A fraction of a second can be the difference between an out and a stolen base.

"Barker's fast ball had been clocked at 96 mph. By the fifth inning his breaking ball was so good, Hassey and Barker decided to stay with it. Barker had two curves: an overhand curve and a three-quarter change-up."

Walker glanced at his notes and continued.

"During the sixth, second baseman Duane Kuiper ranged to his right to stop Rick Bosetti's short-hop line drive. He also had to move to his left to capture a bouncer by Alfredo Griffin in the seventh, and he barely nipped Griffin with his throw to first. Plate umpire Richie Garcia told me in 1992 that Kuiper 'saved the perfect game.'

"Still in the seventh, Jorge Bell asked Garcia to look at the ball. Bell was unhappy with the first called strike. Fans were on their feet and a drum was beating as Bell struck out on a low pitch. Light rain began falling in the bottom of the seventh." Walker continued casually.

"Barker did not hear any of his teammates mention the perfect game, but he said, 'I was thinking about it all the way. But you can't take it all that seriously until the last inning. You've still got three guys to go and any one of them can get a hit: a blooper or something.'

"Barker was nervous in the ninth. 'I was so nervous at the end that I dropped the ball on the mound one time. My stomach was a wreck.'

"Rick Bosetti was the first Jays' hitter in the ninth. Barker threw a ball down the middle of the plate, but luckily Bosetti fouled it off. After a called ball, Bosetti then popped out to third baseman Toby Harrah.

"Manager Bobby Mattick sent in pinch-hitter Al Woods to replace third baseman Danny Ainge. Although 6'5" Ainge had a three-year deal with the Jays, this would be his last season, hitting only .187. He would try his talents at professional basketball with the Boston Celtics, unable to master major league pitching. He would be more successful playing professional basketball with numerous teams.

"Woods struck out on three pitches. But not before he had fouled a ball off Hassey's left leg—the same one hit in the fifth. You can believe that there is severe pain when a catcher is hit by a foul tip, especially when the ball is being thrown around 95 miles per hour. Two outs.

"Pinch-hitter Ernie Whitt (.188) was the last hope for the Blue Jays. The first pitch was a called strike. Then Garcia called ball one. Whitt swung and missed the next pitch. One ball, two strikes.

"Barker checked the signal from Hassey, toed the rubber, took a deep breath, and threw his one-hundred and third pitch toward home plate. Whitt hit an easy fly ball to center fielder Rich Manning.

"The preeminent fireballer had pitched the twelfth perfect game in two hours and nine minutes. No runs, no hits, no walks, and no errors."

Walker smiled in pleasure.

"There were fireworks. Catcher Hassey ran to the mound, but he was pushed aside as teammates mobbed Barker, and many of the 7,290 Tribe fans swarmed onto the field. Several policemen took Barker to his dugout. It was a mob scene in the dugout. Hassey did not become aware of the perfect game until after the game."

During the remainder of the trip Walker and Douglass compared their jobs. Walker explained that audits were scheduled after a comprehensive risk assessment of the entire organization was performed. Thus, the internal auditing organization tried to ensure that important risks were being addressed. Douglass said he wished the FBI worked that way, instead it was forced to constantly react to emergencies.

Fleet went on to describe the individual audit. The first thing you do when you are assigned an internal audit is to set audit objectives. This task is what makes it an audit and not a fishing expedition. Generally, the audit objectives will correspond to the type of audit: operational, financial, or compliance. After the audit objectives are known, then a preliminary survey is done to understand as much about the auditee's operations as possible. This survey entails interviewing key employees, observing operations, and reading or examining documents and records. When the preliminary survey is completed, then an audit program is written, listing the audit procedures that will be done during the audit. A budget is then estimated based on the audit program.

"I approve all audit programs and budgets to ensure that our audits are well planned. Douglass, I know you know all the sayings about poor planning," said Fleet.

"I sure do," replied Douglass.

"Anyway, the auditors now have a good plan to follow. Once they have completed the audit tests, the auditors can review the evidence gathered and reach conclusions which are then reported to management," finished Fleet.

"That sounds pretty thorough, like the FBI," said Douglass.

Fleet added, "Once the report is issued and management responds, then a follow-up visit is made to ensure that the issues identified in the audit report are addressed."

Douglass then asked, "What is the hardest part of the audit?"

Fleet responded, "The hardest part for me has always been the final meeting with management to present our report. The only thing that management sees is that report, and you bet it better be right. In addition, you never know when a situation like that is going to go bad in the sense that management totally rejects what you have found."

"In other words, like a pitcher who just can't get anyone out and is sent to the showers," said Douglass.

Fleet came back, "Exactly, in those situations you want to disappear from the face of the earth. However, fortunately those bad situations are few and far between. If we have done our job as auditors and written a good report concentrating on the significant issues, then there shouldn't be any problems."

Walker told Douglass that the modern internal auditing profession was only about 50 years old. In 1941, the Institute of Internal Auditors or IIA was founded in New York City. The IIA is currently headquartered in Altamonte Springs, Florida, near Orlando. This global organization has over 60,000 members representing nearly every nation. Over half of the members are from outside North America.

The IIA represents the internal auditing profession by issuing standards, offering professional certifications such as the CIA program, holding educational seminars, distributing publications, and conducting research through the IIA Research Foundation.

Douglass said, "Wait a minute. You said CIA agents."

Walker smiled. "Certified Internal Auditor. I like to think that after the fall of the iron curtain, we need more Certified Internal Auditors than CIA agents. Russia even changed the name of KGB. Many of the KGB agents became tax auditors."

Douglass laughed and said, "Do you think that is good for Russians? By the way, you know what we say about CIA agents. They can not follow an elephant with a bloody nose over fresh snow."

Walker continued. "Recently, the IIA Research Foundation published its largest research project to date, The Competency Framework for Internal Auditing or CFIA. The CFIA project was a comprehensive global study of internal auditing."

Walker indicated that the two most acceptable scientific methods for deriving truth are the deductive and inductive approaches. An inference can be either inductive or deductive. Under the deductive approach, there is a direct application of knowledge in the production of new knowledge. Sherlock Holmes was an expert in proceeding from the general to the specific, that is, the inductive approach. Fraud investigators make clinical observations, conduct physical examinations and interrogations in order to draw inferences to arrive at certain conditions.

"The deductive technique involves an empirical approach to truth. One takes a representative sample of the whole in order to predict a probable outcome based upon the sample. Financial auditors use this type of deductive approach. A *fraud auditor* should use both approaches," Walker emphasized.

Douglass interrupted. "Tell me about George Steinbrenner."

Walker just laughed. Everyone knew about George and his frequent firing of managers and public relations directors. Everyone in the organization is afraid of him.

"OK, let's get serious," Douglass finally said. "Are there any similarities between these perfect game pitchers? Why would someone pick perfect game dates to kill fans?"

Walker was silent for sometime. "These games and pitchers are different. I can think of no reason why someone would pick these particular dates to kill someone. But I will ponder your questions. My guess is the killings may involve the players' strike in 1994. There were ill feelings between the players and owners. Better yet, the umpires' union may be involved. Twenty-two umpires were basically replaced by twenty-five minor-league umpires in 1999 during the umpires' strike."

"One of them might be the bad guy. I'm checking all of them out," Douglass said.

Chapter 6

Shea Stadium
and Fenway Park

Internal auditing can add value in only two ways: by reducing the cost of the internal audit function itself, and
by making audit recommendations that add value. These
two approaches are neither dependent nor mutually exclu-
sive. To achieve world-class status, internal audit functions
must pursue both cost reductions and high value audit
recommendations.

Anthony Walz

William Douglass was sitting in the stands in William A.
Shea Municipal Stadium with Fleet Walker watching the game
between the New York Mets and the San Francisco Giants.
Douglass and Walker had taken Subway No. 7 to reach the stadium in Flushing, N.Y.

The stadium was noisy from planes flying over the ball park
to arrive at or depart from LaGuardia Airport. Walker told
Douglass that television and radio broadcasters cannot be heard
when the planes fly over. Walker noticed a few people were
making paper airplanes and throwing them onto the field.

There was also the distinctive smell of a nearby garbage
dump.

Walker was trying to skim a short piece on documenting
audit findings in an issue of *Internal Auditor*. The author, Brian
Schwartz, said that the so-called findings form is probably the
most critical work paper of an auditor. This form provides the

foundation of the outcome of an audit by consolidating all pertinent information relating to a particular audit (i.e., missing a control, a control breakdown). Schwartz said that the most effective format for the finding form has five common elements: the condition, the criteria, the cause, the effect, and the recommendation. Walker thought of the form as something like the scoring sheet that a baseball fan uses to score a game.

"I keep thinking about these perfect games," Douglass tilted his head toward Fleet. "I would think that a perfect game is one in which all batters strike out on three pitches, all of which are called strikes. A called ball by the umpire or a foul is in a sense a flaw," Douglass explained.

"Oh, I doubt that any such game will be pitched," Walker responded. "That would be like a perfect game of golf—18 holes-in-one."

"Well, a number of people have bowled perfect games. I bowl once a week in a bowling league, so I checked on some statistics. Last year about 20,550 perfect games were rolled compared to about 6,000 ten years ago. The real perfection in bowling is to roll three perfect games—hit the pocket 36 times. Several people have done it, but the American Bowling Congress has disqualified them on technicalities—too much oil on the lanes or not a sanctioned tournament. Some people cry conspiracy theory," Douglass explained.

"Too much oil on the lane? How does that affect the bowling ball?" Walker asked with a curious look on his face.

"Oil is put on the lanes to provide traction for the bowling balls. Supposedly adding too much oil gives the bowler a groove that keeps the ball on track. Who knows? At least from the point of view of the ABC, there has never been a perfect-three-game series."

"I can relate to tennis. A perfect game in tennis might be hitting four aces each time you serve during a set. Once in the third set of the 1995 U.S. Open Finals, I saw Pete Sampras serve four straight aces against Andre Agassi, the best returner in tennis," Walker said.

"I'm not into tennis," Douglass stated flatly.

"Well, I hate to say, but over the past decade, the U.S. Open has generated more revenue for New York than Yankee Stadium. For example, New York gets a piece of each hot dog sold at the U.S. Open at Flushing Meadow, but nothing for a hot dog sold at Yankee Stadium." Walker paused.

"Tell me about Bunnings' perfect game," Douglass inquired.

"On Fathers' Day, June 21, 1964, the Philadelphia Phillies were playing the hapless, last-place New York Mets in this stadium," Walker began. "A 6'3", 32-year-old right-hander was on the mound, and his backstop was 6'3" Gus Triandos. Umpire Ed Sudol was calling balls and strikes in the 91-degree humid heat. There was the same huge scoreboard behind centerfield, 86 feet high and 175 feet long with a Bulova clock, and the batters could see large Top Brass, Rheingold, and *Herald Tribune* billboards outside the stadium.

"By the way," Walker continued, "you do know that Bunning is now a Republican Senator from Kentucky."

"Yes, yes." Douglass looked at his cellular phone expecting one of his agents to call with bad news. "Bunning has been putting a great deal of pressure on the President—who in turn is on my boss' back. Bunning was on television last night talking about his perfect game."

"I missed him. Anyway, back to June 21, 1964. The Phillies scored a run in the top of the first inning. In the bottom of the first, Bunning hung two sliders for the first batter, Jim Hickman, but he fouled them straight back.

"Bunning shouted to Hickman, 'You've had your chances. You won't get any more like that.' Hickman struck out three times that day. Bunning would record ten strikeouts during the game.

"The National League Mets were perfect victims for three innings on the grass field in the 90 degree heat, although shortstop Cookie Rojas did jump three feet to catch a liner by Amado Samuel in the third.

"Bunning used an extremely powerful hip and torso rotation with his three-quarter arm motion to power the ball toward home plate. He would follow-through with a sweeping fall toward first base, sometimes to where he was even leaning on the ground with his left glove hand.

"The mound at Shea Stadium was higher apparently than Bunning liked. His mound at Philadelphia's Connie Mack Stadium was intentionally kept low to favor Bunning's sidearm pitching motion. In 1969, the rule-makers fixed the height of the mound at 10 inches to give hitters a better chance for hitting. Much like the way that accounting rule-makers use GAAP for more uniform financial statements."

Walker pointed to the mound.

"In the fourth, right-handed Ron Hunt stroked a long drive to right field, but the ball landed about a foot in foul territory. Part Cherokee, Hunt crowded the plate. In 1971, he was hit by pitched balls 50 times, but this day he would not receive a bruise. He struck out in the fourth after working the count to 3-2.

"Ed Kranepool popped up to Gus Triandos in fair territory, but Kranepool forgot to run to first base. Triandos caught the ball.

"With one out in the fifth, Jesse Gonder lined a ball between first and second. Second baseman Tony Taylor made a diving stop of the hard liner. Picking up the loose ball while on his knees, Taylor threw to John Hernstein on first and easily beat Gonder, who was slow footed. This out was one of only two plays that first base umpire Paul Pryor had to call during the game.

"After the game Bunning said, 'The fifth-inning liner by Gonder was a base hit all the way. What a play that Taylor made!' Bunning beamed. 'What a play!'

"In the Phillies' sixth, Bunning smashed a two-run double. 'It's a wonderful feeling. I still can't believe it,' Bunning said after the game.

"Starting in the seventh, with the Phillies ahead 6-0, the 32,904 formerly hostile fans began to scream for the slender right hander. First baseman Ed Kranepool, nicknamed 'The Krane,' worked the count to 3-2. Bunning threw a close pitch and Sudol called 6'3" 'Krane' out on strikes. Kranepool did not appreciate the strike call and argued with Sudol. Kranepool lost the argument. The side was retired in order.

Walker continued to explain. "Then in the eighth, Hawk Taylor worked the count to 3-2. Taylor was then called out on strikes, but catcher Gus Triandos dropped the ball. Triandos had to throw Taylor out at first. Taylor was angry at Sudol for the called third strike. Triandos was charged with *four* passed balls in one inning while catching for Hoyt Wilhelm with Baltimore.

"The ninth is always the most difficult inning for a perfect game," Walker suggested. "The lanky right-hander forced Charlie Smith to pop out to shortstop Bobby Wine in foul territory back of third base for the first out.

"The next two batters were pinch hitters sent in by manager Casey Stengel, who was the winning manager in the Don Larsen perfect game. Somehow the Mets had to overcome Bunning's spell over them. They had been baffled by his three-quarter motion fast curves and his frequent sliders. George Altman, batting for Amado Samuel, went down swinging, however. Two down.

"John Stephenson, pinch-hitting for Tom Sturdivant, got be-hind in the count 0-2 immediately. He swung at the first pitch and watched the second strike cross the plate. Bunning took his hat off, rubbed his right hand through his crewcut, and then threw two called balls. He fidgeted nervously as he looked to-ward Triandos. His uniform was soaked from perspiration." Gus Triandos signaled for a curve, and imposing arbiter Ed Sudol went into his crouch." Walker slammed his right fist into the palm of his left hand. "'Strike three,' roared Sudol. The rookie left-hander struck out on Bunning's curve ball. The ninth perfect game was complete.

"As with his politics, Bunning was conservative with his pitches. He threw only 86 pitches during the game." Walker paused to collect his thoughts.

"The normally loyal Mets' fans gave Jim Bunning a standing ovation for several minutes. The applause was deafening. Man-ager Gene Mauch and the Phillies mobbed their hero, and when Bunning went into the dugout, the fans began shouting, 'We want Bunning! We want Bunning!'

"Wes Covington was playing left field for Bunning. This was Wes' second perfect game, being the Braves' right fielder during the perfect game of Harvey Haddix. Joe Christopher, the Mets' right fielder was not so lucky. This also was Joe's second perfect game *loss*. He had played left field for Pittsburgh during Had-dix's perfect *loss* game."

At that moment Douglass and Walker watched Mets' out-fielder Bobby Bonilla's home run go over the Diamond Vision video display screen. To the left of the screen was a picnic area. In centerfield behind the fence, a big red apple rose out of a giant black top hat that actually looked like a black kettle. The score was 1-0, in the bottom of the first. Walker made a home run notation on the score card he was filling out.

Walker noticed Douglass looking at his scoring sheet. "Everything in baseball is analyzed. We keep track of minute details, somewhat like internal auditing. Auditors prepare and maintain detailed working papers. On the working papers the auditor uses an assortment of checkmarks, tiny handwritten letters, and geometric figures written next to items relating to specific information in the audit tests. Called 'tick marks,' they represent specific audit tests performed on the listed items."

By the third inning the score was already 5-4 in favor of the Giants. Barry Bonds had hit a two-run home run and second baseman Jeff Kent hit a solo homer over the eight foot right-field portion of the circular fence about 338 feet from home plate.

Walker reminded Douglass that visibility for batters is usually poor in Shea Stadium and 95 percent of the seats are in foul territory.

"Since this repeater hit the fan, I've been looking at some of the scores in the paper," Douglass said. "Why do baseball scores look like football scores now? The Angels beat the Yankees 10-8 yesterday."

Walker smiled and shrugged. "Too many runs. Colorado pitcher Darren Holmes says pitchers should go on strike. Last year, the Red Sox beat the Royals 22-11. Five K.C. pitchers threw 230 pitches. The Dodgers beat the Pirates 19-2. Cory Snyder hit 3 homers and had seven RBIs. Look at Mark McGwire's 70 home runs in 1998. That's 10 more than Babe Ruth's record of 60 homers in 1927. I forget how many Sammy Sosa hit, but Ken Griffey hit 56.

"Toronto Blue Jays general manager, Pat Gillick, says the over-all quality of major league pitching is 'terrible.' Umpire Dave Phillips uses the word 'miserable.' An article in *Sports Illustrated* complains that the pitching staffs are stocked with too many weak-armed nibblers, scattershot rookies and vagabond veterans who have been to more places than Charles Kuralt." Walker shrugged.

"Well, what do *you* think?" Douglass pressed.

"I suppose expansion is partly to blame. In 1960 with eight-team leagues, there were 233 pitchers. In 1993, there were 533 pitchers. Besides, most of the changes in baseball over the past thirty years have helped hitters. We lowered the pitcher's mound five inches in 1969. Then came the designated hitter in 1973, and more and more parks have artificial turf. The new ballparks favor hitters because fans want to see runs.

"Probably the major problem is the small strike zone. Umpires tend to call strikes about seven inches below the letters. As written, a strike goes from the batter's kneecaps to about letter high," Walker explained.

"What should the baseball hierarchy do?" Douglass asked.

"Make the mound taller and call a strike a strike."

Douglass' cellular phone rang. He listened and then motioned for Walker to leave. In the concession area Douglass told Walker that someone was sick in a bathroom on the first base side. By the time they reached the bathroom, medical personnel had arrived and pronounced the young man dead.

A man around 25 years old was lying on the restroom floor near the row of sinks. On the floor was a baseball card. Without touching the card, Douglass noticed that it was damp. Jerry Morales, San Diego Padres. Douglass could smell an odor like garlic on the body.

"Don't touch the card. Save it. It's important."

He turned to the paramedic. "What killed him?"

"I don't know," the young paramedic replied.

"Get the cause of death to me as soon as possible." Douglass ordered. He handed his business card to the medic.

Douglass looked at Walker. "Another San Diego Padres baseball card. This killer must hate the Padres. We need to concentrate on the Padres. Is it a baseball fan? A former player? A former umpire?" Douglass was basically talking to himself.

Douglass looked into the mirror. He saw a narrow face with hazel eyes staring back at him. The eyes were bloodshot. His wife had told him that he looked like a young Harrison Ford. Not tonight. His short, wild hair was not combed. The cowlick on the back of his head was sticking up. He needed a shave. His conservative navy suit on his 5'11½" slender frame was wrinkled.

Before the game was over, Bob Losure on CNN broke the news about the killing at the Mets' stadium.

As the fans left the stadium that evening, many of them saw the police tape around the restroom. The Mets had won, 11-8, in a slugfest.

The headline in the *New York Times* the next day was "Ballpark Killer Strikes Again." There was a photo of Douglass talking to Fleet Walker outside the restroom.

The *New York Times* compared the "Ballpark Killer" with Dr. "X" in 1977. Dr. Mario E. Jascalevich murdered five of his hospital patients in Hackensack, New Jersey, by injecting them with lethal doses of African dart poison, called curare.

Then in 1981, a Los Angeles male night nurse named Robert Diaz was charged with the murder of ten patients by injecting them with a powerful heart drug, Lidocaine. Police found two vials of Lidocaine, a syringe, and morphine in his home. Diaz was found guilty and sentenced to die in the gas chamber.

Dr. Arnfinn Nesset was found guilty in 1983 of murdering at least 22 elderly patients in a nursing home in Norway. The bespectacled doctor killed them by injecting curacit, a derivative of curare, into their veins. The doctor may have killed as many as 62 patients.

There were 134 mystery deaths in a hospital in Vermillion County, Indiana. A former nurse is suspected of using deadly potassium chloride on these patients. A male nurse in Glendale, California confessed to about 45 mercy killings in a hospital in 1998.

★ ★ ★ ★ ★

Same song, second verse, Douglass was sitting with Walker two days later on June 23 in Fenway Park. The autopsy report had indicated that the young man at the Mets' game had died of bug poisoning—savin—mixed with dimethyl sulfate. Douglass also told Walker that the exhumed body of the person who died on May 17 in Yankee stadium was poisoned and did not die from a heart attack.

To try to calm Douglass, Walker asked him if the FBI had ever been called in to look for any confiscated bats.

Douglass appeared surprised. "What confiscated bats?"

"During the Chicago White Sox's game against the Cleveland Indians before the players' strike, Cleveland's Albert Belle, with a then eleven million annual salary, was accused of corking his bat."

"Corking? Why cork a bat?" Douglass asked, with a curious look in his blue eyes.

"A batter can hit a ball about 10 feet further by drilling a hole in the meat end of the bat—say as wide as a dime for 12-inches deep. By decreasing the weight of the bat by about two ounces, the batter is able to swing the bat quicker. Corking the hole dampens the sound of the hollow cavity," Walker explained.

Walker continued. "Back in 1987, Mets' Howard Johnson had his bat seized on suspicion that his bat was corked. In the same year Houston's Billy Hatcher was suspended for 10 days for corking his bat. Each manager can ask to have one bat from the opposing team tested each game. This is, of course, random sampling to obtain an opinion, and then carrying the opinion back to the total population."

"Home-run production of the batters dropped in the 1987 season, inferring that other illegal bats were taken out of use. Back in 1974, Yankees' Graig Nettles was ejected from a game when rubber balls were found in his bat."

"Why call the FBI?" Douglass was still confused.

"Umpire Dave Phillips confiscated Belle's bat so it could be checked for cork. The bat was placed in the Umpires' locker room at Comiskey Park and the door was locked. Sometime during the sixth or seventh inning someone broke into the locker room by going through the ceiling tiles. The person took the confiscated bat and replaced it with a less clean and shinier one. Phillips said that the confiscated bat had vanished. Of course, this could have been management fraud or employee fraud, depending on who really did the dastardly deed."

"So you see, Douglass, not only must the FBI catch killers, but they have to find confiscated bats."

"What happened to Belle?" Douglass smiled and asked.

"The alleged original bat was eventually returned and the American League X-rayed the bat and then sawed it in half. The bat was corked, and Belle was suspended for ten days," Walker said.

"Well, what can you expect from a sport that encourages base stealing and computes a steal per game figure," Douglass smiled. "Why, Rickey Henderson stole 130 bases in 1982 and didn't serve a day in jail."

"Leave it to a FBI agent to worry about crime," Walker joked.

Douglass continued. "Hey, you have players and coaches trying to steal signs. Some teams put spies in the center field scoreboard to steal the catcher's signs. You have batters guarding the plate; there are hit-and-run plays, and the pitcher tries to handcuff the opposing team. Baseball needs police officers, not umpires," Douglass said with acidic humor.

"Now don't forget about the double steal," Walker added with a smile. "There's also a dead ball, say when a batter is hit by a pitched ball or a foul ball is not caught.

"Then there's the emery ball—a ball that's been scratched on one side to cause it to curve more. Kevin Gross was caught on the mound red-handed with sandpaper; Joe Niekro was caught with an emery board. Preacher Roe admitted (after he retired) to throwing a spit ball—a member of the clergy no less. There's crime and fraud in baseball just like the business world."

Walker continued. "I get real uneasy when auditees do not cooperate or try to hide things from me. Sure enough, it's a sign that something serious is wrong. You would think that auditees would wise up. If I wanted to get past the auditor, I would be as nice and cooperative as possible. Then I would try and steer them away from the actual problem areas by focusing them on a relatively unimportant area. You do this by giving the auditors too much information to digest. However, the good auditors know how to cut through the trivial to the important. Just like FBI agents, internal auditors must have excellent interviewing skills.

"I read that Orel Hershiser believes that about 20 percent of all National League pitchers throw spitballs, scuff balls, or otherwise cheat. Orel once said, 'I have a natural sinker already, and I can double the break with a scuffed ball.' It is unbelievable," Walker stated. "To a certain extent, these cheating pitchers are like fraudsters and executives who cook the books."

By the end of the second, the Red Sox were behind the Indians, 2-0. The game was going the way of the Red Sox's season: poorly. Even without a corked bat, David Justice drove a ball to the centerfield fence before Boston centerfielder, Darren

Lewis, caught the ball on the run—almost 420 feet from home plate.

Along left field for 315 feet, Douglass could see the 37 foot-high Green Monster wall covered with hard plastic. A large Citgo sign looms above the Green Monster and the large scoreboard.

Walker told Douglass that before 1976 the wall was made of a framework of wooden railroad ties covered by tin. When the ball hit the wall, an outfielder would have to guess which way the ball would bounce. There is a 23-foot net along the top of the wall to protect the windows on Lansdowne Street—now Ted Williams Way. "Foul territory in Fenway Park is small," Walker added. "The left and center field walls were padded after the 1975 World Series when Fred Lynn crashed into the concrete wall. Now all major-league stadiums have narrow cinder warning tracks along the wall to alert outfielders they are nearing the wall. Fenway Park is considered to be a right-handed hitter's park because of the short distance to the left field wall."

Douglass' phone had not rung by the fifth inning, as the home team threw the ball around the diamond. The infield portion of a baseball field is called the diamond, with four sides each 90 feet in length. The outfield portion of Fenway is grass. Douglass had to admit that the single-deck ballpark was beautiful. Some of the seats are closer to home plate then the dugouts are. He asked Walker to tell him about the Shore perfect game.

"The story actually begins on July 19, 1914, when George Babe Ruth, the son of a Baltimore saloon keeper, was sold by the then *minor* league team Baltimore Orioles, to the Boston Red Sox. Along with Ruth went 6'4", 220-pound pitcher Ernie Shore and catcher Ben Eagan for a total package of $30,000. Apparently, Connie Mack could have bought Babe Ruth, but refused."

"Three years later on Saturday, June 23, 1917, Babe Ruth, the future Sultan of Swat, was scheduled to pitch in hitter-friendly Fenway Park against the Washington Nationals. His opposing pitcher was Doc Ayers. Babe did pitch to the first batter, Ray Walker, in the first game of the doubleheader. No relationship to me," Fleet Walker smiled. "He was white. Anyway, Babe walked the first batter and became angry with Umpire Clarence Brick Owens' calls.

"Babe's arguing and abusive language caused the overweight umpire to issue a warning: 'Get in there and pitch, or you'll be out of here in a minute.'

" 'If I'm out of here, you'll get a punch in the jaw!' shot back Babe Ruth.

"Owens stepped in front of home plate, pointed to Babe, and roared, 'You're through now!'

"Babe rushed to the umpire and swung his left fist. Brick Owens ducked, but was hit behind the right ear.

"Catcher Chet Thomas grabbed Babe, and along with help from other teammates, kept Babe away from Owens. The Boston on-duty police were called on to the playing field. Ruth would receive a 10-day suspension for his aggressive behavior." Walker gave a helpless shrug.

"J.V. Fitzgerald in the *Washington Post* said that Umpire Brick Owens had the reputation of being able to 'lick his weight in wild cats.' If there had been a fight, there was little question that Ruth would have finished second.

"One has to wonder why the baserunner, Ray Walker, didn't just trot around the bases during the commotion. Of course, another umpire might have called time out," Fleet Walker suggested.

"Sox manager, Jack Barry sent his catcher Chet Thomas, with Babe, to the clubhouse. Sam Agnew became the new catcher, and right-hander Ernie Shore became the new pitcher.

"Ernie Shore took his five warm-up pitches, looked at the base runner on first, and threw his first pitch to Eddie Foster, Washington's third baseman.

"Still standing at first base, Ray Walker broke for second base on Shore's first pitch, and catcher Agnew tossed Walker out with a great throw to second base. The 16,158 people in the stands then watched Shore begin retiring batters.

"With two outs in the sixth, Charles Jamieson hit a ball up the middle which bounced off Shore's glove. Shortstop Jack Scott dashed over, picked up the bouncing ball, and threw to first to beat the outfielder by a half-a-step.

"The toughest inning was the top of the ninth," Walker continued. "Boston was ahead, 4-0. After Shore retired shortstop Shanks, catcher John Henry crashed a line drive toward left fielder Duffy Lewis, who came running in to make a nice catch for the second out. With only one more out remaining, crafty Washington manager Clark Griffith substituted speedster Mike Menosky for pitcher Doc Ayres. The 5'8" Griffith, nicknamed Old Fox, had been an imposing pitcher himself and was instrumental in establishing the American League.

"Mike Menosky pushed a bunt past Shore on the mound. Second baseman Barry grabbed the ball, and threw to Dick Hoblitzel at first for the final out.

"Some people maintain that Shore did not pitch a perfect game since he faced only 26 batters." Walker continued quickly to explain. "However, Ernie Shore was credited with the fifth perfect game in the major leagues—at least until 1991 when the statistician committee removed his perfect game from the record books.

"Shore struck out only two batters, but his sinker ball caused six Nationals to hit back to him at the mound. Most of the Nationals meekly hit ground balls to the infielders or lazy flies to the outfielders. A sinker ball is similar to a split-finger pitch, which looks like a fastball but has a late, downward break."

"Do you think Shore could be the bad guy?" Douglass hurriedly asked.

"Nope," Walker tilted his head and laughed. "After retiring from baseball in 1920, Shore went back to Winston-Salem, North Carolina and was elected sheriff of Forsyth County. He chased the 'bad guys' for 34 years, dying on September 24, 1980. Maybe a relative." Walker smiled.

During the seventh inning stretch, Douglass and Walker walked around the concession areas. Douglass talked to several of his agents, but there was no sign of the killer. They both purchased a legendary Fenway frank and a Coke and went back to their seats.

Boston lost, 7-5. Walker said Boston had good hitters this season but no pitching. No one was killed.

Walker told Douglass in a serious tone that the killer knew baseball. The killer knew that the Ernie Shore game was no longer considered a perfect game.

"So when is the next perfect game?" Douglass asked stonily.

"Not good—Yankee Stadium," Walker said quietly. "David Cone pitched a perfect game against the Montreal Expos on Sunday July 18, 1999. I saw most of the game. We have to catch this killer before July 18. That's about three weeks. Can we do it?"

"I hope so. I have agents following all twenty-two umpires that were terminated in 1999. Do you think a losing pitcher from a perfect game could be the bad guy?"

"Doubt it for losing pitchers. No motive; they become at least a footnote in baseball history if they are the losing pitcher. Some of those terminated umpires were experienced—Rich Garcia, Frank Pulli, and Mike Reilly had a combined 58 years

of big-league experience. The twenty-two umpires were replaced by minor-league umpires. Garcia called second base for
David Wells' perfect game in 1998. I'm sure they were angry."

★ ★ ★ ★ ★

By July 18 the FBI had made no progress in catching the
baseball killers. Douglass met with Fleet Walker in the internal
auditor's office in Yankee stadium and both reviewed their
preparations for the game that evening. Walker was naturally
extremely nervous.

Today the Yankees were *not* playing the Montreal Expos, the
team that David Cone pitched the perfect game against on July
18, 1999.

Before 36-year-old right-hander David Cone took the
mound on that Sunday in 1999, former Yankee catcher Yogi
Berra made a triumphant return to Yankee Stadium, ending
many years of ill will with Yankees principal owner George
Steinbrenner. On Yogi Berra day, Yogi used Joe Girardi's mitt
to catch the ceremonial first pitch from Don Larsen. In 1956,
this same Don Larsen pitched a perfect game in the World Series against the Brooklyn Dodgers with Yogi catching. It was
also Yankees manager Joe Torre's 59th birthday.

On that magical day David Cone, 36, would pitch a perfect
game, winning 6-0. He used 88 pitches, 68 for strikes to handcuff the Expos hitters. Montreal were in next to last place in
the National League East, 21 1/2 games back of Atlanta. Cone
had to wait out a 33-minute rain delay with one out in the
bottom of the third. He needed only seven pitches to retire the
Expos in the fourth inning. Only one Expos player came close
to occupying first base. With one out in the eighth, Jose Vidro
hit a hard grounder up the middle. Second baseman Chuck
Knoblauch, who had been erratic in the field during the season,
moved to his right, caught the ball, pivoted, and made a perfect
toss to first baseman Tino Martinez to barely get Vidro.

Today's game against Boston was not as excited. By the end of fourth inning, the Yankees were ahead of the Red Sox, 4-0. The Red Sox were already four games behind the Yankees in the American League East. A loss today at the bats of the Yankees would move Boston five games back of New York.

Nothing happened through the eighth inning, and Walker began to become cautiously optimistic. Douglass and Walker sat down between one of their slow walks around the stadium observing the police officers and FBI agent stationed throughout the stadium.

Douglass asked, "Do you surf the web?"

"Sure," Walker replied simply.

"Last night I was surfing for more information about perfect games. Could you get me some ticket stubs for David Wells' perfect game?" Douglass said this with a straight face.

"Maybe," answered Walker. "Why? How can that solve this mystery? How many ticket stubs do you need?" Walker began to smile.

"Say 100." Douglass answered.

"Is that enough? What are they selling for now?" Walker actually chuckled.

"Someone was trying to sell two ticket stubs from David Wells' perfect game, in good condition, for $400 each. Price negotiable." Douglass said.

"Did you check eBay, the online auction place? So you wish me to give you 100 stubs times $400 or $40,000. You find these clowns, and I'll get you a David Wells stub."

"Tell me a little about Wells' game as we walk around once more." Douglass got up. "I know it occurred one year before the Cone perfect game. Could there be a connection? Two perfect games in two seasons by the same team is unusual."

"You bet it's unusual, but Jim Bunning and Sandy Koufax pitched their perfect games in two consecutive seasons - 1964 and 1965. Anyway David Wells pitched his perfect game on Sunday, May 17, 1998 against Minnesota Twins. Cone apparently sat next to Wells between innings trying to calm him down. Wells is a hefty lefty, at least 240 pounds. One reporter said he looked as if he just climbed out of a 18-wheeler. He had a pierced ear and tattoos of his mother and his son on his chest."

"No kidding." Douglass said as he walked slowly down the stadium hall, eyes darting back and forth.

"During the game, Wells got behind the count on eight of the last nine batters he faced. Paul Molitor, no batting slouch, took a strike on a 3-and-1 count before he struck out. Wells threw 120 pitches, 41 of them balls."

"The biggest scare, as in the Cone perfect game, involved second baseman Chuck Knoblauch. In the eighth inning, Ron Coomer smashed an opposite-field grounder which nearly eluded Knoblauch's glove. Knoblauch knocked the ball down, recovered, and threw out Coomer easily."

Walker paused and continued. "The catching assignments for the Wells and Cone's perfect games are interested. Jorge Posada was the starting catcher in both the 1998 and 1999 seasons. Posada caught Well's perfect game in 1998, but although Joe Girardi caught only 65 games in 1999, he was behind the plate for Cone. Girardi came close to catching two perfect games.

"Six of the Yankees players also had been in the Wells' perfect game the previous year. For both games center fielder Bernie Williams went 4-for-7, but right fielder Paul O'Neill and first baseman Tino Martinez were each 1-for-8."

"After the game, Don Larsen called Wells, and they discovered that they had graduated from the same high school, Point Loma in San Diego."

By the end of this game, nothing had happened. The ball park killers did not strike at Yankee stadium. Walker went home a tired, but happy internal auditor.

Four hours later Walker was awaken by the telephone. The caller was Douglass.

"Sorry to awake you, Fleet, but they hit at the Montreal game at San Diego. Five people are dead, and several more are in serious condition."

"Oh no. They have gone random. We'll never catch them," Walker said.

"We can't assume that they will ignore the perfect game dates. When is the next one?"

"There's good news, and there's bad news," Walker answered. "You have ten days before the next game—July 28." He paused.

"So what's the bad news?" Douglass shrugged.

"There were two perfect games tossed on July 28."

"What? Where?" Douglass almost shouted.

"Los Angeles and Arlington, Texas. I've checked the schedule earlier, and they are both night games. There is two hours time difference between Arlington and Los Angeles, and at least four hours flying time."

"I'll never make both games," Douglass looked perplexed.

"You're right, but there's more good news," Walker added quietly.

"What is it?" Douglass asked earnestly.

"We'll be able to find out if we are dealing with more than one killer." Walker said cheerfully.

"We need to get the airlines to keep a list of everyone flying between Arlington and L.A. that evening. We'll videotape everyone boarding the planes."

"There's more good news," Walker interrupted. "After the July 28 games there are no perfect games pitched in August."

"We're going to catch them on the 28th," Douglass said with little conviction. "Which game should I attend?"

"I don't know. You might as well flip a coin. I often face the same dilemma in my job when I sample. You see, Douglass, internal auditors cannot examine every document or transaction because of time constraints. Therefore, we examine only certain ones (a sample) and base our conclusion on the sample results. This technique saves time, but at the expense of accuracy. We are forced to take a risk, but when I am wrong as an auditor the penalty is not as severe as in this case," Walker mused.

"Also, I forgot but I'll be able to attend the 61st International Conference of the Institute of Internal Auditors. It's in Dallas this year, and I'll be able to check out the Ballpark at Arlington for you. I know some people in their organization, and they'll need some help preparing for these killers."

Douglass did flip a coin and Los Angeles won.

Chapter 7

Los Angeles

By incorporating computer assisted fraud detection techniques into their routine audits, internal auditors can increase the probability that they will detect fraud if it exists. As new technologies enable organizations to become more automated, auditors should also harness the power of computers. With hardware and software becoming more powerful and less expensive, auditors should be limited only by their imaginations.

Nita Crowder

Country Music Television was blaring loudly in the background. Randy Travis was singing, "Baby, please come back before you kill us all," as the man finished brushing clear fingernail polish over his fingers, thumbs, and palms. He had previously covered his hands and arms with Derma Shield. Derma Shield was a non-greasy, non-toxic formulation, which formed an invisible protection against most skin irritants such as paints, grease, sulfuric acids, and blood. He hoped the combination of Derma Shield and fingernail polish would disguise his fingerprints. But after the polish dried, he put on a pair of gloves. He worried that since Derma Shield allowed his skin to breathe and perspire normally, the poison might be absorbed into his skin. He didn't want to take any chances.

On the kitchen table was an open copy of *Merck Index* and *An Instant Guide to Mushrooms & Other Fungi* on several layers of an old *Baseball Weekly* newspaper.

The man known as Sandy was mixing amanitin taken from Death Cap and Panther mushrooms with muscarine taken from Sweating mushrooms. Both amanitin and muscarine are highly toxic and solvent in water. He was tired of using the savin mixture.

According to *Merck*, muscarine causes nausea, vomiting, diarrhea, and circulatory collapse, progressing to convulsions, coma, and death in a few hours. A lethal dose is only 0.23% of a milligram. [LD 50 i.v. in mice: 0.23 mg 1 kg].

Amanitin's lethal dose is 0.4% of a milligram. It causes vomiting, bloody stools, muscular twitching, and convulsions.

The mixture of muscarine and amanitin was placed into a large bottle of dimethyl sulfoxide. Next he added some tubocurarine chloride, taken from the bark of certain trees in South America. Often used for poison arrows by natives, this poison causes complete paralysis of voluntary muscles, including respiration, resulting in death by asphyxia.

He was pleased with the potion, and he filled ten fingernail polish bottles with the liquid. Each bottle was wrapped with tissue and placed inside a Ziploc sandwich bag. Next he used a hypodermic needle to carefully put the mixture inside some peanuts in 12 bags of peanuts. Each bag of peanuts was placed inside a sandwich bag.

He smiled and began to sing his favorite song by the group, Alabama, "Cheap Seats." "We like our beer as flat as can be. We like our dogs with mustard and relish." He emphasized the word relish. "We got a great pitcher. What's his name? Well we can't even spell it. Cheap seats. Cheap seats."

He laughed as he used the needle to place some of the mixture into some little packages of Kraft mustard found at hot dog and hamburger stands. He read the ingredients on the chopped onion packages as he inserted his potion. Ditto for the Kraft Sweet Pickle Relish packages. Alan Jackson was singing

"Who Says You Can't Have It All" on CMT as he inserted the deadly liquid inside some Heinz Tomato Ketchup packages. He really liked Alan Jackson's moustache. Maybe he should buy a white cowboy hat to hide the hair he was losing.

Lorrie Morgan was howling on CMT as he carefully removed the double set of gloves with tissue paper. "This is my night to go crazy just to see how it feels," sung Lorrie. He disposed of the gloves, tissue paper, needle, and newspaper in a large garbage bag.

He picked up his guitar and began picking. His voice was adequate; he had cut several demos, but he had never been able to sell any of the songs he had written. He began singing "Stubborn as a Stump:"

Since she walked out the door
My feet ain't touched the floor
The phone's on her empty pillow in case she calls

She told me that I'd feel better after she's gone
Well I ain't improving
And I ain't moving
I'm as stubborn as a stump in the frozen ground

Next he worked for a few minutes on a 1,000-piece mystery jigsaw puzzle spread out on a card table. Janice had given him "Murder Makes a Call" for his birthday, which was now practically completed. The puzzle had a secret puzzle image. He soon tired, looked at his watch, turned his Mitsubishi television off, opened up a can of Cherry RC Cola, and went to rent a cheap video movie, *The Silence of the Lambs*.

★ ★ ★ ★ ★

"Wait 'til next year" was the statement the old Brooklyn Dodger fans would express after being beaten in the World Series by the New York Yankees. Since their move to Dodger Stadium in Chavez Ravine, the Los Angeles ballpark built on a fault line has been the site of two perfect games. The Dodger

Bums are the only franchise to lose three perfect games—against Tom Browning, Don Larsen, and Dennis Martinez.

The Dodgers were on the winning end of the Sandy Koufax gem. So of the 16 perfect games, the Dodgers have participated in four of them. One other franchise, the Washington Senators/Minnesota Twins, has lost two perfect games (Ernie Shore and Jim Hunter). The Yankees have won three perfect games —Larsen, Wells, and Cone. Two franchises have won two perfect games—the Boston Red Sox (Cy Young and Ernie Shore) and the Cleveland Indians (Addie Joss and Len Barker). The Texas Rangers and the California Angels split two perfect games. Walker called these facts, analytics.

Dodger Stadium is considered to be a pitcher's park. There is a lot of room down the middle, and there are no short porches along the foul lines. A pitcher tries to keep the pitch away from the hitter so that if a slugger hits the ball hard, it'll go into the prescription athletic turf center field.

William Douglass had gone home from Yankee Stadium, kissed his wife, and then flew to Los Angeles. The current convention was that the serial killer would strike again on July 28. Douglass hoped that the adage "the braver the mouse, the fatter the cat" would apply to this diabolical killer. It certainly applied to the finding of fraudsters by auditors, according to Walker.

Douglass was sitting on the third base side staring at the gorgeous, clean ballpark that sits on a hilltop overlooking downtown Los Angeles. Fleet Walker was sitting beside him. They could see palm trees beyond the fences along the foul lines. There was blue padding on the wall around the field and even the concrete was painted blue. On one large tower was a blue Dodgers sign and a large painted baseball. They had a great view of the San Gabriel Mountains on one side and the city skyline on the other.

Chavez Ravine had been gullies, hills, washes, and twisting roads before the stadium was built. The privately financed sta-

dium has 21 terraced parking lots at five different levels allowing fans to park their cars and enter the stadium at the same
level. There is no public transportation to the games. There are
few rainout games and few home runs are hit out of the park.
The scoreboard is in left field and Diamond Vision in left. Although the fans have come late, leave early attitude; it was the
first stadium to draw three million fans in one season.

"Fleet, how was the Institute of Internal Auditors (IIA) convention in Dallas?" Douglass asked.

"It was great. The IIA always does a great job. I enjoy the
networking opportunities and the continuing education ses-
sions. I particularly like one on forensic accounting by a University of Texas professor, Jack Robertson. He is at the fore-
front of forensic accounting. I also liked the presentations on
information technology. However, one trend that I don't particularly like is the emergence of outsourcing practices by the
"BIG FIVE" accounting firms."

Douglass was curious, "what is outsourcing, Fleet?"

Fleet responded, "Outsourcing is the performance of internal auditing services by a third party vendor, such as an accounting firm."

"What's wrong with that? A little competition keeps everybody on their toes," countered Douglass.

"I agree to a certain extent. Outsourcing and corporate cost
cutting have caused all internal auditing departments to get
their act in order or be eliminated. However, I don't feel that
the same CPA firm that performs the annual financial audit
should also perform internal auditing services for the same organization. This situation is a clear conflict of interest and a violation of the CPA firm's independence.

"What do I mean about independence?" Walker answered
his own question. "Often a company being audited has a number of former employees of the CPA firm in the top manage-

ment. The SEC is upset. In 1999, the SEC found that 31 of 43 top partners of PricewaterhouseCoopers had committed at least one violation of owning stock in the company they were auditing. I like what Richard H. Walker, SEC's Director of Enforcement said: 'Cook the books, and you will go directly to jail without passing GO.'

"Outsourcing also raises a loyalty issue and the ability of the outsourcing firm to truly become a part of the organization. I guess an outsourced internal auditing department is better than no internal auditing department, but a good internal auditing department beats an outsourced internal auditing department everytime in my book."

Fleet went on, clearly agitated. "However, you better believe that I pay close attention to making sure the management of the New York Yankees is pleased with my department. That approach is the best way to prevent being outsourced."

"By management, you mean George Steinbrenner." Douglass smiled and changed the subject. "Who is pitching today anyway?"

"Moneybags Kevin Brown," Walker said regaining his calm.

"I know. I'm into baseball now. A seven-year $105 million salary. What is a split-finger fastball?" Douglass asked curiously. "I would split my finger for that money."

"That's a fastball which plunges as it reaches the plate. It's not as bad on the arm as a curve ball. The pitcher grips two fingers across the seams which slows the velocity of the ball without changing the pitcher's arm motion or speed. For example, Orel Hershiser has a big curve like Sandy Koufax and Carl Erskine. A ball can curve as much as 17 inches."

"Really?" Douglass said.

"Poor Lasorda. He's been on the losing end of two perfect games—Dennis Martinez and Tom Browning," Walker said slowly.

Douglass had read Walker's chapter on Dennis Martinez, Mr. El Perfecto. Right-hander Dennis Martinez was a veteran in his sixteenth season during 1991, the acknowledged ace of the Expos starting staff, and the first Nicaraguan to play in the majors. With the Montreal Expos for the 1990 and 1991 seasons, he had been a member of the National League All-Star Team. The 36-year-old ace hurler was starting the third game of this series during "Think Blue" week at Dodger Stadium in Chavez Ravine.

Ron Hassey had caught 52 games for Montreal during the 1991 season, and he was lucky enough to be catching his second *winning* perfect game, wearing bright red shin guards and chest protector. "To catch two winning perfect games is amazing," Walker told Douglass. His competing catcher, Gilbert Reyes, could only watch the game from the bench. Only Ossee Schreckengost caught in two perfect games—he was the losing catcher in the Cy Young game and the winning catcher for Adrian Joss.

With 45,560 fans in the stadium for the Sunday afternoon game in 1991, the 6'1" Martinez, wearing number 32, used control, curveballs, and sinkers to fool the Dodgers. This snapped the Dodgers' 38-inning scoreless pitching streak, tying the Dodger club record in 1966.

With one out in the fourth, Dodger second baseman, Juan Samuel, smashed a ball to the lip of the infield grass, but third baseman, Tim Wallach, made a fine defensive play. During the fourth, Martinez had a twinge in his back, and the Expos trainer came to the mound. The twinge worked itself out, however. With one out in the sixth, second baseman Delino Shields caught Alfredo Griffin's grounder and made a low throw to first base. Stretching to catch the ball, first baseman, Larry Walker, almost pulled his foot off the base.

Alfredo Griffin has truly been jinxed as the winner of the perfect game hard luck award. This Dominican Republic native was on the losing end of both the Browning and Barker perfect games, batting 0-3 in both of them. He would go 0-2 against Martinez, becoming the only person to play in three *losing* perfect games. He has made the most outs in losing perfect games — eight. Reggie Jackson made seven outs in two *winning* perfect games, but on his eighth time at bat he reached base on an error and scored a run in the Mike Witt thriller.

Mike Morgan, the Dodger starter, lost his perfect game in the sixth when Ron Hassey singled, but did not score. Hassey went one-for-four in Len Barker's perfect game and one-for-three in this game — a .286 average.

Then in the seventh, the Expos scored two unearned runs as a result of two fielding errors by hard luck Dodger shortstop Griffin and a triple to right center by Larry Walker.

Martinez helped his own cause in the seventh with a perfect toss to first base on a Juan Samuel bunt to him.

By the end of the eighth Martinez had retired 24 batters, including slugging Darryl Strawberry, Brett Butler, Juan Samuel, Eddie Murray, Kal Daniels, and Mike Scioscia. In 1998, Strawberry would be on the winning end of the David Wells perfect game.

By now the Nicaragua's state-run television network had interrupted regular programming to show the final innings. Later, President Chamorro would declare July 28 a national sports day in Martinez's honor.

Martinez tired in the ninth. Leadoff batter Mike Scioscia hit a fly ball to medium left field, which was finally caught by Ivan Calderon on the run. One out.

Trying to break Martinez's jinx on his helpless Dodgers, manager Tommy Lasorda put in pinch-hitter Stan Javier, who then struck out. Two outs.

With one out from perfection, pinch-hitter Chris Gwynn slowly strolled to home plate. Chris took a called ball by plate umpire Larry Poncino. Left-handed Gwynn hit an outside fast-ball down the third base line barely foul. On Martinez's 1-and-1 fastball, Gwynn hit the 95th pitch of the game toward the gap in right-center field. The ball seemed to hang in the L.A. haze.

At 3:22 P.M. center fielder Marquis Grissom made the final putout. "It was a routine fly ball," Grissom said. "But I had to get over there and get it. I had to forget what was at stake."

When Grissom nervously caught the ball, Dennis Martinez jumped into the air. This was his fourth shutout and first perfect game.

Martinez said afterward, "It was scary. I turned and followed the flight of the ball. I thought it was hit well. Then it went nowhere."

Martinez wept in happiness in the dugout after the perfect game. "I was blank—there was nothing in my mind. I had no words to say. I could only cry. I didn't know how to express myself. I didn't know how to respond to this kind of game." He sent his uniform top, autographed ball, and ticket stub to the Hall of Fame in Cooperstown.

Ron Hassey made history himself as the only man in the iron mask to catch two winning perfect games, his first being Len Barker's on May 15, 1981.

The slender Martinez with short brown hair and a gold chain around his neck continued, "Ronnie knew how to give me a good target. He gave me confidence in my pitches. The way he framed his body, how he spread his legs, and how he swept his mitt and stopped at the spot for me to pitch. The catcher is very, very important to a pitcher."

Vin Scully was watching the perfect game from the Dodger's broadcasting booth. He had also witnessed the Koufax and Larsen perfect games. In the *Los Angeles Times*, Scully compared the three perfect games.

"They've all been different. The tension was unbelievable the day Larsen pitched his because it was in the World Series. I was scared to death," Scully admitted.

How do you compare the Len Barker perfect game with Martinez' game? Hassey was asked. "You really have to compare the pitchers. Martinez is a pitcher's pitcher, and Barker was a thrower—a power pitcher. Both games were obviously exciting to catch and to remember.

"As a young player, I had a great arm for picking off base runners," Hassey remarked. "After I hurt my arm, I was not consistent from day-to-day. I couldn't tell until that day whether my elbow or shoulder would be hurting. My philosophy is as follows: If you don't have a great arm, you have to call a great game."

The nice thing about a perfect game for a catcher is that there are no base runners. He doesn't have to worry about a possible steal.

This day in Dodger Stadium was different. Somewhere in the stands was a serial killer, and Douglass had to catch him. Using his cellular phone he checked with several agents, and then tried to enjoy the game.

After the groundskeepers finished watering the rock-hard crushed-brick infield, the battle between the two teams began. The Dodger infielders are more familiar with the bad hops on the hard infield. The temperature was 70 and there was a 5 mile per hour wind blowing from the north. Along with the normal spitting and the distinctive crotch grabbing by the players, they were constantly slapping at the numerous gnats in the early evening air. Walker suggested, "The gnats are afraid of the dark and will disappear as the night wears on."

In the bottom of the first, Douglass noticed the Dodger third base coach giving many funny signals to the batter, Raul Mondesi. A curve ball caught the corner and froze Mondesi on a first strike. The crowd of 50,880 roared their disapproval of the called strike.

With a beautiful full moon in the sky the dreaded phone call came in the fourth inning. Kevin Brown was pitching to Astros Jeff Bagwell, the 1994 National League MVP, as Douglass and Walker hurriedly stood up and walked to the concession area. The crowd roared as Bagwell struck out. Bagwell is paid $6.875 million annually.

Brown was the winning pitcher. He scattered eight hits over seven innings to send Los Angeles to a season-high seventh straight victory. The Dodgers scored two runs on one passed ball by the Astro catcher. Shane Reynolds was the losing pitcher.

But Douglass was looking at peanuts. Peanuts were scattered around the body of the teenage girl lying on the concrete floor. Apparently the killer had put poison in the peanuts.

The news from the Ballpark in Arlington was also grim. A lady had been poisoned in a restroom with oleander shrub poison mixed with dimethyl sulfate. Was this a copycat killing? The other killings had been in men's restrooms. Everyone had assumed that the killer was a male. Assuming these killings were related, there must be two or more suspects. One killer was a woman — or at least someone who dressed like a woman.

So Douglass had lost. The killers had won. The resulting media coverage for the next week rivaled the O.J. Simpson matter. One headline: "Ballpark Killers Strike Twice in One Day." Plus Senator Howard Mestere delivered a blistering attack on baseball owners, accusing them of gutting the Commissioner's job, lying to Congress, and breaching the faith of fans, during a 2 ½ hour hearing aimed at examining the game's baseball antitrust exemption.

This week had not been good for baseball. The press was in a feeding frenzy. Since the Arlington killing was in a woman's bathroom, the *Wall Street Journal* ran a story on the increase of the female serial killer. There have been more than a dozen female serial killers, including Florida's ex-prostitute, Aileen Wuornos. She confessed to robbing and killing five men after posing as a hitchhiker. Sometime companion Tyria Moore was the state's star witness against Wuornos.

North Carolina has had two prominent female serial killers. In Robeson County, Velma Margie Barfield, a Sunday School teacher and nurse, poisoned her Mother, her fiancée, and patients in order to "do God's work on earth." She poured arsenic into her Mother's soup *and* coke. Prosecutor Joe Britt said at her trial that "she enjoyed the funerals, the grieving, and the murders."

Burlington County, N.C. also produced the Black Widow serial killer, Blanche Taylor Moore. This human predator was the subject of a television program, "Black Widow Murders: The Blanche Taylor Moore Story" in 1993.

The *Washington Post* ran a series on 16 couples who killed, starting with Bonnie and Clyde. Raymond Fernandez would romance lonely widows and 300-pound Martha Bech would murder them.

Another killing couple was Frederick and Rosemary West in Gloucester, England. The British police unearthed the remains of eleven women at or near the couple's Gloucester house of horrors in 1994. Aside from five murder charges against Rosemary, she was charged with the rape of an eleven-year-old girl and the assault of a seven-year-old boy.

Chapter 8

Rhode Island

Today police departments are often unable to take on many of the investigations that they would have in the past. That's particularly true where there is a need for a forensic accountant. It used to be that the police would engage and pay the forensic accountant. Now, some police officers are telling corporations that they can't afford that anymore—and if a company wants the police to investigate a case that requires a forensic accountant, then the company should pay for those skills.

Norman Inkster

"Douglass here, what can I do for you?"

"I'm the one you're looking for concerning the perfect game murders."

"Sure. Sure. What's your name?" Douglass muttered sarcastically.

"I want you to install an unlisted cellular phone and a CB in Fred Campbell's car—the forensic accountant. You are to put three million dollars worth of diamonds inside a briefcase, which should be put inside a silver metal suitcase. Also put $200,000 in small, unmarked bills in the suitcase.

"The diamonds should be one-to-two carats, at least eye clean,—e.y.e—and I color. No junk. No CZs. Put combination locks on both the suitcase and briefcase. This suitcase should be marked #3. You are to have two other identical suitcases—labeled #1 and #2. On each suitcase have the following

139

warning: 'Caution: Radioactive Material Inside.' Put the suitcases in the trunk of Campbell's blue Chevrolet. No tracing device in the car or suitcases. We'll call him sometime during August and tell him what to do with the suitcases."

"Look Mr. Anonymous, we've received at least 100 extortion calls. How do I know that *you* are the real killer?" Douglass replied sternly.

"Agent Douglass, I warn you. If you do not put the diamonds in Campbell's trunk within six days, we will release anthrax at a future game. Also, do not follow Campbell by car or helicopter. Do *not* put a tracing device in his car," warned the voice.

"Please sir, you must provide me with some evidence that you are the real killer and not a copycat," Douglass pleaded.

"SK has been printed on three of the San Diego baseball cards left at the crime scenes. Now, we'll call you in six days to see if the diamonds are in the trunk, and you can give us Campbell's car phone number and the combinations to the locks. Do not put a paint bomb in the suitcase.

"Remember, Agent Douglass, you cannot outsmart us. Tell Commissioner Selig that we can destroy baseball. It's worth a mere three million to stop the damage now. We'll be back next year at random ball games. The price will then be four million," the voice explained

"You said anthrax..."

The line went dead. "So it's a ransom plot by a terrorist group," Douglass said softly with a scowl across his face. "That's why we couldn't fit the person into a serial killer profile."

Douglass called Bud Selig, Commissioner of Baseball, and told him about the extortion demand and anthrax threat. Douglass explained that bioterrorism weapons using anthrax or other bacteria are easier to make and distribute than nuclear weapons. Anthrax, an animal disease, is a rapid and highly effective killer. Germs and nerve gas are the newer weapons of choice, and a major attack from terrorists in the U.S. is inevitable. They had been putting savin on the baseball cards, so they have some knowledge of poisons.

Selig said he would call a meeting of the owners of the teams to decide whether to pay.

Douglass told Selig to keep the extortion demand as quiet as possible. "We don't need this on the front page of every newspaper." Selig agreed.

Next Douglass called Campbell and told him about the killer's request. "I'll send someone out to install a cellular phone, a CB, and a tracing device. We'll try to be close to you at all times."

Campbell was shocked.

The Commissioner called a hasty meeting of the owners of the 28 major league baseball teams. Most of the owners or their representatives met around 8:30 on the next evening in the O'Hare Hyatt, where other important baseball conferences had been held. The executive director of the Baseball Players Association was in attendance.

Commissioner Selig called the group to order and introduced Special Agent Douglass. Douglass had asked Fred Campbell and Fleet Walker to attend the meeting.

Douglass calmly told the assembled baseball barons about the extortion phone call, emphasizing that the male caller knew about SK printed on three of the baseball cards. There was an almost universal gasp as he mentioned the anthrax threat.

Douglass told the group that the world has entered into a new stage of terrorism. The number of people with knowledge of how to synthesize culture and chemical bacteria is increasing, and a biological weapon attack is possible. For example, an Arkansan has been publishing a ricin cocktail for years. Recin, extracted from the castor bean plant, has no antidote and is

6,000 times more toxic than cyanide. The castor bean plant can be found in Southern California.

Douglass also told the group that anthrax, smallpox, and plague were the greatest threat because they have the potential to spread quickly and cause huge number of deaths. The signs of a virus may not be apparent for days or weeks. Health officials may misdiagnose the illness as flu. The United States has not vaccinated against smallpox since the '70s, and there are only enough vaccine for 7.5 million people.

Bill Giles, who had paid $30 million for the Philadelphia Phillies in 1981, asked about the mechanics of the pay-off. "Will this killer not be at maximum risk when he first gets his hands on the diamonds?"

Douglass replied, "We believe so. We will do what it takes to catch the killer at the time of the pay-off."

George Steinbrenner wished a discussion of the so-called perfect game theory of the killings. "Look, Don Larsen pitched a perfect game in Yankee Stadium, and I believe we will be in the World Series this year. We cannot have a bunch of sociopaths running around with anthrax grenades."

Several people nervously laughed. Peter Angelos, owner of the Baltimore Orioles, said, "I doubt that you'll make the series, George."

Douglass asked Fleet Walker to talk about the perfect game connections. Walker outlined how there had been a murder or attempted murder on the dates and at the approximate locations of 11 of the perfect games. "Look, this pattern cannot be a coincidence. Somebody is systematically killing people on perfect game dates."

The Los Angeles Dodgers' representative almost shouted, "Look, we have to do something. The next perfect game was pitched by Sandy Koufax on September 9. Earthquakes, fires, floods, O.J., and now a ballpark killer. Our attendance is falling.

We'll have more reporters and television people in our stadium on September 9 than we'll have paying customers."

Walt Jocketly, the general manager of the St. Louis Cardinals, replied, "Tell Bill Russell that we're willing to trade market shares."

There were a few laughs. The group was worried, however.

Walker paused and continued. "The individual may be a former player, umpire, or manager who now hates baseball. I hope you will search your files and let us know of anyone affiliated with baseball who has a motive."

Someone whispered "Pete Rose." Former manager of the Cincinnati Reds and a potential Hall of Famer, Rose spent some time in jail and was permanently suspended from baseball by the then Commissioner Pete Ueberroth for gambling problems. Like Darryl Strawberry, Rose also had been accused of not paying taxes on autograph income.

Since the killer has asked for diamonds, Douglass asked the ball clubs to compile a list of current and former players or employers who were jewelers. "Anyone with training in gemology should be a suspect," Douglass suggested. "Send the names to me."

Colorado Rockies owner Jerry McMorris informed the group that last year during a ballgame a fan had been poisoned by a pesticide—possibly in food—in his ball park. When Douglass asked, McMorris did not know the type of poison.

At that point, someone mentioned Marge Schott, the controversial ex-owner of the Cincinnati Reds. Described as baseball's female George Steinbrenner, she was temporarily suspended from baseball for racist and bigoted remarks. Then on May 18, 1994, she stated that "Only fruits wear earrings. I was raised to believe that men wearing earrings are fruity." Baseball's Executive Committee sent her a letter of reprimand and asked her to make a large donation to a charity.

After her controversial "fruity" statement, the L.A. Dodgers came into Riverfront Stadium for a three game series. Dodgers' Brett Butler, age 37 and going gray, Raul Mondesi, and other players wore all sorts of garish women's earrings dangling from their left ear lobes during the series. The Dodgers won two of the three games.

Leonard S. Coleman, Jr., president of the National League, declared that he was against paying the extortion demand. "We cannot start paying extortion demands. Never."

A voice vote was taken, and by a wide majority the owners voted not to pay the demand.

Baseball Commissioner Bud Selig told the group that it was extremely important that everything said and done should remain in this room. "We must try to minimize publicity at all costs."

After the meeting, one person who Douglass did not recognize, said that five team owners had agreed to pay $300,000 to the terrorist. "We'll have the money to you in two days. Maybe the small sum will slow the maniac down or cause him to make a mistake. However, we will deny that any money came from baseball."

On the flight back to New York City, Douglass discussed with Fleet Walker the vote of the owners. Walker told Douglass that the five teams were probably the L.A. Dodgers, Cincinnati Reds, Texas Rangers, Cleveland Indians, and the New York Yankees, since these teams were the remaining perfect game parks.

According to Walker, most of the owners of the small market teams voted against a pay-off.

"Okay, can you tell me about baseball cards?" Douglass asked. "Is there a connection between baseball cards and the terrorists?"

Walker merely shrugged, and said, "Well, interest in baseball cards exploded in the United States in the late 1970s, and baseball card collecting became the number one investment in the '80s. Baseball cards moved from bicycle spokes and shoeboxes into safe deposit boxes and investment portfolios. What was once a child's hobby is now a $2.5 billion industry."

"Some vintage cards with unusual histories now sell for huge prices, almost regardless of their condition. For example, a creased T-206 Honus Wagner card from a 1909 set sold for a record $120,000 in 1988. In 1991, another T-206 Honus Wagner card was purchased for $410,000 by Bruce McNall, the former owner of the Los Angeles Kings hockey team. These amazing prices are a function of scarcity more than adoration of the Hall of Famer, and the Pittsburgh Pirate shortstop, nicknamed "The Flying Dutchman.""

"Four hundred and ten thousand for one baseball card," Douglass looked confused. "I'm in the wrong business. Why is his card so high?"

"Less than 40 of the cards are known to be in existence. There are two theories to explain the small number of Wagner cards. One school holds that Wagner, an ardent nonsmoker, obtained an injunction to prohibit the card's manufacturer, the American Tobacco Company, from distributing it. The other school maintains that Wagner had the cards recalled, because he was never paid to appear on them. Nevertheless, these cards are scarce, expensive, and the dream of every collector."

Douglass thought for a moment and a curious look appeared in his blue eyes. "So you are telling me that this killer is leaving old, valuable cards at the scene of the crime? I'm confused."

"Oh no," cautioned Walker. "There are thousands of cards that have values of far less than these collectible cards. Most players do not distinguish themselves in a discernible manner and, consequently, the values for their cards do not rise much. These so-called common cards often sell for less than $10. For example, a 1964 Topps common card in mint condition sells for around $5 or less; a 1984 Topps common card in mint condition sells for about 5 cents.

"Then there's the factor of rookie cards. Rookie cards are a major leaguer's first appearance in a regularly issued, nationally distributed card set. There is probably no other sports memorabilia item that is so typical of the hobby as the rookie, or first issue, card of a player," Walker explained.

"Why is the rookie card more valuable?" Douglass seemed puzzled.

"Unknown potential is probably the reason. No one can predict which first year player will develop into a superstar. Each year the draft is full of first-round turkeys and late-round superstars."

"Are all rookie cards of stars valuable?"

"A rookie card is a milestone for a professional player. It is proof that the individual player has made it from the minor league to the major league level. Interestingly, the rookie card is the most sought after card of any player. It is similar to the first edition of a book or the first print in a series," Walker continued to explain.

"The rookie cards of older baseball players—those who entered the big leagues prior to 1948—are not in as great a demand as those of modern players. The rookie cards of Babe Ruth and Lou Gehrig are not the most popular cards for these players. The rookie cards of other famous players from before 1933 such as Ty Cobb, Honus Wagner, and Christie Mathewson are not eagerly pursued, probably because they were well-established stars when their cards were first issued.

"The two most popular rookie cards are those of Mickey Mantle and Willie Mays. The 1951 Mantle and Mays cards issued by Bowman represent the earliest cards of major superstars to be issued *before* they were superstars," Walker emphasized.

After 1951, complete sets of baseball cards were issued on an annual basis. Many famous players emerged from the newly issued complete sets. For example, the 1954 Topps set includes Henry Aaron's rookie card and Ernie Banks' rookie card. The 1955 Topps set includes the rookie cards of Roberto Clemente, Sandy Koufax, and Harmon Killebrew. The 1957 Topps set includes the rookie cards of Don Drysdale, Frank Robinson, and Brooks Robinson. These cards have become classics. To the baseball purist, first cards of these players are truly amazing. To see the rookie cards of a teenaged Hank Aaron, Sandy Koufax, or Frank Robinson is incredible for the true baseball fan—a step back in time," said Walker admiringly. "At one time, Nolan Ryan's rookie card was worth $1,500. It's between $600 and $900 now."

Douglass slowly shook his head. "I remember Nolan Ryan. I've seen him in a Dairy Queen commercial." Douglass waved his right hand indifferently and said, "Enough. So we have a killer running around randomly killing people in or near baseball parks with baseball bats and poison baseball cards—cheap, common baseball cards. Anything else?"

"Well, the players selected by the killer all played for the San Diego Padres—a National League team. He knows baseball history and poisons."

"We receive several anonymous tips to check out John Rocker as a possible suspect. Apparently he was suspended in 2000 for 45 days of spring training and 28 days of the regular season. What do you think?" Douglass asked.

Walker thought for a moment. "Maybe. Rocker was suspended for an interview he gave in *Sport Illustrated*. He was fined $20,000 and forced to undergo sensitivity training for his politically incorrect remarks about minorities, homosexuals, and immigrants."

"Really," Douglass said. "Suspended for speech."

"Right. This was the first time a player was disciplined for speech since New York Yankee outfielder Jake Powell was suspended for 10 days by Commissioner Kenesaw Mountain Landis in 1938."

"Should we follow Rocker?" Douglass asked.

"No. He was sent to the minors when he later threatened the reporter, but he came back to Atlanta after only a few weeks. I'm sure there are many other players who get mad when they are fired or go through arbitration and don't get what they wish," Walker suggested softly.

"Well, sending people who make unpopular statements to involuntary counseling worked quite well in the Soviet Union," Douglass joked.

Walker did *not* laugh.

★ ★ ★ ★ ★

From New York City, Douglass got a flight to Quantico.

The headline in *The Chicago Tribune* the next morning was "Baseball Owners Huddle." In the write-up an unidentified source spoke of an extortion demand from the "Ballpark Killer." Over the next several days the print media and television had a feeding frenzy. The coverage was almost as great as the Clinton impeachment in 1998-99. Lawyers were bringing class action lawsuits against baseball, including the players themselves. The players had the deep pockets.

Two days later Douglass received the $300,000 from an anonymous carrier, and he flew to Providence. The three suitcases were placed into the trunk of Fred Campbell's Chevrolet, and Douglass kept the car watched by round the clock guards. He would stay in Providence until the pay-off. It could be almost five weeks, because no perfect games had occurred in August. All of his phone calls were routed to Providence.

On August 7, Douglass received the phone call from SK. He told SK that the extortion money was in Campbell's possession.

The phone call was traced to a phone booth in Providence, but SK was not at the phone booth when four FBI agents arrived. Early in the morning on August 11 at 6:45, Fred Campbell received the expected phone call from SK. The polite voice told Fred to get into his car and drive north from Providence on Route 146. "Stop in Manville and wait for a phone call." Fred called Douglass and left for his trip. As instructed on the phone, Fred set his CB on Channel 16. Douglass traced the phone call to another pay phone in Providence. Douglass was in one of the five cars tracking Fred Campbell. Douglass had told Fred to do exactly what the killer told him to do. "Your safety is most important."

The phone on Fred was working so well that Douglass could hear Fred breathing. Fred was breathing faster when he pulled into and stopped at a service station in Manville. He pumped gas, paid his bill with a credit card, and waited in front of a Coke machine. He bought a Coke and waited some more.

After about 30 minutes a voice came over the CB. "Hello Fred, Glad you could make it. Please step outside your Chevrolet and take off the phone. I'm sure the FBI has wired you. Drop it outside so I can see you. Then remove the tracer from your car."

"If there's a tracer on my car, I don't know where it is," Fred answered.

"Okay, step out and take off the phone on your body. You are not to phone out to anyone. Set your CB on Channel 31 now. Channel 31." Then silence.

Fred turned the CB to Channel 31, opened his car door, took off the phone on his body, and dropped it on the ground. He looked around, and got back into his car.

"Fred, if you get lost or forget your instructions, stop your car and call me on Channel 16 every five minutes. Channel 16. Sweet 16. Please go North on Route 146 and stop at the

Exxon station on the right, outside Manville. Park your car near the telephone booth and wait for my phone call."

Again Fred followed instructions, stopping in front of the phone booth. His hands were sweating inside the surgical gloves he had put on before he left the safety of his home. Sure he had been involved with some fraud cases and some weird husbands and wives. Some of the friendly divorces too often became acrimonious. Tracking down hidden assets of a spouse could become interesting. As a forensic accountant he was not a mere bean counter. But never had he dealt with a mass killer who used deadly poisons.

"Hello Fred," said a friendly voice. "Please go inside the phone booth. There is an envelope and a listening device taped to the bottom of the shelf in the phone booth. Turn the listening device on and keep it on. Please read my written instructions."

On the front of the white envelope was typed: "Fred, do not use your phone or in any way contact the authorities. Keep your car radio off and speak as little as possible. Open and read."

Fred nervously opened the envelope and read the following typed instructions:

Turn your CB to Channel 23.

In an emergency, call me on Channel 16.

Turn around and drive back to Manville on 146.

Never drive faster than 50 mph. Break no traffic laws.

Turn right on Route 120 (west) to Primrose.

Turn right (north/west) in Primrose to and thru Mapleville.

Turn south on 102 to Chepachet.

Turn east on 44.

About 2 miles turn on road to Smith and Sayles Reservoir — go to 101.

Turn west on 101 to North Foster.

South on 94 to Foster, then toward Clayville via 102.

Thru Clayville to 14 (turn right) east to Waterman Four Corners on to I295.

I'll give you further instructions.

There was a map of the area taped to the bottom of the legal-sized paper.

Typed under the map was a warning:

"Do not attempt to relay these instructions to anyone. Please don't forget to turn on the listening device and put it on your front seat."

Fred turned on the listening device, got into his car, and placed the device on the instructions to keep the paper from blowing around. He turned his car around and headed back to Manville.

Just before Primrose the voice was on the CB again. "I'm back, Fred. What do you mean by forensic?"

Fred was startled. "Forensic refers to that which is used by the courts. It's an adjective attached to the branches of certain sciences — chemistry, pathology, geology, anthropology..."

"Did you see the movie *Speed*?"

"No," was Fred's only remark. He was becoming more frightened. He had seen *Speed*. He could still see the explosions in the movie.

"No matter, Fred. As President Clinton says, I feel your pain. Just stop in Primrose, turn your motor off for five minutes, put suitcase number 1 in your front seat, and then continue along the route as directed. Don't signal anyone. Don't talk to anyone," the voice warned. "Turn your CB to Channel 27 now. Channel 27."

After waiting in Primrose for five minutes Fred continued along the route toward Mapleville. About three miles *after* Mapleville, the polite voice was back. "Fred, shortly you will cross Chepachet Basin. Go to the south side of the bridge and toss suitcase number one into the water. Then continue along your route. Change to Channel 29 now. Have a pleasant drive. Don't drive faster than double nickels."

Fred did as instructed and threw the silver suitcase into the water at Chepachet Basin. He saw no one. He drove through Chepachet, North Foster, and Foster. On the outskirts of Clayville, the voice was back.

"Fred you are doing fine. Please stop in Clayville, transfer both suitcases to the inside of your car. Wait five minutes. Change to Channel 14 now."

"Look," Fred asked cautiously, "what is your name?"

"Now Fred, you can call me Sandy, the Terrorist. Turn your CB to Channel 14 please. I know where you live. I've seen your beautiful wife with your two daughters. I've read about forensic accounting on the internet. Do you know the three facets of proving the guilt of a fraud suspect?"

"Please leave my family alone. I'll do anything you wish. Motive, means, and opportunity, I believe."

"Well, Fred, I'll tell you my motive. I want the diamonds. That's all. Deliver them, and you'll be fine."

"I'm here to serve you. I'm only the messenger."

Silence until Fred turned right on to Route 14 and had driven about three miles.

"I'm back, Fred, just like Freddy Krueger." He laughed. "Shortly you will cross Scituate Reservoir. When you get to the east side of the bridge, stop your car. You will see on a sign a number 2 or number 3. Throw the appropriate suitcase on the right shore, near the water. Then continue your leisurely drive. Turn your CB to Channel 31 now. Drive slowly across the bridge. Channel 31."

Fred came to the bridge and started across at around 30 MPH. At midway the CB came alive. "Stop Fred. Throw number two suitcase into the water to the person in the boat on the right side. Do it now! Throw the direction paper and the listening device into the water."

Fred was so astonished that he slammed on his brakes without looking into his rear view mirror. Luckily there were no cars on the bridge. Fred grabbed number two suitcase and threw it into the water toward the boat. He heard the motorboat leave as he climbed back into his still running Chevrolet. He continued across the bridge quickly.

The motorboat was less than 200 yards from the bridge when two helicopters appeared on the horizon. A black Bell Ranger police helicopter arrived first, followed by a Blackhawk helicopter. A loud voice came from the police helicopter. "Stop your boat. This is the FBI. You are under arrest."

The man with a straw hat in the boat stopped the engine and put up his hands. Two divers dropped from the Blackhawk helicopter into the water and swam to the boat.

The man known as Sandy saw the commotion with Army binoculars from a good distance away. He was not a happy camper.

Chapter 9

San Pedro

The efficiency and effectiveness of most audits can be significantly increased through the use of computer assisted audit tools and techniques (CAATTs). Auditors can use CAATTs to select a sample, perform 100 percent verification, examine trends, or conduct detailed analyses of financial, personnel, inventory, and other types of data. However, the reliability of the results obtained through the use of these CAATTs obviously depends on the integrity of the data itself and the analyses performed by the auditor.

David Coderre
Jim Kaplan

After questioning the man in the boat for six hours and checking his alibis, Douglass was convinced that the fisherman who had picked up the suitcase was merely gullible and was not directly involved with the extortion plot. He operated a bait and fishing supply shop on the Scituate Reservoir, and was an occasional fishing guide.

According to the grey-headed fisherman, a tall man named Sandy had hired him for several days. Then the tall man had asked him to pick up a suitcase that would be thrown into the water by the boyfriend of his ex-wife. Sandy had promised him $500 for retrieving the suitcase.

A careful investigation at his bait and fishing supply shop uncovered no fingerprints or other evidence to help identify the mysterious Sandy, the Terrorist. Nothing. The listening device was not found in the water.

Douglass knew that the FBI had blown the drop. Sandy and the terrorists would be mad. What would the group do now?

Two days later, *The New York Times* had the following headline: "FBI Botches Extortion Drop." The accompanying article spoke of the extortion demand from the "Ballpark Terrorist." Anonymous sources were quoted. The FBI was blamed for not following the fisherman to the people behind the extortion demand. The newspaper ran a long article on profiling violent crimes.

Three days later the fisherman with his straw hat appeared on David Letterman's show. He said he had been hired as a consultant by a movie company working on a movie about the ballpark killers. Letterman gave his top ten reasons the FBI cannot get their man:

#10. *The Untouchables* series was canceled.

#9. Baseball players make more then FBI agents.

#8. They are still looking for Hoffa.

#7. They wear jackets telling who they are.

#6. The FBI is still looking for Elvis.

#5. J. Edgar Hoover is still alive.

#4. The Pink Panther has been hired to reorganize the FBI.

#3. The Men in Black took over.

#2. FBI stands for Federal Blunder Institution.

#1. The FBI is not perfect.

Over the next week the news media again had nonstop coverage. Like the French paparazzi following Princess Diana in Paris, reporters followed Douglass and Fred everywhere. One night Larry King had Jack Godwin on his show discussing the importance of profiling criminals. Author Godwin stated that nine out of ten profiles are vapid. "Profilers play at blindman's bluff, groping in many directions in the hopes of touching a sleeve. Look the police need hard data—fingerprints, names, faces, locations, dates, and times. These dull and tedious psychiatrists cannot provide hard evidence," Godwin said.

Another author on King's show, John Levin, asserted that psychological profiles are useless in identifying a killer. "Profiles are inherently limited in their ability to solve crimes." The week was bad for the FBI. The supermarket tabloids provided a number of stories about the various terrorist groups behind the extortion demand. One person stated that the National Basketball Association was behind the killings. "The NBA wishes to destroy baseball. They are trying to recover from their players lock-out." The increased publicity initially increased attendance at many of the baseball stadiums.

The President called the Director of the FBI and told him, " Do whatever it takes, no matter what it costs, but catch this murderer. I've had pressure from ex-presidents living in Georgia, Texas, and California. My pollsters tell me that we can lose 25 more House members in November if we do not stop this killing."

The Director was instructed to inform the President every morning at 7:30 a.m. of any progress in the case. Pressure was transferred to Douglass naturally. Douglass called Fleet Walker and convinced him to come to Providence to help with the case.

Barbara Walters on *20/20* had a rare interview with Sandy Koufax, who pleaded with the person or group to stop killing innocent people at baseball parks.

Barbara asked Sandy about his first year in the major leagues. "I believe you were a bonus baby, meaning that you had to be kept on the Dodgers' roster. Your bonus was $14,000. What famous person did you replace on the Dodger roster?"

Sandy smiled and replied, "Another southpaw pitcher, Tommy Lasorda. Tommy was sent back to the minors to make room for me. Tommy became a Hall of Famer in 1997."

"Lasorda, of course, was until 1996, the Dodgers' long-term manager," Barbara interjected. "Tell me about your first year in the major leagues," Barbara asked in a friendly tone.

"I'll never forget my first year," Koufax replied. "I didn't know what I was doing. I was scared to death. I had just turned 19, and there I was in spring training with the greatest names in baseball—Reese, Snider, and Robinson. I had no right being there. They gave me money, and every time I threw I could feel someone watching me. So I tried to throw a little harder, just to prove that I was worth the money. I ended up hurting my arm. For two weeks I was combing my hair and brushing my teeth right-handed."

"That's right," said Barbara, "you were a lefthander like Tom Browning, who also pitched a perfect game—for the Reds, I believe. Why were you so wild when you first came to the majors? Duke Snider said that taking batting practice against you was like playing Russian roulette with five bullets."

"Oh, I have to give credit to catcher Norm Sherry. He sat next to me on a plane ride to a B-squad game in Orlando around 1961. He told me to stop throwing my fastball so hard. Try some more curves and change-ups."

"That day I pitched and Sherry caught me. Every time that I would just rear back and throw, Sherry walked out and made me use change-ups and control. I pitched a no-hitter that day. That season—1961—I won 18 games and struck out 269 batters, breaking Christy Mathewson's National League record of 267."

"I was told that you pitched two perfect games—not one."

"Well, you're talking about my third no-hitter. I pitched my first no-hitter in 1961, my second one in 1963, and my third no-hitter against the Phillies in 1964. This third no-hitter was about 17 days before Jim Bunning's perfect game."

"Anyway, I walked Richie Allen in the fourth, but he was caught stealing second. So I faced *only 27 batters* during the game. If Ernie Shore is credited with a perfect game, then an argument can be made that I pitched two perfect games. Shore faced only 26 batters, and the one batter walked by Babe Ruth was thrown out stealing in the first inning. I believe a baseball committee eliminated Shore's perfect game from the record books in 1991."

Barbara laughed. "So tell us about your official perfect game on September 9, 1965. How well did you pitch that day against the Chicago Cubs?" Barbara asked.

"Just average for the first few innings. My first pitch to Don Young, the first batter, hit the dirt about three feet in front of the plate. I threw mostly curves during the first two innings, and started throwing fast balls in the third. My control was good. My curve was the best I had the whole season. In the last three innings the fastball was my only pitch."

"Is there anything else about the game you remember?"

"Well, Cubs pitcher, Bob Hendley, also threw a great game. He allowed only one hit, he walked only one player, and there was only one Cub error. A classic 1-0 nail biter. Our duel was the most perfect game in modern times—only one hit, one walk, one error, and one unearned run."

"Sandy, I greatly appreciate the opportunity to talk to you. In closing, I would like to quote a piece by Jim Murray of the *Los Angeles Times* describing your pitching:

What makes National League Sandy Koufax great is the same thing that made Walter Johnson great. The team behind him was the ghastliest scoring team in history. They piled up runs at the rate of one every nine innings. This was a little like making Rembrandt paint on the back of cigar boxes, giving

Paderewski a piano with only two octaves or Caruso singing with a high school chorus. With the Babe Ruth Yankees, Sandy Koufax would probably have been the first undefeated pitcher in history.

★ ★ ★ ★ ★

Another man known as Sandy had planned to do some scuba diving after the disappointing diamond drop. He flew to Miami, and took a TACA 767 jet to Belize City. From Philip S.W. Goldson International Airport he and Janice took a small Tropic Air prop plane to San Pedro, a small town on an island off the coast of northern Belize.

Belize is a small Central American country with an extensive coastline bordering the western Caribbean Sea, approximately 750 miles from Houston or Miami. Bordered by Mexico to the north and Guatemala to the west and south, the 9,000 square miles of land is slightly larger than Massachusetts with a population of approximately 200,000 English-speaking people. Along the coast is the longest continuous barrier reef in the Caribbean. The 180-mile reef is surpassed in size only by Australia's Great Barrier Reef system.

Along the coast are many cayes (pronounced *keys*) in comparatively shallow water beyond the barrier reef. There are more than 200 cayes and inlets along the 180-mile coast, and the most developed is the Ambergris Caye, which is near San Pedro. San Pedro itself is a quaint little town where no buildings can be erected taller than a palm tree.

With more than 200 types of fish and hundreds of invertebrates to observe, Sandy soon forgot some of the disappointment. But he was still plotting and thinking. Should he discontinue his campaign or try for one more extortion drop?

His first murder had been the worst, when he had experimented with the poison on the baseball card last season at a Colorado Rockies game. He had felt remorse for weeks. He was mowing his lawn one-day, and he noticed a large black bird following him around. The bird was catching the bugs that he was disturbing. Several days later he saw a city worker mowing the grass along the roadway. Hundreds of white birds were around the large mower looking for the disturbed bugs. He suddenly rationalized that the innocent people that would be killed in his campaign against baseball were simply unlucky. They were merely a price to be paid to meet his goals.

After a few more killings, he had become de-sensitized. However, he did not seem to have the typical triggering factor, which drove most serial killers to commit murder over and over. A killing frenzy did not come over him. He did not seem to be addicted to the act of murder as if it were a drug. He thought he could stop, but he did get a sense of power as he continued to outsmart the FBI and the local authorities. If there were to be another extortion drop, it would be exceedingly dangerous for him.

He had been diving only about 30 times, so he was still an amateur. He had decided to learn how to scuba dive when he saw George Brett's Ben-Gay commercial. Brett played third base for the Kansas City Royals for 17 years. In the commercial Brett advertises Ben-Gay for arthritis in a scuba suit and then falls backwards from a boat into the water. There is a beautiful underwater shot of fish and a coral reef.

On his first day they made three dives. At the first dive site, Hoi Chan, there were a number of snorklers near the boat as he entered the water. His mask fogged early and both his buoyancy control and kicking were poor. Movement underwater is mostly done with your legs, and arms should move as little as possible. The water was warm, the current medium, and he saw a number of colorful fish. The maximum depth for his dive was 28 feet.

After lunch they dove the Cypress dive site, where they saw fewer fish, but there was much better scenery. When he neared the surface he ran out of air, and he panicked. Janice came up behind him and gave him some air. Afterward he discovered that his room key had fallen from his pants pocket under the water. He later realized that his diving buddy also had taken some money from his pants pocket during the dive.

Where he was staying was a dump of a room, which normally had no hot water. But he was paying only $40 per night, and he had to walk only 75 feet to the pier to get on the boat.

Later that evening the group dove the Tackle Box site, and he saw his first shipwreck and two moray eels. Bambino, his dive master, had taken a bucket of fish, and he fed the eels. At one point one of the eels swam from behind him through his legs. Yes, he was frightened.

That night they ate at the Island Grill, which had a sign "No shirt, no shoes, no problem." The building had a thatched roof, and there were a number of coconut trees surrounding the grill. Early the next morning while they were eating breakfast, a tall, thin beach bum with a faded blue baseball cap (turned to the right side with a clothes pin) asked Sandy, "How are the pancakes?"

Sandy said, "Do you want them?"

"Yes."

Sandy gave the black man the pancakes, and then threw him a plastic bottle of syrup. After eating the pancakes, the bum washed his hands in the saltwater.

There was a beautiful blue sky with white clouds. A number of black seagulls, with white strips down their breasts, were flying over the white sand. From the grill Sandy could see a bar called the Purple Parrot and Joe Miller Photography: Underwater camera rental.

The early morning adventure was the Victoria Canyon dive site. Divers generally make their deepest dive the first dive during the day. At a depth of about 95 feet the group went through a tunnel about four or five body lengths wide. There were numerous colorful fish and very deep canyons. This was Sandy's most comfortable dive. As they made their one minute safety stop at about 15 feet below the surface of the water, a boat came over them.

Afterward, Sandy's dive master said that Sandy was probably "narced" at the deep depth. Scuba divers should not go much below 100 feet because the deep depths cause narcosis. Inexperienced divers have been known to be in such a "happy" state that they continue on down to their death. Of course, the deeper the dive, the fewer minutes a diver can safely stay underwater. For example, on your first dive at a depth of, say 50 feet, you can safely stay down about 78 minutes. But at a depth of 100 feet, the maximum dive time is 20 minutes. Many divers wear dive computers which automatically provide critical information such as maximum depth, bottom time, surface interval time (when you can dive again), safe-to-fly, nitrogen level, and other relevant facts. An audible/visible alarm even warns the diver when the air supply is low—an example of an internal control.

The afternoon dive at Hoi Chan Canyon was worth the whole trip. As they descended to a depth of about 40 feet, a school of five graceful manta rays passed overhead. The scenery was magnificent, and the colorful fish were indescribable. However, after about 15 minutes into the dive a three-to-four foot fish that looked like a shark began following Sandy. The fish began to attack Bambino, who would hit at the fish, and then the fish would attack Sandy. The fish would try to attach to Sandy's bare legs. This battle went on for about 20 minutes until Sandy decided to go to the surface. He forgot to make his safety stop, which could have caused the bends—or decompression sickness, known as nitrogen narcosis or caisson disease. This condition causes paralysis and pain as a result of bubbles of nitrogen forming in the blood. Bends is caused from moving from an atmosphere of high pressure (under water) to air of ordinary pressure on the surface. A diver also should wait about 24 hours after diving before flying on a plane to avoid the bends.

Sandy was fine, but he had round suction marks on his legs where the fish had tried to attach to him. On the boat Bambino was laughing at him. "That was not a shark. It was a sharksucker or remora. This fish attaches to sharks. It was, of course, looking for its host."

"The monster looked like a shark to me. I could see its teeth," Sandy complained.

By the fifth day Sandy was practicing with an underwater scooter and a closed circuit rebreather. A normal scuba diver uses a buoyancy compensator on which a tank of air is strapped to the back. As the diver swims underwater, bubbles are released from the regulator and they float to the surface. The rebreather allows a diver to swim underwater for up to six hours as deep as twenty feet without producing bubbles.

Sandy and Janice decided to give baseball one more chance to pay them.

One of their last dives was the Blue Hole, a cylindrical reef formation about 780 feet in diameter and 480 feet deep. The Blue Hole is the remnant of a terrestrial cavern formed when the sea levels were much lower. There are stalactites hanging from the ceiling at 130 feet down. This dive was the highlight of the trip.

On his return to the states, Sandy watched a Connie Chung interview on CBS with Fleet Walker, an internal auditor for the New York Yankees. Walker, as an expert on perfect games, was helping the FBI in their search for the ballpark killer. Sandy decided to go to Cooperstown to begin the preparation for the next diamond drop.

Cooperstown, New York, named for the pioneering parents of novelist James Fenimore Cooper, is a small town at the southern end of Lake Otsego near the middle of New York state, southeast of Utica and Syracuse and directly west of Albany. The National Baseball Hall of Fame and Museum, drawing over one-half million visitors a year, was dedicated on June 12, 1939 at Cooperstown. Baseball immortals such as moonface Babe Ruth, Cy Young, Connie Mack, and tall Walter Johnson gathered at the brick building for the dedication. Life-sized wooden carvings of Ted Williams and Babe Ruth greeted Sandy as he entered the museum. Plaques of baseball players and cases of baseball mementos were on display in the first floor exhibition room.

While touring the Hall of Fame Gallery, Sandy was impressed. He read the bronze plaque of Tyrus Raymond Cobb: "Led American League in Batting Twelve Times and Created or Equalled More Major League Records Than Any Other Player. Retired With 4,191 Major League Hits."

Sandy knew that Ty Cobb had dominated the game. Cobb was driven and once said that baseball is like war. He had a violent temper and once went into the stands and beat a handicapped fan who was heckling him. Many of the players hated Cobb, but they went on strike when Cobb was suspended. This was probably the first strike.

There was George Herman (Babe) Ruth: "Greatest drawing card in history of baseball. Holder of many home run and other batting records. Gathered 714 home runs in addition to fifteen in the world series."

There was Hank Aaron who broke Babe's career home run record on April 8, 1974, in Atlanta with his 715th home run.

Sandy was aware of Addie Joss, nicknamed "The Human Hairpin" because Joss pitched with an exaggerated pinwheel motion. He pivoted away from the batter before his pitch, and then threw sidearmed with a "jump" ball. Hitters thought that his ball dipped, flattened out, and dipped again. Playing nine seasons with the Cleveland Naps, he pitched a perfect game in less than one hour and forty minutes against the Chicago White Sox during the heat of a tight pennant race. *Sporting Life* called it the greatest pitchers' duel in history.

Addie died at the young age of 31 with spinal meningitis after pitching only nine seasons. He was cut down during the prime of his baseball career, yet he was elected to the Hall of Fame in 1978, even though the rules require 10 seasons of play. During Joss' brief tenure, the Wisconsin native compiled the second lowest lifetime earned run average, 1.88, in the history of baseball. ERA refers to earned run average. The analytic ERA could be compared to earnings per share of a business. They both compare how well one is doing on a per unit basis. A higher EPS is better, but a lower ERA is better. Actually, price/earnings ratio is a better comparison. In general, the lower the price/earnings ratio of a stock, the better.

Aside from the 10-year experience rule, a player must get 75 percent of the votes of the Baseball Writers Association of America. Just like other areas in life, such as Oscar winners, this process is haphazard and some excellent players do not receive a 75 percent vote. Thus, there is a Special Veterans Committee which may consider eligible players retired for 25 years. This committee elected Addie Joss to the Hall of Fame.

In the World Series Room he viewed the glove used by Willie Mays for his famous catch in 1954. He saw Yogi Berra's catcher's mitt from Don Larsen's 1956 perfect game. On this floor he looked closely at the T-206 1909 Honus Wagner baseball card. He watched a baseball movie in the library's 48-seat "Bullpen Theater."

Chapter 10

Los Angeles and Cincinnati

Fraudulent disbursements account for about $300 billion losses annually, and the most expensive tend to be fraudulent disbursements through billing schemes. Therefore, internal auditors seeking to get the biggest bang for their investigative bucks should begin by making sure company vendors are for real.

Joseph T. Wells

Sandy found a pay phone that was not equipped to receive incoming calls, because Douglass probably had Call Trace (★57), which for ten dollars a use, will record a caller's phone number in a computer and forward it to a police department. Or Douglass might have Call Return (★69) which automatically returns the last call made to the telephone.

"Thrill me," was the curt response from Douglass. The Ballpark Killer was taking a toll on him. To waste all the manpower and resources at the Dodger Stadium and again at Cincinnati without any results was true pressure.

"*Deja vu* Douglass. Have you missed me?" the voice asked. "I was upset that you arrested the poor fisherman with my diamonds. He has probably made more money from the tabloids than you and I."

Douglass interrupted, "That was a terrible mistake on our part, Sandy."

"You are so right, Mr. FBI Agent, and we will give you a demonstration of our determination within the next week or two."

"There's no need to kill anyone. What is the name of your group?"

"Shame on you Douglass. After our next activity, you will go through the same drill as last time, except we wish $4 million of diamonds, $300,000 of small bills, *and* the 1909 Honus Wagner baseball card from the Baseball Hall of Fame in one aluminum suitcase, no larger than two feet by three feet. Silver color. No tracer. No paint bomb, please." Sandy warned. "I'll tell you when to put the suitcase in Fleet Walker's *blue* Saturn.

"You'll give me his car phone number and the combination to the lock on the suitcase. I don't wish to damage a good suitcase. Install a CB in his car, also. Thank you Douglass. This venture will be your payoff pitch."

"Wait a minute," Douglass shouted. The line was already dead. "Why Fleet Walker?"

Payoff pitch? Douglass made a mental note to get a baseball dictionary. He called the Baseball Commissioner and told him of the new extortion demand. Bud Selig said he would call another meeting of the owners. "Please keep the extortion demand from the press. The coverage is just beginning to taper off, and we don't need another panic."

Douglass checked his list. It was September 19. The next perfect game was pitched on September 30, at Arlington Stadium. Well at least he had some time to get ready. But would the group strike at Arlington? They might pick a random ballpark.

From the 17th floor at 350 Park Avenue, New York City, the Commissioner called another meeting of the owners for Denver. Fewer owners were at the Denver meeting, and several of them complained of the decline in attendance, and a severe decline in the sale of beer and drinks. Fans were afraid to go to bathrooms. But the vote outcome was the same: do not pay the diamonds. John Morris, owner of the San Diego Padres, summarized the position of the majority of the owners. "We cannot pay extortion money to everyone who hates baseball."

Astros owner, Drayton McLane, Jr., seconded Morris' motion to "refuse to pay the extortion demand."

Douglass was told by the same person to use the money given to him previously by the carrier in this second extortion drop. Same ground rules: Baseball would deny giving anything to anyone.

In coordination with Douglass, the FBI began accumulating names of former players that might have a reason for disliking baseball. There were many names. The 1994 baseball strike had forced teams to cut staff across the board. Maybe some ball players were still angry because of the owners' demand for a salary cap.

As a result of the 1994 strike, eleven players did not reach the necessary service time to qualify for free agency. This group of players, including Jim Abbott and Jack McDowell, could have been quite upset.

Another example was the Chicago White Sox, who trimmed payroll by refusing to offer four players arbitration. The Detroit Tigers also declined to offer salary arbitration to Tim Belcher, Eric Davis, Storm Davis, and Bill Gullickson. Or consider Chris Gwynn, a former Dodger and Royal outfielder. The owners claimed that the strike days did not count as service time, which left Gwynn one day short of the required six years. "I would check out all the players who were damaged by the strike," Walker suggested, "especially anyone with jewelry experience."

The list was not productive. In fact, August was not productive. No perfect games have been pitched during the month of

August. No one could provide an explanation for this long dry spell from July 28 to September 9. Walker said it was the dog days of summer. The hot weather and humidity affected pitchers more than batters. But who knows?

However, September 9 arrived and Douglass, Walker, and thirty other FBI agents were in Dodger Stadium. There were more television, radio, and newspaper people in the stands than fans. Fans were afraid to attend the game. A CNN poll at the beginning of September found that 94 percent of the U.S. adult population were aware of the "Ballpark Killer." There were rumors that some of the players were considering calling in sick. They were worried about an anthrax attack.

To make matters worse, today was a double header between the Dodgers and the St. Louis Cardinals. The Cardinals had won yesterday, and Walker told Douglass that the Dodgers were in their typical slide from first place after the All-Star Game. The Dodgers had been in first place by 4 games at the All-Stars Game break, but were now in third place behind San Francisco and San Diego.

Douglass was in the stands early enough to watch a Cardinal coach conduct fielding drill for his players. The coach would toss a ball in the air and hit ground balls or fly balls to the fielders with a bat with a long thin handle. Walker called it a fungo bat.

After the "Star Spangled Banner" was sung, the first game of the double header began. Matt Morris pitched a one-hitter, allowing only a single in the third inning by Eric Karros. Morris retired the final 20 batters after Karros singled in the third. He tied a career-high with eight strikeouts and walked one in a fine shutout. The Cardinals routed the Dodgers 10-0. Cardinal homerun king Mark McGwire had three hits, including a three-run homer and a double, drove in three runs and scored three times. The ballpark killer did not strike in the first game.

The second game of the doubleheader was even more nerve-wracking for Douglass. He was constantly scanning the crowd with his binoculars. What was he looking for in the colorful crowd? Maybe a white male with a painted sign which said: "I'm the killer."

He tried to pass the time with questions about Sandy Koufax. "How good was Koufax?"

Walker quoted Pittsburgh Pirate Willie Stargell, who said, "Hitting against Koufax was like eating soup with a fork."

Douglass asked about the tradition of teammates not mentioning a no-hitter or perfect game.

"Apparently Koufax's teammates did not speak to Sandy about the perfect game. After each inning, Koufax would sit on a stool in the runway of the dugout and watch the game in taut silence." Walker said.

"When Koufax headed to his stool in the seventh, according to *Newsweek*, he saw 6'6" Don Drysdale occupying his perch. Drysdale awkwardly jumped to his feet, worried that his blunder might jinx the game.

"Dodger broadcaster Vin Scully was not worried about jinxing the pitching performance. He kept reminding his audience 'Koufax has a perfect game. If you know any red-hot baseball fans, you'd better call them up and get 'em on the other end of this one.'

"Apparently during Kenny Rogers' perfect game he also sat in the same seat when his team was batting," Walker stated. "But the TV announcers of the Rangers game kept telling listeners about the potential perfect game."

"Kenny Rogers, the singer?" asked Douglass curiously.

"No, Kenny Rogers, the Rangers' pitcher. He later played for the Yankees. Let me continue the Koufax game.

"Ernie Banks, a wrist hitter, said after the Koufax perfect game, 'The man was just great. It was beautiful. The first five innings he was getting the curve over real good. Then he got tremendous momentum. I thought he'd be a little less tough, but he just kept throwing the ball right on through.'"

Walker was worried also, so he asked, "Do you think the terrorist group has anthrax?"

"Maybe," was Douglass' soft response. "I hope it's a bluff. But an obscure sect of New Age fanatics in Japan produced anthrax, botulin toxin, and various other nerve agents, including the sarin used in the Tokyo subway system. They had planned similar attacks for New York City and Washington, D.C. The Tokyo attack killed only 12 people in the subway, so delivering huge casualties can be difficult.

"President Clinton's friend and fund-raiser Charles Trie orchestrated the sale in 1993 of a huge medical fermentation device to a pharmaceutical plant in China suspected of manufacturing biological and chemical agents for military use."

Douglass paused. "In 1993, Canadian border agents found a quarter pound of white powder in a plastic bag in an American's car. The substance was ricin, a lethal toxin, and they would have died of respiratory failure and paralysis if they had opened the plastic bag."

Walker frowned slightly and said, "Ricin makes the phantom double play chicken feed in the total picture of the universe."

"What is a phantom double play?" Douglass asked seriously.

"Oh, let's watch. Infielders cheat on double plays. When a shortstop takes the throw from the second baseman on a double play, most often the shortstop will not touch second base. Cuts down on injuries to shortstops. The player coming into second base will attempt to 'take out' or knock down the infielder to prevent him from completing the double play. Internal auditors have to be like a shortstop. They have to find the fraud and still keep the auditee happy. Tough job.

"Back to Koufax," Walker apologized. "At least 29,139 fans saw a remarkable duel between stubble-chinned Koufax and Bob Hendley, age 26. The Cub pitcher did not allow a Dodger hit until the seventh inning—a bloop double to the grass outfield by Lou Johnson. The lone hit did not result in a score.

"The Dodgers scored their only run in the fifth. Sweet Lou Johnson walked, went to second on a fine sacrifice bunt by Ron Fairly, stole third, and scored when catcher Chris Krug's throw to third baseman Ron Santo was too high.

"Lou Johnson would get the only hit, the only walk, and score the only run for the entire game. Ironically, although now a Dodger, he had been voted the best Cub rookie in spring training three seasons before he was traded.

"Plate umpire Ed Vargo told me that he became aware of the perfect game at the top of the eighth. He had called Sandy's third no-hitter. Koufax struck out the side in the top of the eighth, including sluggers Ron Santo and Hall of Famer Ernie Banks. In the ninth Sandy struck out Cub catcher Krug, after he fouled off two pitches."

Walker paused to collect his thoughts. "Pinch-hitter Joey Amalfitano was disposed of quickly—three swinging strikes. Next, manager Lou Klein sent pinch-hitter Harvey Kuenn up to the plate, and he went down swinging. Poor Kuenn, a lifetime .303 hitter, also made the last out in Koufax's 1963 no-hitter against San Francisco. Sandy was so happy that he danced a little jig on the mound.

"His Dodger teammates mobbed him after the last strike out. The Dodger Stadium crowd gave him a tremendous ovation. Dodger owner, Walter O'Malley, gave Koufax a miserly $500 bonus." Walker grinned.

"This duel was the most total perfect game played in modern times—only one hit, one walk, and one error. From the point of view of hitting, however, it was probably the worst game in history. Ignoring the two perfect games in 1880, Chicago may have been the worst hitting team to be on the losing end of a perfect game," Walker acknowledged.

"This Koufax-Hendly pitching struggle is reminiscent of the first perfect game, which was settled by an unearned run. Worcester's Lee Richmond, also a lefty, beat big Jim McCormick in the first perfect game in 1880. Cleveland's McCormick allowed only 3 hits and 1 base on balls, but his second baseman, Fred "Sure-Shot" Dunlap made a double error to allow the winning unearned run.

"Koufax said afterward that no one talked about the perfect game. 'Nobody on the bench said a word to me. At least I didn't hear anything. The Cubs also remained silent.'

Walker chuckled as he continued. "Jim Gilliam must have had mixed emotions. He had played second base for the Dodgers in Don Larsen's World Series thriller, going 0-for-3 at bat. Playing third base for Koufax, he was again 0-for-3, but at least he was on the winning end of a perfect game."

"During his career, the reticent Sandy won three Cy Young awards, during the time when only one was given per year. Each vote was unanimous. He was voted into the Hall of Fame in 1972, one of the youngest players ever selected. He fulfilled six years of a NBC contract broadcasting Saturday games. Sandy then retired to privacy. Braves' pitcher Greg Maddux has won four Cy Young awards and has a five-year contract of $57.5 million."

During the entire game, Douglass and Walker continued their discussion of internal auditing.

Douglass began, "I just don't understand how we blew that drop. We had everything planned."

"I know how you feel. Internal controls work that way also," Fleet added.

"What are internal controls, Fleet?" asked Douglass.

"Internal controls are the policies and procedures an organization adopts to provide reasonable assurance of meeting its objectives. Internal controls fall into five categories: control environment, risk assessment, control procedures, monitoring, and information/communication. These five types of control must be evaluated in terms of the organization's operations, financial reporting system, and compliance with government laws and regulations," Fleet said.

"What do you mean by reasonable assurance?" asked Douglass.

"Remember that the cost of a control should not exceed its benefit. In other words, there is still some risk that cannot be mitigated. Like the drop. That is why you should not beat up yourself too badly, Douglass," Fleet offered.

He continued, "I can also sympathize with your media problems. It is very similar to when a fraud occurs in a corporation. Everyone asks where the auditor was. Often we previously have made a recommendation which was ignored. Regardless management is often looking for a scapegoat."

The Dodgers today were able to salvage a split in the twin bill, beating St. Louis 7-5. Gary Sheffield's three-run double capped a five-run rally in the eighth inning. The Dodger reliever was finally able to hold a lead. Los Angeles' beleaguered bullpen had blown 25 of 44 save chances this season.

The news media were disappointed. There had been no explosion or killing. Douglass and Walker were relieved. But the next perfect game date was soon—September 16 in Cincinnati.

★ ★ ★ ★ ★

At Cinergy Field, formerly Riverfront Stadium, the huge white sterile saucer on the bank of the Ohio River, Douglass and Walker went upstairs to find their seats. Here in Riverfront Stadium in August 1987, Pete Rose looped his single into left field to beat Ty Cobb for the most hits. On April 4, 1974, Hank Aaron hit a homerun at Riverfront Stadium that tied Babe Ruth's record. Since it was still early, Walker took Douglass to the upper rows of the upper deck in right field. Douglass could see the Cincinnati skyline. Cinergy Field is a circular stadium with artificial turf. Today's game was a night game like the September 16 perfect game.

Back at their seats Douglass reviewed Walker's write-up of the reason he was sitting on the third base side in Cinergy Field/ Riverfront Stadium.

On Friday, September 16, 1988, 6'1" Thomas Leo Browning almost did not get to pitch at Riverfront Stadium, on the bank of the Ohio River in downtown Cincinnati, Ohio. There was a rain delay of two hours and twenty-seven minutes at the start of the Los Angeles Dodgers and Cincinnati Reds scheduled game. The day was wet and dreary, and Browning was looking for his first win against the Dodgers in five starts. The Dodgers had won 9 of the 15 games with Cincinnati so far in the 1988 season.

The 1988 Dodgers were *not* a last place team. They were leading the National League West division by 7 games ahead of Atlanta and 8 ½ ahead of Cincinnati. The Dodger Blue would beat the New York Mets in the seventh game of the playoffs, and go on to beat the Oakland Athletics in four out of five games in the World Series. This would be a fabulous season for the Dodgers.

In Riverfront Stadium, a ball can be hit out anywhere, and a pitcher has to worry about letting anyone hit the ball hard. This night, with the 10:00 p.m. start the Dodgers would be impotent, however. The 28-year-old left-hander had little trouble with the Dodgers. There was one threat in the fifth, when third baseman Chris Sabo grabbed a hard-hit grounder by Dodger right fielder and skinhead Mike Marshall. Sabo's throw to first baseman Nick Esasky was high, but umpire Mark Hirschbeck signaled that Esasky put his foot back on base in time for the out.

Similarly, Tim Belcher, an Ohio native, had allowed no hits and issued only one walk, to Eric Davis in the second, until the sixth. Belcher lost his no-hitter and shutout in the sixth as a result of Barry Larkin's double with two outs and Dodger Jeff Hamilton's throwing error after fielding Chris Sabo's bouncer to third. His throw hit the dirt at first base and Mickey Hatcher was unable to come up with the ball. Larkin scored the lone unearned run of the game. Sabo was then picked off at first by a throw from Belcher. Belcher would pitch a three-hitter.

According to Belcher, "During the game, I'm as intense as anyone, just hoping for a walk or anything. But you're there watching it unfold. It's something you fantasize about, putting yourself in that position. Just being a part of a game like this is special. I'm not bitter. I had no control over anything." This year was Belcher's second season, and he had hit his first home run off Browning earlier in the season.

Browning was complimentary of Belcher. "He was pitching as well as I was pitching. He pitched a hell of a game. That helped me maintain my intensity, because we were only ahead 1-0. Any mistakes might have cost us the game."

During the seventh, Kirk Gibson, who takes a lot of time at the plate, struck out for the second time, and he was not happy with plate umpire Jim Quick's calls. After some words were exchanged, Quick tossed Gibson from the game. Tommy Lasorda and Belcher had to restrain Gibson, and second base umpire John Kibler was finally able to get Gibson to leave the game. Alfredo Griffin in the first inning had argued with Quick about his calls, also.

Tom did not realize he was pitching a perfect game until the eighth. "When I got to the eighth inning, I felt a little bit antsy," the Casper, Wyoming native said. "I don't know how to explain it. Everything fell my way. It was just one of those days where everything worked, and every ball was hit right at people."

The first batter in the ninth, catcher Rick Dempsey, smashed a fly ball to left field. Paul O'Neill raced across the artificial turf and caught the ball at the warning track. One out.

Next up was the dangerous, but slumping, Steve Sax, who is a contact hitter. He grounded out to shortstop Barry Larkin. Two down. The Dodgers were down to their last out.

To try to break Browning's spell on his hapless Dodgers, silver-haired manager Tommy Lasorda sent up pinch-hitter Tracy Woodson. Recently acquired Jeff Reed, the catcher, hung the sign and Browning tossed his first pitch to the right-hander. Woodson fouled it off.

Woodson watched the second ball sail inside. He watched an outside pitch go by for ball two. On the next pitch Woodson grounded a foul ball toward the Dodgers' dugout. Two outs, two balls, and two strikes. Everyone in the stadium was standing.

On Browning's one hundred and second pitch, right-handed Woodson struck out. There had been 27 Dodger outs in a row. The one-hour, 51 minute masterpiece was finished. Fireworks exploded.

The Reds rushed on to the field to celebrate this magical moment and jumped on Browning to form a pile of bodies. This was the first perfect game for the Cincinnati franchise.

"I was just happy to complete a game," Browning said later. "The next thing I know the dog pile comes out. It's a great feeling. When I got up I was a little teary eyed."

After the dog pile, some of the Reds put Browning on their shoulders, and he gave them a series of high-fives. Pitcher Danny Jackson brought Browning a bottle of champagne. As Browning left the field, the crowd of 16,591 gave him a standing ovation, and he sprayed some of the jubilant fans with champagne.

Reds manager Pete Rose said, "He pitched perfect. I guess that's the best way to describe it. He pitched perfect."

Of Browning's 102 pitches, 72 were strikes and only 30 were balls. No batter got more than two balls. He tossed first-pitch strikes on 21 of the 27 Dodgers, and struck out 7 of them. With these analytics, Browning had attained the highest heights in the baseball profession.

After the game, a Hall of Fame representative asked for Browning's hat and an autographed ball.

Later he said, "My lucky hat? Sure I'm going to give them my hat." Winking he continued, "and they aren't getting the ball either; not the one I struck Woodson out with. They'll get one of the other ones."

Douglass stopped reading as Cincinnati Denny Neagle began his first windup to Atlanta's first batter Chipper Jones. "What was the connection between perfect games and the killings? There had to be a connection."

"I do not know." Walker then showed Douglass a Cincinnati newspaper article which rehashed the five Cincinnati killings in 1966 by an unknown suspect. All five women had been found in their home raped, with a lamp cord tied around their necks.

Action came quickly today in the bottom of the first in Cincinnati. Cather Eddie Taubensee's bases-loaded single keyed a five-run first inning off of four times Cy Young Award Winner Braves' Greg Maddux. The Braves' bullpen was roughed up for six more runs in the next three innings by the time Douglass received the phone call.

On the first base side, a police officer had found an ice chest with a typed note to Douglass:

Dear Bill Douglass,

Since you are such a nice guy, today's demonstration is just a warning. We could have placed a deadly VX grenade in this ice chest. To paraphrase Al Capone, kind words and a bomb will get you more than kind words. Baseball must be prepared to pay.

"The Ballpark Killers"

P.S. Tell Fleet Walker hello.

Douglass whistled a sigh of relief. "VX is a nerve gas more toxic than sarin. Its damages occur much more rapidly, and it is dangerous in contact with the skin. Iraq has about 80 chemical weapons factories and about 100 germ warfare factories. At least there would be no killing today. Let's go get a cheese coney, which is a hot dog with Cincinnati chili and shredded cheese." They walked to one of the eight Gold Star Chili stands.

Walker pointed out that there was no baseball card in or on the ice chest.

During the early innings Walker told Douglass about Marge Schott, the controversial ex-owner of the Reds. "Mrs. Schott is an excellent example of the need for top down auditing—basically auditing management," Walker explained. "Management is responsible for everything. Management can destroy an organization."

"Marge Schott was then the only female controlling owner in major league baseball. In 1993, Major League Baseball hit her with a one-year suspension in February for making racial and ethnic slurs. She also was fined $25,000 and forced to take a 40-hour sensitivity-training course. Would you believe that team policy requires her to sign any check of more than $50?"

"Pretty low," was Douglass' only comment.

"Her partners sued for controlling interest in order to keep her out of the spotlight. She spent a half-million dollars in legal fees to keep control. She came back and had a habit of rubbing hair from her late St. Bernard, Schottzie, on the uniform shirts of her players.

"In 1997, a reporter discovered a swastika armband in her home and asked, 'What is this for?' Marge said it was just a memento and explained that Adolph Hitler was a perfectly nice guy, who just went astray."

"Wow. The forty-hours of sensitivity training must have helped her a lot," Douglass laughed.

"Anyway, after she made remarks to a *Sports Illustrated* reporter that were insensitive to Asian-Americans and working women, the baseball owners threatened to suspend her again. On June 12, 1997, she agreed to give up daily control of the Cincinnati Reds through the 1998 season. She keeps her partnership shares as 43 percent controlling owner, but can not speak for the team. She basically stepped down as CEO of the Reds. Then on October 2, 1999, she was compelled to sell her controlling interest after she made a remark on ESPN that Hitler was good when he came into power."

"Could she be doing these killings?" Douglass was serious.

"I doubt it," Walker replied. "She's still wealthy. She owns two Cincinnati-area car dealerships and several other Midwest businesses. But General Motors alleged that she falsified sales records of 57 cars at her Chevrolet dealership. Where are the internal auditors when you need them?"

Walker's earlier observation was prophetic, because in the eighth inning a fan died while eating a hotdog. Never assume in baseball and internal auditing. One must assess the efficiency and effectiveness of information and evidence. Oral evidence is worthless to an internal auditor. A typed note was found on the table where the fan had put tomato ketchup on his hotdog:

"Douglass, it ain't over 'til it's over."

"A Berraism," Walker explained. "Yogi Berra, the catcher for the New York Yankees for many years is credited with a number of comical, yet wise statements. He caught Don Larsen's perfect game."

A San Diego baseball card was found on the table.

"Why did the killer skip the Koufax game?" Douglass asked almost to himself.

"Maybe it's merely money or lack of travel time. Can he afford to fly around the country?" Walker suggested.

"Good point," Douglass said.

The Cincinnati news media compared the "Ballpark Killer" with Donald Harvey, a Cincinnati nursing attendant at Daniel Drake Memorial Hospital. Harvey pleaded guilty to the murder of 24 people over a four-year period; a list of the 24 names were found behind a picture in Harvey's apartment. He admitted to poisoning with arsenic, cyanide, rat poison, and hepatitis germs. He suffocated others with plastic bags or injected air into their veins to cause blood clots.

The article said that the FBI estimates that there are at least 500 serial killers currently at large.

Douglass shook his and said, "Too many," when he read the piece. "More like 100."

The next day Commissioner Selig offered a $500,000 reward for anyone providing information leading to the arrest and conviction of the "Baseball Killers."

That night Douglass watched three rerun episodes of "X-Files" which his wife had taped for him in his absence. But the shows could not keep him from worrying about the Ballpark Killer. He tried never to underestimate his opponent. But he never accepted at face value what an opponent gave him.

★ ★ ★ ★ ★

Walker made it to Baruch College by subway on the No. 6 line with a little time to spare, exiting at 28th and Park. He was a "subway stop professor" twice a week at CUNY. His internal auditing class was at 7:30—one and a half-hours, twice a week. Walker walked to the 26th street building and entered on the Park Avenue side.

Upon entering the building, Walker showed his identification card to the security guard. The card must be carried at all times, and no one enters a Baruch building without a card which is magnetically coded each semester. A unique aspect of Baruch life is that almost all facilities are accessed by elevators, so students and faculty often spend a great deal of time waiting in long lines to go up. Tonight was no different, but Walker made it to the seventh floor to get his mail in the accounting department in Room 725 and then to his office on the same floor. Walker shared an office and a phone line on the seventh floor with another assistant professor—Tim Lembke. On their door was a statement: A regular auditor is like a watchdog (e.g., a bulldog); a forensic accountant is like a bloodhound; and an internal auditor is like a seeing-eye dog (e.g., monitors and guides top management).

Walker liked to teach, especially internal auditing, because the students in the class were senior undergraduates or graduate level students. The vast majority of Baruch students work at least part-time, and there is a large night student population. There were some business people from the community taking his course. These part-time students brought into his classroom many of the more practical aspects of auditing.

Walker's course was a part of the Endorsed Internal Auditing Program or EIAP at Baruch. Only thirty or so other universities and colleges in the United States had internal auditing programs. These were endorsed by the Institute of Internal Auditors (IIA) and promoted among chief auditing executives who tried to hire their graduates.

As he was gathering the material for his class, there was a knock at his door. "Come in, please," Walker said.

"Fleet, I would like for you to meet Jim Welker. He is in New York City to present a paper at NYU." Walker looked up at Nick Iyer, who was in the office next to him.

Walker got up and walked over and shook Jim's hand. "Glad to meet you, Jim. Nick has talked about you and your research often."

"Oh, no. I hope it was good," Welker smiled.

"What are you talking about at NYU?" Walker asked.

"Something that should interest you." Welker handed Fleet a paper. "I would like for you to read it and tell me what you think. My title is 'What Impact Supervisory Pressures Have On Internal Auditing Decisions.'"

"Great topic!" Fleet said.

"We have questioned over 200 internal auditors with respect to certain decisions they have to make on the job. One group is the control group, who have no pressures from a supervisor. Another group has pressure from an audit manager to make an improper or unethical decision. A third group receives pressure from the audit director."

Welker paused for a moment, and Fleet pulled out and looked at his silver Lenin pocket watch. Fleet liked pocket watches. He had purchased this raised side profile of Lenin in Red Square on one of his visits.

"We divided the internal auditors into authoritative and nonauthoritative personalities. We found that the audit directors caused the nonauthoritative auditors to break more rules."

Nick interrupted. "Jim, we have to let Fleet go to class. Welker could talk all day about his behavioral research."

Fleet told Jim and Nick good-bye, picked up his classroom materials, and rushed downstairs. He did not have time to stop off at the fifth floor cafeteria.

Walker looked around his classroom, mentally noting the pre-class activities of his students. Many were talking, some were reading the New York Times, or The Ticker (the bi-weekly student newspaper), and two were even reading their internal auditing book.

He began his lecture with a review of his key to the internal auditing world. No one had any questions about the overhead that he had covered last week.

"Today I wish to cover the analytical auditing procedures in 'Statement on Internal Auditing Standards #8.'" Fleet put a second overhead transparency up which summarized Standard #8.

"Who wishes to tell us a definition of analytical auditing procedures? No one raised a hand. "Okay, Charles Clark, would you give me a definition?"

"Analytical auditing would refer to the use of the techniques which you have listed in the overhead under techniques; such items as interperiod analysis, budget comparisons, industry comparisons, regression analysis, and other techniques fall under the category of analytical auditing."

"Why do we use these techniques, Charles?"

"To gather evidence to be used to improve audit efficiency and effectiveness," Charles replied.

"Right, Charles, to gather evidence. Auditors and people in general tend to be overconfident in their judgments, so we use analytical methods, such as reasonableness tests, to gather evidence to support our audit judgments. Standard 420 requires auditors to collect, analyze, interpret, and document evidence to support audit results."

Walker continued. "The quality of audit evidence varies. Of course, evidence from parties independent of the audit is more objective and less subject to distortion by the auditee. By the way, fraud occurs more often in the fourth quarter. If a company announces that it's missing earnings estimates in the fourth quarter, you can bet that the auditors found something they didn't like. Auditors do the bulk of their scrutiny in the fourth quarter before they bless the financial statements. And watch the stock plummet when the company announces that they are missing the estimates."

"For investors, my colleague George Sorter at New York University believes that with fewer CPA firms today, there's a greater likelihood of blown audits. The accounting firms are under tremendous time and cost pressure, and it's as if they are not looking for fraud. These permissive professionals say 'you can do this' rather than 'you should do this.' As high-tech companies become increasingly complicated, the outsider auditors are increasingly working blind. Thus, internal auditors can not expect the external auditors to catch the fraud, so internal auditors must do their job and catch the fraud."

Walker put another overhead transparency on the projector listing the various types of evidence and continued, "Evidence is the information auditors use to reach conclusions. Evidence must be sufficient (enough) and competent (right quality).

Enough evidence must be gathered to persuade. This hurdle is much lower than legal or scientific thresholds."

A student raised her hand and asked, "What is the right kind of evidence?"

Walker answered, "Evidence should be objective, free from bias, and relevant. In recent years, auditors have begun to discount much documentary evidence because technology has enabled false documents to be created relatively easy. That is why we need analytical evidence to tell us if transactions make sense. The other types of evidence that are still valid are physical and testimonial."

Walker continued, "Evidence is gathered by means of audit procedures such as interrogation, examination, review, inspection, etc. The proper order is to set audit objectives, evaluate the evidence needed to meet the audit objectives and then to select the audit procedures necessary to obtain that evidence."

Fleet finished class by assigning a case study, requiring the students to evaluate a fact situation and write an audit program to meet the audit objectives stated in the fact situation. He was a hard professor.

Chapter 11

Arlington

The allure of numbers, to most of us, is like the excitement of settling sand—a narcoleptic surety. Crafty criminals prey on this boredom. They pile on the numbers, spewing meaningless records in false books.

Cory Johnson

He had walked toward the Ballpark at Arlington from Motel 6 where he had parked his RV the night before. The old Arlington Stadium where 6'7", 185 pound Michael Atwater Witt pitched the thirteenth perfect game during his fourth season was gone. This former stadium had been one of the worst in the majors, and the 24-year-old California Angel hurler's pitching gem had been tossed in front of only 8,375 Texas Rangers fan on the last day of the season in 1984. The little Arlington stadium had been built in 1965 for a Double A team and was originally called the Turnpike Stadium. Texas Rangers' president Tom Schieffer had called it "a backwater stop, the worst facility in baseball."

As he walked toward the massive Ranger red brick and Sunset Red granite exterior stadium, he saw wrapped around the facade bas reliefs of longhorn cattle and scenes depicting the state's rugged history, including stories that tell of the Alamo, the oil boom, the cotton and cattle industries, the space program near Houston, the Texas Rangers' call for volunteers and two scenes honoring the state's two professional baseball teams.

The clay bas relief subjects were selected from 40 suggested sketches. Located in the granite work near the smaller arches, the reliefs measure 4 feet by 19 feet and are reproduced nine times each to fully wrap around the building. Each cycle takes up more than 190 feet of viewing space because pillars space the work in between.

Although a night game, the Texas sun was still hot as he neared the home plate entrance to the Ranger's red brick "Ballpark." This place with green metal roofs is one of the hottest parks in the majors, with temperatures soaring into the 100s. Thus, even Sunday games are scheduled at night.

To his left he could see the Texas Giant and the Six Flags Towers across two six-acre man-made lakes. Bisecting the lakes and winding alongside the ballpark is Nolan Ryan Expressway, named after baseball's strikeout king. As he gave his $16 Texas Rangers' ticket to an employee, he noticed several policemen and someone taking a video of everyone walking through the turnstiles. He was glad he had disguised his appearance. He put the red, white, and blue ticket stub into his shirt pocket to keep as a souvenir of the game.

After purchasing a program, he walked slowly around the stadium, noticing the blue section signs held up by Rawlings bats. He was amazed by the 9 by 10 feet panels hung in the entrances to the park's luxury suites. At least 30 of these paintings were visible as he walked around the ballpark's main concourse. The paintings had the appearance of old photographs, which seemed to capture the nostalgia of the game.

The paintings of Joe DiMaggio, Ty Cobb, Babe Ruth, Mickey Mantle, and Nolan Ryan seemed to capture the idiosyncrasies and playing style of each of the players. There were paintings of Eddie Mathews, Catfish Hunter, Duke Snider, Sandy Koufax, Willie Mays, Lou Gehrig, Stan Musial, Hank Aaron, Frank Robinson, Lou Brock, Johnny Bench, and many others. He tried to go upstairs to get closer to the murals, but the guard at the top of the escalator said no. "You don't have a 200 number ticket."

He did see the baseball-shaped lamps along the outer wall, but two strolling police officers caused him to descend the stairs quickly. He passed Bambino's Pizza, but instead he bought a Decker hot dog and a Dr. Pepper.

After being fortified with some energy, he continued his tour into the center field area. Here was a four-story office building where a person could watch the game from an office window. There was a retail area and an amphitheater area to boost the bottom line. He passed the Short Stop, Red River BBQ, and many other food vendors.

After walking around the Rangers' dugout on the first base side of the park, he went back to the third base side to check out his faux wood green folding chair. The plastic seat was excellent—section 14, row 5, seat 8. All the seats are angled toward the mound, and no smoking is allowed in the seating bowl. His seat had a cup holder.

He could now see the arched windows, exposed green girders, and wall-to-wall advertising—Bud Light, Southwest Airlines, FINA, Budweiser, What-A-Burger, Dallas Morning News, Dr. Pepper: A Texas Original, and Friday's Front Row Sports Grill.

The field itself was a lush green carpet—real bermuda and rye grasses. The outfield dimensions were not symmetrical, a feature common to parks constructed in the early twentieth century. These quirky corners, odd angles, and high walls give the home team an advantage, because the more time an outfielder plays in the stadium, the better he will know the corners. According to Will Clark, "when we figure out how the bounces come off, we'll have an edge."

The right field corner foul pole is only 325 feet from home plate, and the fence is only 8 feet high. Which brings up the age-old question: why is a ball *fair* when it hits a yellow *foul* pole? Maybe it's a defective internal control? The left field foul pole is 332 feet from home plate, with the deepest point 407 feet in right center. Both yellow foul poles had been taken from the Arlington Stadium, according to the Rangers' program. Fans sit close to the field itself. The first rows of seats on the first and third base sides are just 57 feet from home plate. Fans sit only 44 feet from first and third bases, respectively. Thus, fewer foul balls are caught, and there should be slightly higher batting averages in this stadium—not good from the point of view of a pitcher.

The relentless sun was still hot, so he decided to go to the bathroom. There was a police officer near the closest bathroom, so he walked to the center field area. He found a bathroom, walked inside, and then, using tissue from his pocket, he opened, entered, and then locked the door to the far stall.

Using his right foot he knocked the cover down on the white commode. The killer began to prepare his deadly potion. The prey was anyone. Just as in the green jungles of the rain forest, the hunter was also the hunted.

He sat down on the commode without dropping his tan pants. He pulled out a small, black garbage bag, put on some surgical gloves, and took out a clear nail polish bottle from the bag. From inside the brim of his red Rangers hat he took out a baseball card. He spread the plastic bag over his lap, put the baseball card face down on the round, white toilet paper holder, and carefully opened the bottle. He brushed some of the deadly liquid on the back of the card, flipped it over, carefully, and brushed more liquid on the front of the card.

Next he placed the bottle on the white tiled floor, stood up, and opened the cover of the commode. Then he brushed some of the liquid on the seat of the commode. He slid the bolt on the door open and then carefully wiped some poison on the bolt handle. He closed the bottle tightly and then wiped the bottle off with toilet paper. He carefully removed the rubber gloves using toilet paper. After flushing the toilet paper, he carefully folded the garbage bag with the bottle and gloves inside, and put it in his front pocket. He left the card inside the stall, using toilet paper to push open the stall's door. He washed his hands carefully, always using toilet paper to touch anything, including the water faucet. He put the used toilet paper in his pocket, smiled at his bearded image in a mirror and exited the bathroom without touching anything.

He went through the same ritual in a bathroom on the first base side of the stadium, and then purchased a $3 Bud Lite on the way back to his seat in time for the first out of the game. The Rangers were in the field with their white uniforms with red lettering, red shoes, and red hats with large white Ts.

The visiting team, the Baltimore Orioles, took the field wearing grey uniforms, black lettering, black hats and shoes. This American League East team also has a new classic park at Camden Yards.

The Rangers were in the disgraceful American League West, and five teams were in the American League Central as a result of the realignment of the two leagues in 1994. With the Rangers in the West are Anaheim, Seattle, and Oakland; only Oakland has ever played in a World Series. Many experts predicted all four teams would lose 100 games during this season.

The realignment had been driven by economics because the format calls for an extra round of playoffs, two best-of-five series in each league involving the three division champions and the second-place team with the best record. The winners advance to the best-of-seven League Championship and then to the World Series.

At the end of each half-inning, police officers came down the aisles and stood at the wall separating the stands from the field. At first the police made him nervous, but he did not even notice them by the middle of the game.

There was little excitement during the first three innings other than a loudmouth fan behind him harassing Orioles'

Jerry Hairston, who committed several errors at second base. After the top of the second inning, an American Airlines jet banked around the home plate side as it left Dallas/Fort Worth airport. During the third inning a small plane pulled a sign advertising "Fantasy Ranch. No cover with ticket stub." The electronic scoreboard said "Thanks for making it a Blockbuster night."

He checked the pitching rosters of the Rangers and Orioles in the "Game Day News." Not a single knuckle ball pitcher on either team, he thought.

A fastball may rotate as many as eight times as it goes toward home plate. A knuckle ball with no more than a half-rotation will move erratically up, down, or sideways as much as 11 inches.

When he had pitched in the early seventies, he had held the ball so it was released with little spin. The air rushes past on the side of the ball without stitches, and the ball feels a deflecting push from the smooth side toward the stitched side. The less spin, the more the deflection, and the more movement. Even catchers had a hard time catching *his* knuckle balls.

In the top of the fourth, with a runner on first base, he heard the sirens at the same time that Will Clark hit a home run into the left field seats. The fans began to shout, "Throw it back. Throw it back." Someone did throw the ball back onto the field. At the Rangers' park visiting team's home run balls are often thrown back onto the field. 2-0 in favor of the visitors.

More excitement occurred at the bottom of the sixth— What-A-Burgers' dot racing on the scoreboard. Red, yellow, and green dots raced around a diamond with the fans shouting for their favorite color. The red dot won. The fans went wild.

After the seventh inning stretch which features the song "Cotton Eyed Joe" rather than "Take Me Out to the Ball

Game," Juan Gonzalez, with a five-year, $30.7 million salary hit a home run into the right field seats. The score was 2-2 going into the eighth.

There was little excitement in the eighth except for the blue and white Blockbuster blimp flying around the stadium. No player came close to hitting the sign in right field which says, "Hit it here and win a new suit. 501 ft." Also no player hit the Target sign in left field. The Rangers scored a run in the bottom of the ninth on another Hairston error.

As Sandy left, he walked around the first base side of the stadium and saw the classic yellow police crime scene tape around the entrance to a bathroom. To be safe he hurriedly walked to the center field area and removed his red baseball hat, sunglasses, and fake beard. He kept on the moustache and put on a pair of wire-rimmed glasses. As he exited the center field gate, he followed closely behind a tall man and a fat woman. He noticed two men on each side of the gate frantically trying to observe the departing fans. Probably FBI agents, he thought. The hunter had struck again.

While walking back to Motel 6, he turned to observe the ballpark at night under a full moon. A magnificent structure. He spent about an hour in the Exchange/A Strip Show, next to Motel 6. He slept in his hot RV that night rather than risk staying another night in the motel. He did not see the police officer trying to get inside the Motel 6 office at 3:10 a.m.

Super-sleuth William Douglass had twenty-three FBI agents in the Ballpark. There were many extra police on duty, many in plain clothes. The goal was to catch the killer, or at least to stop another killing. At fifteen-minute intervals, an agent or police officer checked the stalls in all of the men's restrooms. A video was secretly taken of everyone entering and leaving the restrooms.

At the beginning of the second inning, Douglass was elated. One agent found the baseball card in the bathroom in the center field area *before* anyone picked it up. About twenty-five minutes later the second baseball card was found on the first base side. Again no one was killed. Another 45 minutes elapsed before he could review both videos taken of the people entering and exiting the two bathrooms. Only two people had entered both bathrooms—a small boy and a tall man with a beard.

The bearded man wearing the Ranger hat had to be the killer. By now it was the bottom of the eighth so Douglass hurriedly called all of his agents to view the film of the suspect. At least one agent was sent to every exit. Douglass was sure they would get the killer.

Douglass tried to run around the inside of the stadium frantically searching the sea of faces exiting the stands. He was constantly bumping into people, who cursed him. Fleet Walker went the other direction around the stadium. There were too many people. Douglass passed Walker four times before the crowd thinned. Nothing.

Around 11:30 the stadium was virtually empty, except for employees, FBI agents, police officers, and news reporters. Douglass used the FBI agents to search the entire stadium. Again nothing.

Armed with a sketch of the bearded man, Douglass sent the police officers to all hotels and motels in a three-mile radius of the ballpark. Douglass remained at George Bush, Jr.'s old office to coordinate the search for the suspect.

At 5:46 in the morning Douglass received the phone call from Officer O'Hare. O'Hare was excited. "We have his name. Sandy Kojak. He has a Missouri license—Kansas City. He stayed at Motel 6 two nights ago. I've sealed off the room."

"Great," said Douglass. "Fax me a copy of his license. Pronto." Douglass gave the officer the fax number. "I'll send the forensic team over. I want everything saved from the room —fingerprints, hairs, and the bathroom sink."

Reviewing the fax copy of Sandy Kojak's photo on the Missouri license, Walker told Douglass, "I'm not sure that Sandy Kojak is his real name."

"Why?" Douglass asked.

"Sandy Koufax. Sandy Kojak. It's probably an alias. Sandy Koufax pitched a perfect game."

"We'll soon know. I'll get the K.C. office working on the matter."

★ ★ ★ ★ ★

Over bacon and eggs later that morning in Ponder, Texas Sandy perused the *Fort Worth Star-Telegram*. On the front page in large letters was this headline: FBI, 0; Ballpark Killer, 0. He read the related article:

The Rangers won the ballgame last night under heavy surveillance by local police and at least 25 FBI Agents. The ballpark killer left at least two poison baseball cards in two men's bathrooms, but no one was hurt—except maybe the collective ego of the FBI. Authorities found two deadly baseball cards in two stalls within minutes after the serial killer left them in the bathrooms. However, even though the FBI now have a video picture of the suspected killer, they were unable to arrest the man at the Ballpark in Arlington last night.

The FBI took videos of everyone entering and leaving the men's restrooms, and had officers or agents check the restrooms every 15 minutes to look for the deadly baseball cards. There is now an all points bulletin out for a suspect, Sandy Kojak, from Kansas City, Missouri. The FBI has made available the following photograph of the suspect. (Photo of a bearded white male was shown.)

Some authorities are questioning the handling of the operations at the ballpark last night. Arlington Council member Bunky Harvey stated that "The FBI used fans to bait a trap for the killer. Someone could have been killed. We were very lucky last night." Council member Harvey stated to a local television station. "Fans should have been warned of the danger of going to the bathroom. Fans should have been told not to pick up any baseball cards."

Apparently a serial killer has been killing someone at ballparks on the date that perfect games were pitched. The killer or killers had more narrow escapes than Bill Clinton. Last night was the date that Michael Witt pitched a perfect game against the Rangers on September 30, 1984, in the old Arlington stadium.

There was a picture of Special Agent William Douglass talking to an expert in baseball, a Fleet Walker. Walker is an internal auditor for the New York Yankees.

Ponder is a town of 438 people north of Fort Worth. Sandy had eaten a huge steak there the evening before in the Ranchman's Café. The Café had a sign over its open door as follows: "We know who lives in a Barn."

Sandy liked another sign on the Café's wall: "It's our money, Not Theirs." IRS was in red movie letters. Newspaper clippings showed that a Bonnie and Clyde had been filmed in the Café.

After breakfast he was on the road early. When he was near the border of Texas, he stopped the RV on the side of the freeway and removed the brown wig and mustachio. He also removed the cummerbund stuffed with old socks to make him appear larger. He did not remove his plastic-like bulletproof vest. As he removed the earring he said, "I don't understand how any guy could wear such a thing. They would have to be nuts."

He recalled reading where Hall of Famer Rick Ferrell said that you would be joked out of the league for wearing earrings and gold chains. There was a different sense of manliness in the

players in the '20s or '30s. Players would not drink water during the game even in the worst heat, and players did not eat
snacks on the bench even during a doubleheader. Ferrell was a
lightweight fighter before his 18-year catching career.

Garth Brooks was singing "Friends in Low Places" as Sandy
headed the RV back on to Interstate 30. He had to be in
Cleveland by the second of October. At least Cleveland would
be cooler than Arlington. He adjusted the brown prescription
sunglasses. He kept humming "Bonnie and Clyde; Sandy and
Janice."

For some reason the Garth Brooks' song made him think
about the high salaries paid to some of the franchise players. If
it had not been for that one umpire, he would have pitched a
perfect game. He would have been in Baseball's Hall of Fame.
He knew that *if* he had pitched that perfect game, he would
have stayed in the majors more than three years. "If" is a big
word, of course. But that one umpire blew three called strikes
—not just one.

That one umpire made him a poor man—a lifetime of selling cars, selling insurance, and selling securities. Sure, some forgettable characters have pitched perfect games. Mike Witt had
lasted nine seasons—winning 109 games and losing 104 games.
But he had been better than string bean Witt. Witt only had a
fastball and curve—not a knuckle ball.

He continued to get madder as he thought about Darryl
Strawberry. Here was a former Dodgers player with a five-year,
$20.5 million contract. The Internal Revenue Service was con-
stantly after the outfielder because he allegedly did not pay taxes
on his earnings from baseball card shows. Strawberry played for
the Yankees for several years, but he was suspended for one year
in February 2000 for testing positive for cocaine a third time.
Steve Howe had seven drug violations before the then Commissioner of Baseball Fay Vincent exiled him from baseball for-
ever. Howe had been Rookie of the Year with the 1980

Dodgers, but his chronic cocaine problem caused him to drift in and out of baseball over a decade. But his "adult attention deficit disorder" contention could not save him from the righteous Fay Vincent. Eventually Steve Howe came back.

The large salaries paid to franchise players have caused a downward mobility for middle-level veterans. Quality players were replaced by younger, mediocre players in order to meet salary caps. Salary caps are about 5 percent of deferred revenues.

Tom Reich, a baseball players' agent, said it succinctly. "Get below the market for major players, and you're into the Kmart. This is like Hollywood now. The bankable stars get all the money, and everybody else in the picture scuffles for a living wage."

Sandy came up behind an older car with two bumper stickers. One stated "Discourage Inbreeding; Ban Country Music." The other sticker said: "I live dangerously during the week; then I go bushhog racing."

Sandy laughed and said out loud. "If I was a real serial killer, my victims would be drivers who have stupid bumper stickers on their cars."

Without a disguise, Sandy's face had gained some lines since the days he had been a pitcher. He still had dark black hair, slate-blue eyes, and a strong square jaw. His hairline was slowly receding.

As he drove Sandy remembered when he hatched his crazy scheme. His wife had divorced him, he lost his second job of the year, and he became depressed. After watching a movie starring Michael Douglas called "Falling Down," he went back to his car and drove to his hometown: Crawford, Nebraska.

Crazy times. He drove throughout the night and arrived in Crawford early in the morning. Crawford is a small town in the northwest corner of Nebraska. With no place to go, he had driven 19 miles to Toadstool Badlands Montrose Park—three miles of paved road and 16 miles of dirt road.

He still remembered the park from his childhood, even though he had moved to Denver with his parents at age seven. Northwest of Crawford, Toadstool Park is a moon-like landscape, mostly volcanic ash and brule clay, that was sculpted by wind and rain after an earthquake exposed the area.

He had slept in his car for several hours because of the fear of rattlesnakes in the area. As the sun came up he turned on his radio and got out of his Ford to stretch his aching bones. A group called Pirates of the Mississippi were singing "Now I lay me down to sleep. I pray the Lord my soul to keep. If I die before I wake, feed Jake. He's been a good dog."

"I was a good pitcher, too," he mumbled. "If the Florida Marlins could pay Gary Sheffield $10.62 million each year, surely they will pay a small extortion fee to me."

There in the early morning he wrote his song "A Hole in my Sole:"

She threw me out this morning, seven weeks ago,
And I've been walking since that day.
She gave me directions with no place to go.
Step by step by step, I'm on my way.

Oh, these old boots are falling apart.
Not much for keeping out the cold.
I know that she meant to break my heart,
And now she's wearing a hole in my sole.

Toadstools. As a boy scout he had studied the difference between some poisonous and non-poisonous toadstools. Toadstools and mushrooms are the fruit of fungi which grow in weblike networks underground. When it rains enough, the fungus reproduce by sprouting above the surface and releasing spores. They can be colorful and weird looking. Some of them reminded him of colorful paper parasols.

How could he get revenge for the bad calls in his perfect game? How could he bring baseball to its knees? He knew that most serial killers were caught, so how could he be sure to be labeled insane? He could write a best-selling book, earn a few million dollars of royalties, and get out of the funny farm in a few years.

The killings had to be outrageous and bizarre. The toadstool formations and his goals caused him to focus upon the simple idea: kill someone on the dates of each perfect game at the appropriate stadium. The genie was out of the bottle. He decided to use poison from mushrooms to avoid the problem of being near the killing scene. He also wanted the person to die with a baseball card.

He used the outside smelly toilet at the park and checked out the sod house. The sixteen-mile dirt and rock road followed railroad tracks. He did not pass a single vehicle along the dusty road. He stopped at a Sinclair station in Crawford to get gas, and noticed the Crawford Hot Air Balloon Company on the outskirts of town. He saw farmhouses, fenced green fields, cattle, decorative mailboxes, and large round bales of hay on his slow drive through Nebraska. One mailbox looked like a tractor. He saw a beautiful pheasant along Route 77.

The road through Nebraska was straight, but poor. Nonworking windmills and small cattle ponds dot the landscape. He drove into Wyoming toward Lusk. There were many wooden snowdrift fences, and he passed Lost Springs, population 4. At Orin Junction he took a left on Interstate 25 toward Cheyenne with his future life in focus. He remembered a Shakespeare saying: "The evil that men do lives after them; the good is often interred with their bones."

Although he had never been a reader, he began to devour everything he could find about serial killers, such as *The Blooding, The Red Dragon, The Third Deadly Sin, Prime Witness, Silence of the Lambs*, and *The Butcher Theater*. He reviewed many *FBI Law Enforcement Bulletins*, and copied any articles about serial killers. Soon he was reading articles in the *Journal of Forensic Science*. He wanted to be smarter than his hunters. He hoped to avoid the fate of Ted Bundy, Jeffrey Dahmer, Doug Clark, Randy Woodfield, Arthur J. Shawcross, Jerry Brudos, the Boston Strangler, John Wayne Gacy, Chris Wilder, Ken Bianchi, Wayne Williams, Ed Gein, Carol Bundy, Henry Louis Wallace, Frank Potts, and other captured violent offenders. He read *The Serial Killers* by Colin Wilson and Donald Seaman, and *Serial Killers* by Joel Norris on several occasions. He loved Patricia Cornwell's early novels.

He especially enjoyed the succinct Chapter 6 in *Profiling Violent Crimes* by Ronald M. Holmes. This chapter entitled "Profiling Serial Murders" provided a table outlining the types of serial killers and their crime scene traits. He outlined on paper a series of crime scene characteristics which would depict his acts as a mixture of the visionary, mission, comfort, lust, thrill, and power/control killer. He worried that most serial killers had a sex motive for their killings. But with the discovery of genetic fingerprinting in 1984, he had to be extremely careful. Genetic fingerprinting allows authorities to analyze semen, blood, and skin tissues and match a murderer. Everyone knew about DNA after the O.J. Simpson trial. Killers now shaved their private parts before raping and killing to avoid detection through DNA analysis. Besides, many of his kills would have to be swift.

Sandy was especially interested in the sixty unsolved murders in the Kansas City area. Since 1977, at least 60 black, drug-using prostitutes have been murdered in waves. Somehow a serial killer or copycat killers have escaped detection. Sandy wanted to be just as successful. He infrequently visited his mother in Kansas City, and he scrutinized the Kansas City papers for details of the killings.

After returning from his trip to Crawford, Nebraska, he applied for and began working as a maintenance person at a local university in Denver. He had access to keys to the chemistry department, and during his night duties he was able to gradually obtain two poisons from the chemistry laboratory. Surprisingly, security was lax for most poisons, other than narcotics. One professor was performing experiments with pesticides. With a sufficient supply of both savin and malathion, he began to experiment with the animals in the lab at night. He found that rats and rabbits would die if some savin or malathion was absorbed through their skin, but the amber liquid malathion had a distinctive odor. Then he read about dimethyl sulfate, a colorless and odorless liquid which can be absorbed by skin or eye contact. He located a bottle of dimethyl sulfate, and he began experimenting with a mixture of the dimethyl sulfate and savin on the animals. It worked rapidly.

He found several oleander shrubs on campus, and he put the narrow leaves, milky sap, and pink blossoms in a mustard bottle to soak. Each night for twenty days he would mash the items with a large screwdriver. He read that oleander was used as rat poison in Europe. He mixed the resulting water with dimethyl sulfate. His potion killed the rats and rabbits in the university laboratory. He was almost ready for his reckless experiment. But first he went for his daily jog. He had always been a loner. He liked to run. In high school he had been on both the track and baseball teams.

While jogging he thought about the fact that he did not fit the patterns of the typical serial killer. A serial offender normally fits four of six behavioral characteristics by the age of 12:

Animal Torture
Enuresis
Pathological lying
Fire setting

Chronic daydreaming
Violent fantasy

Okay, so he did daydream some.

He did not kill for sex. His first murder was not between age 25 and 30. He was not from a broken family. His father or mother had *not* abused him, and he had not abused his wife. He was not an O.J. Simpson. True his marriage had failed, but he did not use drugs or drink heavily. Well at least he was a white male. Many serial killers were white males, although he had read about the unsolved murders of about eight female prostitutes left within three miles along the west bank of the Mississippi River. Apparently a black male was strangling the victims with his bare hands, then raping them.

Another recent black serial killer was silky-voiced Henry Louis Wallace, a radio disc jockey at WBAW-FM in Barnwell, South Carolina. He was charged with murdering at least 10 women over two years in South Carolina in 1994.

How could he fake insanity if he was caught? He decided that if he was caught, he would confess to the murders of John F. Kennedy, William McKinley, and Elvis Presley. Duck Liuas had confessed to killing Kennedy and McKinley in Columbus, Georgia during the search for the Columbus Stocking Strangler. Eventually Carlton Gary was arrested for the raping and killing of a number of elderly women in Columbus. Gary had been one of the few captured black serial killers.

On his job at nights he also had discovered some hand props in the drama department. The glove-like props fit over a person's hands and lower arms, and they looked almost real when wearing a long-sleeve shirt. Over a three-month period he took two pairs of the hands. He needed them to disguise his fingerprints. He wanted to be a master of disguise like Albert DeSalvo, the Boston Strangler.

Since Sandy worked on essentially the late shift, he became friends of a young business professor in the other building in which he worked. The untenured professor was in his fourth year and struggling with his teaching and research. According to Dr. Dean, the restructuring of universities like corporations, and the elimination of tenure through post-tenure review, made getting tenure at even an average university difficult. Soon higher education will be taught by what the *New York Times* calls migrant laborers—nontenured track, low-paid part-timers.

In order to obtain tenure, a professor must publish a number of esoteric research papers. The more esoteric and less understandable in the real world, the more valuable the research. Even if you want to primarily teach, the educational system is out of control. Grade inflation is unbelievable. At Stanford, the Doc said, they give 90% A's and B's. "At most private universities now, if a student pays his or her fees, they get their B's." The Doc had a funny laugh. "It's not much better here," Dr. Dean complained. "I believe in Vince Lombardi's philosophy: The best motivator is fear. But few teachers believe in teaching any more. There's only a few dinosaurs like me left."

One evening the professor was reviewing his student evaluation of teaching results. He called them SETs. He was folding them into airplanes and trying to toss them into a trashcan on the other side of the desk. Few of them went into the round filing cabinet.

"Look at this one," Dr. Dean said. "Dr. Dean is the worst professor I *evry* had. He *embarrased* me in the classroom *bye* asking questions about my homework. He *incist* on giving *tought* exams, and he gave about 15% of his last semester's classes C's. He should be fired. He's *to ole* fashion to be teaching in a institution of higher education."

Dr. Dean had circled some of the student's misspelled and incorrect words. He folded it into an airplane and threw it towards the trashcan. It missed.

"I take it you never played basketball," Sandy laughed.

"Look, some of these remarks are libelous. I should be able to sue, but the students don't have to sign their names. The teaching profession is the only profession that doesn't have due process," the Doc muttered.

"Grade inflation is caused by these damn SETs. They are required everywhere. Look, Sandy, if you call someone stupid, the person will not evaluate you highly on an *anonymous* questionnaire. Most professors are simply buying grades in our department. Look at these grade distribution averages for my department with their SET scores. The higher grades a professor gives, the higher is his SET score. How can we educate students when we give them a loaded gun. Administrators are stupid!"

"Just give them all A's," Sandy suggested. "Why fight the system?"

"You are, of course, right," the Doc said. "Of course, my department head likes Beth Moore better than me. He's trying to get her tenured so he gives her better classes—banker's hours we call it. Since the better students register first, they select her classes. Since I'm stuck with the late classes, I get the dumb students; so how can you give them A's? It's hard to make up an exam that they can pass. Many students simply don't attend class and study any more."

"Do you want me to sell your exams beforehand, Professor, so they can make good grades?" Sandy asked half seriously.

"That's really not a bad idea," the Doctor replied. "I've heard that Beth Moore gives her students 100 true-false questions a week before the exam, and she then makes up her exam from these questions. Look at her SET score, 4.82, and her grade distribution, 3.59. She's giving more than one-half A's.

"The higher education business is really unbelievable. Other than the casino business, it's the only business where you can make money despite a lack of striving for a better product. Like casino operators, most universities understand their stakeholders' psychological needs—good grades—and just offer the opportunity to fulfill them. An L.S.U. law school dean says that students are the only customers who wish less.

"Every semester we teach in auditing courses that analytical auditing procedures are ineffective and inefficient if there are many influencing factors. A professor from Florida found 132 factors which determines the opinion that a student has of his or her professor."

"What are analytics?" Sandy asked.

"Well, analytics are various techniques, such as regression analysis, trends, ratios, and other tests used by auditors to gather evidence to improve audit effectiveness and efficiency. Batting averages for baseball players and ERA averages for pitchers are examples of analytics."

The doc tossed another airplane and missed the trashcan. "Sandy, do you know what is an internal control?"

"Sure," Sandy replied. "A door lock to keep people out."

"Right. There are many types of internal controls. A door lock could be considered a preventive control, along with credit checks or a night watchman. But a preventive control works only when the people or functions perform their roles."

"There are detective controls, such as bank reconciliation's or observing payroll distribution on a test basis. A detective control can be less expensive to apply than a preventive control."

"I get it," Sandy said. "A fire alarm could be a detective control."

"Correct. Now a corrective control corrects the problem identified by the detective control. The fire sprinklers or a computer exception report would be examples of corrective controls.

"Now a directive control is designed to produce positive results. For example, management of a university may instruct department heads and deans to hire part-timers to save money. Our department now has about 60 percent of the classes taught by migrant workers. Migrant workers in higher education cause negative results. It's called impression management."

Another airplane flew through the air and hit the trashcan. "Two points. These SETs are an accounting internal control system. The administration asks the inventory—the students—to hire and fire professors. Students are *not* customers; they are inventory—raw material. It's much cheaper to have the students evaluate the professors, rather than to measure learning. The teacher who teaches the most learning to the most students is the best teacher. SETs measure whether the students like you—not if you are educating them. Most auditing and cost professors teach that you get what you measure and reward. Unless the characteristics of a service or manufacturing process are matched with the desired outcome (i.e., more learning), the signals from the control system can cause dysfunctional behavior and destroy the process. Professors modify their behavior based upon the organizations culture."

An airplane missed the trashcan. "This teaching internal control system has wrecked higher education. It causes professors to operate dysfunctionally. They deflate coursework and inflate grades. SETs are the most dysfunctional accounting control system in the U.S.

"Years ago professors were able to give grades based upon a bell-shaped curve—about as many D's and F's as A's and B's. Grade inflation has caused grade distributions to be positively skewed.

"Today the D and F students are getting B's and A's. These same students are building our bridges and buildings, working on our elevators, dispersing medicine, operating on patients, and flying airliners."

"Not a happy thought," Sandy said. "But I have to go. This internal control has to do some work."

"Wait, look at this." The doctor wrote on his blackboard: There's a strong positive correlation between grade received and overall course rating (N = 468, r = .42, p < .0001).

Sandy just threw his hands up and left scratching his head.

With the large amount of free time in the evenings, Sandy would use his passkey to enter offices to look for incriminating stuff about the professors. When he did something wrong he would say "internal controls" and laugh. He found condoms, love letters from mistresses, pornographic literature, threats from gamblers, alcohol, drugs, guns, knives, hate literature, and many other items. He bought a camera and began taking photographs. Beth Moore became his enemy, so he began to plan how he could get her denied tenure. He could only find one piece of incriminating evidence in her office.

There was a letter from the department head telling her to give easy grades. "Remember you are in competition with Jim Dean. The higher grades you give, the better your evaluations will be. I'll give you the better classes and give him the late classes or the 8:00 a.m. classes. But you must help by pampering the students."

Sandy made a copy of the note and gave it to Dr. Dean. Sandy said, "Kind words and a gun will get you more than kind words. Al Capone." Sandy wanted to be a dysfunctional internal control or defective internal control.

Sandy then checked Beth's personnel file in the department head's office. Nothing much, except for an unsigned note: "Hope I can see you tonight. Love." He would have to manufacture something and put it in her personnel file. She was married. He made copies of her signature and the department head's signature. Sandy felt that there was something other than professional behavior between the two. Maybe he would plant a bug in the office.

By using the computers in the professors' offices, he was able to search the Internet for material about serial killers. He was able to find a number of interested sites about the various serial killers. He would print the sites and carry them home to read at his leisure. He wished to avoid the mistakes made by these monsters. He liked the Criminal Psychological Profiling web page by Joseph A. Davis in California.

When Sandy first realized that there were two perfect games on the same day, he had decided to go to only one game. He was afraid to fly from Dallas to Los Angeles or vice versa on the same day. He assumed that the authorities would be monitoring the flights. Two kills in two parks by the same person was almost impossible, and certainly highly risky.

Then he met a woman at a single's group in Denver. She was newly divorced like him, so she was in her "crazy times" also. Some experts believe that divorced people go through a time period of one to five years where they do crazy things. Sandy had even read that white males are more likely to have an accident or a health problem within a year of a divorce. Sandy began to exercise regularly after reading that fact.

Janice had been dumped by her ex-husband for a younger girl. She was left with two small children with little money from her waitress job. Sandy learned that Janice had been a battered wife and had been arrested for shoplifting. One night she confessed that she had briefly considered killing her ex-husband and his girlfriend.

Sandy explained to her that such an action would be unwise. "The cops will get you. You have a motive, and most murders are committed by someone close to the victim."

Slowly and carefully Sandy was able to convince Janice to help him with his scheme. "Get even with him by becoming wealthy." He took her to see *Natural Born Killers*, a movie about a male and female mass murderers of 52 people. Janice did not like the movie, and she left around the middle of the movie. "There was too much violence and blood. The plot was not realistic," she said.

He didn't like the movie either. He had disliked killing the two people with baseball bats. Too much blood. But he had to get the authorities' attention. They had not noticed his earlier killings with poison. Using poisons to kill reduced his guilty feelings. They were merely random, unknown people. He had to admit, however, that killing was addictive. He enjoyed the massive attention in the news that his campaign against baseball was creating.

He had to keep his emotions under control. Murderers are caught because they stop worrying about the details. He had written on an index card what Ted Bundy said: "You learn what you need to know to kill and take care of the details, like changing a tire. The first time you're careful; the 30th time you can't remember where you put the lug wrench." Good advice for internal auditors?

She eventually agreed to help, but only with the July 28 games and the extortion drop. He had given her detailed instructions about preparing the kill site at the Ballpark in Arlington.

Sandy had read that most serial killers were solitary persons, but some have bonded to become group killers. The most infamous group was the Charles Manson family. The Hillside Strangler team, Kenneth Bianchi and Angelo Buono, took women to Buono's home to torture and murder them. Bianchi was a private security officer and an applicant for a police department. The duo of Leonard Lake and Charles Ng murdered at least 25 people, and Lake kept two five hundred-page journals of their exploits. Ng was the son of a wealthy Hong Kong family and had been educated in a private school in North Yorkshire.

The homosexual team of Henry Lee Lucas and Otis Toole left a bloody trail through the Midwest. Becky Powell became Lucas' mistress, helping in some of the killings. Eventually, Lucas killed Becky Powell too. Sandy wondered if he would eventually have to kill Janice. After all, she could turn state's evidence and get a reduced sentence. Time would tell, Sandy thought. It would have to be an accident. He did not wish to draw any attention to himself. Maybe he could arrange a diving accident. Janice was a better diver than he, however.

Chapter 12

Cleveland's Jacobs Field

Auditors come in after the battle and kill the wounded.

David B. Hannuksela

Douglass was reading a piece by Walker entitled "Fraud Auditing Profiling." Walker had handed him the article and had marked a portion.

There are three factors of fraud: motive, opportunity, and lack of integrity (or rationalization). If the three factors are present in an organization, fraud will probably occur. An economic *motive* may be the simple need for money to pay hospital bills, for drugs, for gambling debts, or for alimony payments. The absence or lapse of internal controls in an organization is a tempting open door or opportunity for fraud. Finally, the lack of integrity or ability to rationalize criminal behavior completes the pyramid and allows an individual to engage in fraudulent activities.

Fraud profiling involves an educated attempt to provide auditors with specific information as to the type of employee who could commit a major fraud. The purpose is to provide an auditor with a personality composite of an unknown employee that will aid in the discovery of fraud and apprehension of the perpetrator. Constructing a fraud profile from the audit evidence can effectively aid in the discovery of the fraud, suspect development, and investigative strategy. Fraud profiling can be used to develop trial strategy. Profile characteristics can provide

215

attorneys with information about the strengths and weaknesses of the opposition's case, cross-examination techniques, nature and quality of audit evidence, motivation, and fraudsters' state of mind during commission of the fraud, and expert witness information.

The typical perpetrator of occupational fraud is an intelligent, college-educated white male. For example, in 1979, a former college professor, Stanley Mark Rifkin, learned of the computer access codes while visiting the Security Pacific National Bank. He then called the bank, posing as a branch manager, and transferred $10.2 million using the codes to his Swiss bank account.

Other characteristics of occupational fraudsters are as follows:

Egotistical
Inquisitive
Risk taker
Rule breaker
Hard Worker
Under stress
Greedy
Financial needy
Disgruntled or a complainer
Big spender
Overwhelming desire for personal gain
Pressured to perform
Close relationship with vendors/suppliers.

However, given the right pressures, opportunities, and rationalizations, many employees are capable of committing fraud.

Douglass didn't respond. The killings were depressing him. The medical reports indicated that the killer was mixing a type of pesticide—savin—with dimethyl sulfate. Savin had been used in the Tokyo subway cult attack that killed 12 people. In the same mixture the killer had placed a potion taken from oleander shrub. The dimethyl sulfate caused the potion to be rapidly absorbed by the skin. Most veterinarians have dimethyl sulfate. The mixture was deadly. But why include fingernail polish remover? Was it a woman?

Sandy Kojak did not exist. The driver's license was a fake— a real Missouri license, but the address was fake. The copy of the birth certificate was fake. No leads. Zero.

The battle on the field today between the Cleveland Indians and Kansas City Royals was insignificant when compared to the battle between him and the "Ballpark Killer" or killers. The confrontation was now personal. The killer was sending him notes, tantalizing him. As he looked through his binoculars, he felt that someone in the stadium was looking at him. He had to be in personal danger. How about Fleet Walker?

The ice chest at Cinergy Field had caught him off guard. Could he have saved the innocent fan from the hot dog death? How would they strike today? Would they kill today? Would they really leave a bomb? What type of mind would randomly kill someone from afar? Certainly not the typical serial killer. What would happen if he did not catch the killer when he made the second extortion drop?

Questions. Nothing but questions. This killer was not the typical repeater. No leads. Douglass had read Walker's description of Adrian Joss' perfect game so many times that he knew it by heart. A perfect game was elusive. The Ballpark Killer was an elusive phantom. But was the killer trying to be caught with the notes and telephone calls?

Richard Herrins, a serial killer in Chicago in the early sixties, wrote in lipstick on a dressing-room mirror: "Catch me before I kill again." The victim's head was under the message.

What could the perfect game on October 2, 1908, have to do with these murders? The Cleveland Naps and Chicago White Sox were trying to catch the American League leading

Detroit Tigers. Eventually, Detroit would win by one-half game over Cleveland and 1 ½ games over Chicago.

Edward A. Walsh was on the mound for the visiting White Sox looking for his forty-first win. Big Ed had been pitching almost every day to keep the White Sox in the pennant race. If they would win today, they would remain in the pennant chase.

However, Big Ed's great catcher, Johnny Kling, was injured, and replacement Ossee Schreckengost, the losing catcher in the Cy Young perfect game, was behind the plate. During the bottom of the third, Joe Birmingham was on first with a single. Big Ed threw to first to pick the runner off. Birmingham realized he was picked off, so he broke for second. As Birmingham ran toward second, a fill-in first baseman, Frank Isbell, hit Birmingham in the back with his throw. As the ball rolled away, Birmingham trotted to third base. The report in the *Cleveland Plain Dealer* indicated that Birmingham intentionally took a big lead to get the throw to first in order to steal second.

Big Ed struck out the next two batters, George Perring and pitcher Addie Joss. With two strikes on Cleveland's leadoff hitter, Wilbur Goode, Walsh threw a spitter which broke catcher Ossee Schreckengost's index finger and the ball rolled back to the grandstand.

Birmingham scored the only run of the game on the wild pitch. Walsh then struck out Goode on the next pitch. Goode struck out four times during the game. Big Ed struck out a total of 15 batters in 8 innings. He walked only one and allowed four hits.

Poor Big Ed. The opposing pitcher for Cleveland, 6'3" Adrian Joss, had already pitched three perfect innings. Nine batters had not reached base. Joss, a former University of Wisconsin native born in the same year that the first two perfect games were thrown, was working on his 24th victory. His catcher was 5'10" Nig Clarke, who was wearing shin guards like those introduced the previous year by catcher Roger Bresnaham. Bresnaham was a detective in off-seasons.

The player-manager of the White Sox team, center fielder Fielder Jones worked long-armed Joss to a 3-and-2 count. After the next pitch crossed the plate, Jones dropped his bat and headed to first base.

However, Umpire Tom Connolly shouted "Strike three!" This out was one of only three strikeouts that Joss recorded that day.

Cleveland manager and second baseman Napoleon Lajoie made several phenomenal plays on slow-hit balls on the right side of the diamond, turning sure base hits into routine outs. Lajoie handled 10 chances without making an error and went 1 for 3 at bat.

In the eighth inning, leadoff batter and left fielder Pat Dougherty (.278) smashed a hard hit grounder toward right. Frenchman Lajoie caught the ball and gracefully threw out Dougherty. Dougherty had played left field for Boston when Cy Young pitched his perfect game.

Playing shortstop for Chicago was another athlete participating in his second time perfect game. Freddy Parent had played shortstop for Cy Young's flawless game, batting 2-for-4. In this losing game, Parent would go 0-for-3.

One writer said the following about the pressure-packed top of the ninth: "A mouse working his way along the grandstand floor would have sounded like a shovel scraping over concrete."

Trying to stop the perfect game, manager Fielder Jones, a former civil engineer, put in three pinch hitters. The first pinch hitter, Harry White, grounded out, and the second, Jiggs Donahue, popped up to first base.

John Anderson, nicknamed "Terrible Swede," was the last pinch batter in the ninth. He would not go down meekly.

Norwegian Anderson was big and powerful, but a slow runner. He lined the first pitch to left field, but the ball curved foul at the last moment. On the next pitch, he smashed the ball down the third base line. Bill Bradley grabbed the ball and threw it toward first base.

George Stovall stretched to catch the low toss, but the ball fell from his glove. He picked it up at about the same time Anderson's foot hit first base. Umpire Silk O'Loughlin signaled the runner out, and the Chicago players did not complain.

Addie Joss had pitched a perfect game in less than one hour and forty minutes before a crowd of 10,598. *Sporting Life* called it the grandest pitchers' duel in history.

Joss and Lee Richmond were neighbors, as a result of Richmond teaching a mathematics class at Scott High School in Toledo. Joss's son, Norman, went to his first class in plane geometry after his father had pitched a perfect game.

His geometry teacher said, "Now look. Your father pitched a perfect game. Well, so did I. And it doesn't mean anything here. The fact that your father did the same thing isn't going to help you with plane geometry." The world is small.

Today, the Indians were playing in the American League Central Division in a new, state-of-the-art ballpark, not the nearby dark, old Cleveland Municipal Stadium. Jacobs Field is a contemporary marvel with its white color and steal beams. The vertical light towers match the smokestacks and skyscrapers visible from the stands.

Dennis Martinez, a previous perfect game pitcher, had appeared on Larry King Live the night before, talking about his perfect game, and pleading with the killers to "stop their campaign against baseball." Martinez was not on the mound today. He had retired in 1997. Instead, Bartolo Colon was the starting pitcher for the Indians, and Pat Rapp had the starting nod for the Royals. Jacobs Field is a hitters' park, with 42,400 seats.

Before the game Douglass and Walker walked to Indians Square and the Bob Feller statue in the right-center field area. More than 6,000 loyal fans and businesses paid $100 to have their names chiseled into the bricks that pave Indians Square. The proceeds paid for sculptor Gary Ross' 10-foot statue of the Indians pitcher with the most wins; Bob Feller won 266 games. Next they checked on the personnel guarding the 40 re-strooms—two of which were unisex restrooms for patrons with small children and for handicapped people.

The game today would not be a low-hitting affair on the Kentucky bluegrass, asymmetrical field. Center fielder Kenny Lofton hit one of Cleveland's five home runs and also tripled, as the Indians beat the Kansas City Royals 11-3.

Douglass saw first baseman Jim Thome homer twice into the bleachers and drive in a career-high five runs. Several balls were hit into the three quirky corners in the outfield wall. No one hit the scoreboard, however. The Cleveland Indians were no longer the laughing stocks of baseball.

During the seventh inning, Douglass and Walker walked around the concession area and talked with some of his agents placed throughout the stadium.

At the close of the seventh inning Douglass saw employees removing something from the turnstiles at the gates. "What are they doing?" Douglass asked, pointing to a turnstile on the third base side of the stadium.

"Internal controls," Walker explained, "to stop the home team from cheating on gate receipts and attendance. The visiting club has access to the self-registering turnstiles after the end of the seventh inning. The visiting team can request a count of the ticket stubs also."

"How much of the gate receipts does the visiting team receive?" Douglass asked.

"Depends," replied Walker. "In the National League, about 14 percent; in the American League, 20 percent," Walker stated.

Jacobs Field is an urban ballpark, sitting on only 28 acres. Douglass could see the 90-degree angle of the three decks down the right field line, which follows Carnegie and East Ninth Streets. The nineteen 200-foot light poles are toothbrush shaped, and there is exposed steel and concrete architecture.

In left field is the world's largest scoreboard and a 19-foot mini-Green Monster which produces unpredictable caroms. An out-of-town scoreboard is contained inside the green wall. There is an open pavilion in center field, and a playground for children in right field. A person can actually buy a peanut butter and jelly sandwich. There is an interactive area which allows children to have their picture taken with cutouts of various players and have them made into personalized baseball cards.

Douglass and Walker walked past the 425-seat chrome-and-glass restaurant in the left field side, but settled for fajitas from the concession stands that are in the middle of the concourses, and not against the walls.

To Douglass' joy, nothing happened in the stadium during the game. However, minutes after the last out Douglass heard the sound of emergency vehicles. When the information became available, he learned that at least two people had died of the savin poison and one was critically ill. Someone had painted the poison on the door handles of cars in an open parking lot on East 9th Street and Carnegie Avenue.

The diabolical killers had carried out their threat. By noon of the next day, almost everyone in the United States knew about the killings at the ballparks. In a poll taken by CNN, 66 percent of baseball fans would not go inside a bathroom in a baseball park. Forty-three percent of the polled people were afraid to go inside *any* public bathroom.

The Commissioner of Baseball increased the reward for the capture of the killer or killers to $1 million.

The *Cleveland Plain Dealer* rehashed the exploits of the "Cleveland Torso Killer" in the mid-1930s. The Mad Butcher of Kingsbury Run killed and dismembered at least a dozen people, mostly prostitutes and derelicts. On two occasions two victims were killed at the same time. The killer mixed the dismembered parts of the bodies together. The killings stopped in 1938, and the "Torso Killer" was never captured.

Chapter 13

Top of the Ninth

The two greatest threats to secure e-mail messaging are spoofing, where one machine or user masquerades as another to send a message, and sniffing, where hardware or software is used to receive data intended for someone else. E-mail spoofing and sniffing are surprisingly simple processes.

L.R. Garceau
Jack Matejka
S.K. Misra
Etzmun Rozen

The phone was ringing at 6:30 on Friday morning, and Fleet Walker picked up the receiver

"Hello" Fleet mumbled.

"Good morning, Fleet. How are you?" said the strange voice on the other end.

"Sleepy," replied Fleet. He was in Cooperstown, following Sandy's instructions.

"Today's the day for the payback pitch, Fleet. I'm Sandy. You have been expecting my call. I want you to get up, dress, grab a bite of breakfast, and climb into your car."

Fleet was now alert. He was dreading this phone call.

"Please go to the entrance to Doubleday Field in Cooperstown. Facing the entrance under the flagpole, turn left and you will see the white ticket window. Under the window you will find instructions. Set your CB on Channel 16. Drive slowly, and don't break any traffic laws. Channel 16. Don't contact the authorities. Bye for now."

After calling Douglass, Walker drove to the center of Cooperstown to Doubleday Field on Pioneer Street, just a few steps from Main Street. The annual Hall of Fame Game is played on Doubleday Field, named after Abner Doubleday, the father of baseball.

Douglass was staying at Otesaga Resort Hotel and had played a game of golf on the Leatherstocking Golf Course the previous afternoon. He shot a poor 96 on the course. Douglass arrived at the entrance of the field about 30 seconds after Fleet arrived. The call from Sandy had been made from a pay phone in nearby Bowerstown.

Fleet found the instructions taped under the ticket window, along with a two-way radio. The air was cold.

Douglass mumbled "Not good," when he drove up and saw the two-way radio. "We'll be close behind, so don't worry." Douglass read the instructions out loud.

Put CB on Channel 16.

Take Route 28 south toward Bowerstown.

Go east/north on I88.

Exit south on 145.

Right (south) on 30.

Left (east) on 23.

Cross I87, thru Catskill, Hudson.

At Great Barrington, south on 7 to New Milford.

Take I-202 to Danbury.

You will receive further instructions.

Do not relay instructions to anyone.

Douglass said, "Your radio is working. Both of them. Break a leg."

Walker's drive toward Bowerstown was uneventful, until he reached the outskirts of Bowerstown.

A pleasant voice came over the two-way radio. "Fleet, please stop at the next gasoline station on the right up ahead and wait in front of the telephone for someone to call. Switch to Channel 20 now on your CB. Channel 20."

Walker followed instructions and waited near the telephone. When it rang, Sandy told Walker, "Please take off any radio and drop it outside your Saturn. Once you've dropped that radio, please remove any other radio from your body or the car. Drop the second one so I can see you. Pick both up and put them in the trash can near the gas pumps."

Walker removed both radios and dropped them on the ground. An attendant inside the gasoline station was watching him as he put them in the trash can.

As he was about to get into his car, the voice was back on the two-way radio. "Fleet, turn your CB to Channel 22. Channel 22. Put the suitcase in your back seat. Lock your doors."

Once Walker was through Bowerstown and driving along I88, the voice was back. "Fleet, did you see the movie *Rollercoaster*?"

Walker answered no.

"Too bad," Sandy replied. "Inside the two-way radio is a ricin bomb. Don't open it; there's a tamper switch. I have the detonator switch. If there is another radio on you or in the car, stop and get rid of it."

"I don't believe there's another radio in my car," Walker almost shouted.

"OK, I trust you, Fleet. You *are* an internal auditor. Is there a tracer on your car?"

"I don't know," Walker said.

"Remember the bomb, Fleet. Do not pass along any of my instructions. Ricin is very lethal."

The drive seemed like eternity. Walker thought about his good life, his wife, his kids, and his job with the Yankees. And George. He turned the radio on softly to pass the time. There were no instructions from Sandy over the two-way radio. He became worried that the radio was broken; then he remembered the CB and his car phone.

More driving. Boring. He crossed over I-87, through Catskill, and crossed the Hudson river.

"Stop, Fleet. Turn around and go back across the bridge slowly," came the voice over the two-way radio.

Walker obeyed.

Near the middle of the bridge the voice said, "Fleet, go to the end of the bridge and stop your car. Take the suitcase to the bridge, and you'll see two ropes tied to the bridge railing. One rope is tied to a rowboat. Tie the suitcase to the other rope and lower the suitcase into the rowboat. Then untie the rope to the suitcase, and then untie the rope holding the boat. Drop the ropes into the boat. Remember, untie the boat rope *last.*"

Fleet parked his Saturn at the end of the bridge, took the suitcase and two-way radio, and walked to the ropes. He lowered the aluminum suitcase into the boat, untied both ropes, dropped the ropes and the two-way radio into the boat, and walked *quickly* to his car. He actually squealed his tires as he drove away. He heard no explosion, but within 30 seconds he heard the helicopters.

Under the bridge a figure in a dark diving suit took the suitcase from the boat and put it inside another suitcase. He put a similar aluminum suitcase into the boat and allowed it to start floating down the river. He was careful to stay under the bridge in case a satellite was photographing the drop.

He calmly placed a lift bag around the suitcase, tied the suitcase to a rope around his waist, pulled on his mask, began breathing through his regulator, and disappeared under the water. The underwater scooter had carried Sandy about 150 feet from the bridge when the helicopters arrived. Sandy was blowing his nose inside his mask in order to equalize the pressure under water.

Douglass was in the lead helicopter. "What is wrong?" Douglass asked the agent with the detector.

"The signal has disappeared," the agent shouted.

"I can see the suitcase," replied Douglass loudly.

The boat was slowly floating down the Hudson River.

"Get some divers in the river. Maybe a switch has been made," shouted Douglass above the sound of the helicopter.

The four divers captured the loose rowboat, and one diver pulled the boat to the shore at the end of the bridge. Once his helicopter landed on the road, Douglass looked at the suitcase. "It's the wrong suitcase. Get under the water," Douglass shouted to the three divers still in the water.

Three of the divers went under the water immediately.

Douglass told the fourth diver to search under the bridge.

Shortly the diver under the bridge surfaced and said that she had found a galvanized steel wire attached to a sand anchor under the bridge.

"Follow the wire quickly," Douglass ordered.

The female diver dove again, and in about 30 seconds there was a loud explosion. Douglass saw the diver float to the top unconscious.

Upstream Sandy heard the sound of the first explosion. He smiled.

As Douglass jumped into the water to save the unconscious diver, he saw the three other divers surface holding their ears. Sound travels well under water.

Sandy had developed three underwater distraction grenades. He had purchased inert grenades from an army surplus store. He then filled the grenades with a bursting explosive, installed a detonator, and then sealed the grenade with fiberglass. He planted the grenades along the steel wire, tying several long, thin strings to the grenades' rings. Apparently one of the divers had jerked one of the strings. The grenades would produce shrapnel, causing some minor injuries.

Douglass was able to get the stunned female diver into the helicopter. The three other divers then followed the wire at a safe distance as Douglass walked down the bank of the river. They were able to avoid the other explosive devices. About a quarter of a mile downstream the wire stopped at a point where there was a small dirty road. There was a fresh tire mark, made by some type of dirt bike. There was some scuba gear left near the river. There were footprints leading from the river to the tire marks.

Douglass phoned the helicopter, telling one to follow the road, one to go up the river, and another one to go down the river. "Look for a dirt bike. Look for a suitcase or a briefcase."

Depression began to build in Douglass. What would the group—or killer—do when they discovered that the diamonds were merely CZs? Would they be satisfied with $300,000? There was no valuable baseball card in the briefcase. There were only two days before October 8, the date Don Larsen pitched his perfect game.

At that moment Sandy was looking at his lighted underwater compass. The underwater scooter would carry him about six miles up the river. The closed circuit rebreather would allow him to stay under water for up to six hours. There were no tell-tell bubbles floating to the surface as he traveled about 12 feet below the surface. His sonar gun allowed him to navigate up the river to his parked car.

He would not have to worry about decompression sickness because he was swimming only seven to twelve feet under the water. Breathing air under water pressure increases the absorption of nitrogen throughout the body. If a diver rises too quickly from depths of 30 feet or lower, bends, or decompression sickness can occur.

Under the bridge Sandy had placed the aluminum suitcase into a larger suitcase. He had covered the inside of his suitcase with copper screen wire, aluminum foil, and a thin sheet of lead. No tracing signal could get through the combination—he hoped. He also hoped that the FBI would be fooled by the tire marks and the scuba gear Janice placed downstream the evening before. He hoped the distraction grenades should slow them up.

★ ★ ★ ★ ★

At 4:20 the next morning Fleet Walker called Douglass at his home. He was excited.

"I know who did it," Fleet shouted. "Milt Pappas is doing it."

"Who is Milt Pappas?" a sleepy, tired FBI agent asked.

"He pitched against the San Diego players that are on the cards left at the killings," Fleet explained.

"Didn't many pitchers pitch to these players over an entire season?" reasoned Douglass.

"True, but Pappas had an *almost* perfect game against these players. He retired 26 players and then walked the twenty-seventh player."

"Doesn't sound like a likely suspect to me," Douglass yawned.

"But one of the people killed was the umpire that called the Pappas game—Moose Phommin. Pappas was extremely upset after the game. He said that the umpire called *at least two* strikes as *balls*. Besides, the score was 8-0."

Douglass understood the motive. A player felt that an umpire had cheated him out of a perfect game—a chance to be in the Baseball Hall of Fame. "Is Pappas a member of the Baseball Hall of Fame?"

"No. But he won 209 games and lost 164. Don Drysdale had a 209-166 record, but he *was* elected to the Hall of Fame. A perfect game *might* have put Pappas into the Hall of Fame. Look, I'll fax you the write-up of the game. I'll try to send you his address. *We* can stake him out."

Douglass smiled at the word *we*. For an auditor, Fleet was a good detective. What courage to deliver a suitcase to a terrorist group thinking that he was talking to a ricin bomb in a two-way radio. There had been no bomb in the radio.

"When he skipped the David Cone perfect game date on July 18, he still sent us a signature. He hit in San Diego, when the Padres were playing Montreal. David Cone beat Montreal *and* Pappas played for San Diego."

"So those murders in San Diego were not random. Good work Fleet. Fax me a write up of the Pappas game."

Douglass was in his office before the fax arrived, and Walker called Douglass on the phone to provide the address of Milt Pappas. Within 30 minutes, five Chicago FBI agents were checking on Milt Pappas.

Douglass reviewed the Phommin killing and found that in interviews with authorities, Phommin's wife said that someone had sent Moose free tickets to some baseball games. Moose attended one of the games and was killed with poison. Someone stuck him with a needle of poison while he was in the restroom.

Douglass read the piece for a second time. He believed Fleet Walker had found the killer—Milt Pappas, a former Chicago Cubs pitcher.

Almost Perfect

by

M. Fleetwood Walker

Randy Huntley was crouching behind home plate on a cold, windy day. Moose Phommin was calling balls and strikes behind him. Milt Pappas was the Chicago Cubs' pitcher on the mound on September 2, 1972. Day baseball at Wrigley Field starts at 1:20 p.m.

By the ninth inning, twenty-four batters had faced Pappas at the National League's Wrigley Field, trying to hit a ball to the ivy vines clinging to the outfield brick walls. Balls lost in the ivy are ground-rule doubles. Twenty-four San Diego Padres had been unable to reach even first base in the "Friendly Confines." Sure the Padres were in last place, but a perfect game is a perfect game.

Only in the first inning had 33-year old right-hander Pappas thrown three balls to one batter—to Leron Lee, a left-handed hitter with a .300 batting average. Lee then grounded out.

There had been a scare in the fourth inning from Enzo Hernandez, a .195 hitter. Hernandez pushed a fine bunt down the third-base line, and would have beat it out if third baseman Ron Santo had not allowed it to roll foul. Then Hernandez proceeded to strike out. The small foul territory benefits hitters, not pitchers.

Later in the fifth inning, Nate Colbert slapped a one-hopper between short and third, but shortstop Don Kessinger made a magnificent play on the wet field.

After two outs in the eighth, Pappas knocked down Derrel Thomas' sharp liner, scrambled after the loose ball, and threw out the speedy runner at first.

The crowd of 11,144 gave Pappas a standing ovation when he came to bat in the eighth. With the crowd on its feet for the top of the ninth, Huntley suggested to Pappas that he should take something off his slider to get an off-speed pitch. Pappas' change-up pitch couldn't find the plate. Both knew that unexpected wind currents can turn routine flyball outs into home runs.

Huntley's legs hurt from squatting behind the plate. He must be ready to spring up and snag an errant pitch from Pappas. But Huntley was worried. Would Phommin remember Huntley's disgusted gesture he had made earlier when he had flied weakly to the outfield? Phommin had shouted to Huntley, "Do that one more time, and you're out of the game."

Pappas would face two right-handers, John Jeter and Fred Kendall plus a probable pinch-hitter for the pitcher.

As Pappas took the first sign from Huntley, he felt his bad cold even more. He had almost told his manager, Whitey Lockman, that he did not wish to pitch today. But his wife urged him to pitch. So, here he was going into the ninth pitching a perfect game in his sixteenth season with a commanding lead of 8-0.

Jeter swung and missed the first pitch for a strike and then took a ball. Jeter hit the third pitch in the air to center field; Bill North slipped, fell, and lost the ball in the sun. Miraculously, left-fielder Billy Williams, a future Hall of Famer known more for his hitting than his fielding, ran over and caught the ball. "Sweet Billy." One out. Luck is necessary for a perfect game.

Kendall came to the plate. Huntley signaled for a slider, which is a cross between a curve and a fastball. About 5 mph slower than a fastball, a slider has a late, lateral curve to the left. Kendall crushed the hanging slider down the first-base line—foul. On the next pitch, Kendall grounded out. Two outs.

Only one more out to immortality. Pinch-hitter Larry Stahl, a left-handed veteran hitting .226, came to the plate. Huntley signaled, Phommin went into his crouch, and Stahl swung and missed the first pitch for strike one.

Next Pappas threw an outside ball. On the third pitch Stahl swung and missed. Two strikes and one ball was the count.

The fourth pitch, a slider, was called a ball by Phommin.

Crouching again, Huntley put down one finger for a fastball and set his mitt as a target. Pappas went into his wind up, threw the ball, and Stahl took the pitch. It passed low over the corner of the plate, in the strike zone accordingly to Hurtley.

"Ball three," Phommin shouted.

Stahl seemed surprised that he was not called out.

Huntley considered complaining, but he recalled the threat from Phommin to eject him. Huntley merely signaled for another slider. After all, Pappas had issued only 29 walks in 195 previous innings.

Pappas knew he had to throw a strike. "But doggone if I'm going to give into Stahl and take a chance of losing my no-hitter." The pitch came toward the plate. Stahl did not swing. The pitch was close, but low.

"Ball four," Phommin screamed.

Stahl trotted down to first base with a freebie—the only Padres baserunner. Pappas had missed a perfect game by *one* strike.

There had been two low, close pitches that could have easily been called strikes. Maybe they were strikes to another umpire. On bad days some umpires allow trusted catchers to decide balls and strikes. Suppose Huntley had been more aggressive and complained about the third called ball?

The next hitter, Garry Jestadt, popped out. Announcer Jack Brickhouse said, "Pappas is the only guy I ever saw throw a no-hitter and be angry."

According to Pappas, "It didn't sink in until 11:00 that night what Phommin did to me. Then I was ready to kill him. I still feel it was a perfect game."

But plate umpire Moose Phommin had a different view. "Was the pitch close? They're all close, but I don't call pitches close! It's either a ball or a strike. Those pitches were well below the knees."

In the game of baseball, the umpire is the final arbitrator—just like management in a company. Management can overrule an internal auditor. Internal auditing reports are *not* made public like external audit reports. Likewise, there is no instant replay in professional baseball. However, in both instances, subtle political forces are at work, which tend to prevent the most outrageous wrongs from happening.

Umpires who blow too many calls will get into more than the usual amount of arguments with managers until they are disciplined by the commissioner's office. Likewise, in the corporate world, the audit committee will become concerned if audit comments are not implemented. Eventually they will take action to ensure that the audit comments are implemented. However, in both instances serious wrongs may occur to a player or an internal auditor before action is taken.

Pappas spent only one more season in the major leagues. He came within one game of winning at least 100 games in both leagues.

There have been four other perfect games spoiled with two outs in the ninth. Hooks Wiltse (New York), who got his nickname from his elongated nose, hit the opposing pitcher in 1908 with a 0-2 count. Tommy Bridges (Detroit), Milt Wilcox (Detroit), and Billy Pierce (White Sox) each had his perfect game spoiled by a clean hit on the first pitch to the twenty-seventh batter he faced. Also, Minnesota Twin Jack Kralick walked the 26th batter on a 3-2 pitch in the ninth on August 26, 1962. George Aluski, of the Kansas City Athletics, was the only batter to reach base that day.

Of course, Pedro Martinez of The Montreal Expos pitched a perfect game for nine innings on June 3, 1995, but was taken out in the tenth inning when Bip Roberts got a lead off double. Martinez settled for a 1-0 victory after Mel Rojas relieved and retired the next three San Diego batters. A reliever or bullpen pitcher is analogous to technical support auditors.

Douglass set the article about Pappas aside and called Chicago. He had to get some agents following Pappas quickly.

Chapter 14

The House that Ruth Built

Immaterial fraudulent financial reporting—that which occurs at the branch or division level—can grow into a serious problem if it becomes widespread. Unfortunately, a high level of integrity at the senior management level, or an impeccable "tone at the top," cannot guarantee employee integrity in the field or organizational divisions.

Courtenay Thompson

In 1973, George Steinbrenner and a syndicate of limited partners purchased the New York Yankees from CBS for $10 million, absorbing a $1 million loss. Using the free agency mechanism, George purchased Catfish Hunter, Reggie Jackson, and other stars to rebuild a pennant winner. In 1988, Steinbrenner sold the Yankees' local cable television rights through the year 2000 to the Madison Square Garden Network for $500 million—a cool $490 million profit above what he paid for the Yankees.

The Yankees in 1973 were in a state of decline since their last pennant in 1964. Of course, the Yankees are best known for success, such as the year 1956. That year, World Series' fever was gripping the nation. All ears and eyes were focused on the battle between the two archrivals, the Brooklyn Dodgers and the New York Yankees, who were meeting for the fourth time in five years. The Dodgers had beaten the Yankees the past year. The Dodgers had a team batting average of .258 and the Yankees' average was .270.

Like Charlie Robertson, a tall, handsome Hoosier by the name of Don Larsen was an unlikely candidate to pitch the first and *only* perfect game in World Series history. His Yankee teammates called him Gooney Bird because of the flaky things he would do.

Two years before the 1956 World Series, 6'4" Donald James Larsen was a 3-21 hurler for the Baltimore Orioles. The undistinguished right-hander was traded to the Yankees and had respectable 9-2 and 11-5 seasons in 1955 and 1956. However, Larsen changed his pitching style near the end of the 1956 season.

Coach Del Baker of the Boston Red Sox told the Michigan City, Indiana native that he always knew in advance what type of pitch Larsen was throwing. Larsen gave it away with his wind-up.

So Don switched to a no-wind-up delivery. He explained, "It gives me better control. It takes nothing off my fast ball, and it keeps the batters tense. They have to be ready every second, and don't forget, no coach can read the pitch in advance."

Tense or not, during the second game of the World Series the Dodgers' hitters crushed Larsen early. He was removed in the second inning after two outs with the Dodgers ahead 1-0. The bases were loaded. Maybe the colorful Casey Stengel, who became a Hall of Famer in 1966, took Larsen out too soon, but at the end of the second inning, the Dodgers were ahead by 6-0. A total of four runs were charged to Larsen. The Flatbush fans were happy.

Casey, nicknamed "The Old Perfessor," had faith in Larsen. The Yankee Skipper and former dentist once lectured, "See that big fellow out there: He can throw, he can hit, he can field, and he can run. He can be one of baseball's greatest pitchers any time he puts his mind to it."

With the Series tied 2-2, Larsen was the starting pitcher on October 8, 1956, a beautiful autumn day. The sun was shining brightly. Larsen would face four future Hall of Famers—shortstop Pee Wee Reese, third baseman Jackie Robinson, catcher Roy Campanella, and outfielder Duke Snider. Snider nicknamed the Silver Fox, hit four home runs in both the 1952 and 1955 World Series. Roy Campanella won Most Valuable Player awards in 1951, 1953, and 1955.

Number 8, Yogi Berra, a 1972 Hall of Famer, was the catcher for Larsen behind the plate. Babe Pinelli, a National League umpire, was the arbiter behind the plate.

The villainous Dodger pitcher Sal Maglie, who was nicknamed "The Barber," had a constant five o'clock shadow. Maglie received his nickname "The Barber," because with his excellent control, he could give hitters a close shave without hitting them. Maglie had late in the 1956 season pitched a no-hitter against Philadelphia.

Alvin Dark said that "Maglie got by on meanness. He was the only man I've ever seen pitch a shutout on a day when he had absolutely nothing."

Did 27-year-old Larsen do anything the night before to prepare for the important game? "Why no," was his response, "I did just like I always do. Had a few beers and went to bed around midnight or so."

This game would illustrate the role luck plays in the achievement of a perfect game. Four batted balls came close to being hits. In the second inning, Jackie Robinson smashed a grounder off third baseman Andy Carey's glove. But the ball ricocheted toward shortstop Gil McDougald, who back-handed the ball and threw fleet-footed Jackie out at first. This would be

Robinson's last game; he retired after he was traded to the Giants at the end of the 1956 season.

Although Casey may have had faith in Larsen, Jim Turner, the Yankee pitching coach sent blue-eyed, strawberry blond Whitey Ford to the bullpen in the third inning. As Larsen went out to pitch Turner told lefty Whitey, "Go down there and be ready because we never know how many innings we're going to get out of this guy. We may need you." Only eight years later Casey Stengel would be the losing Mets manager for the Bunning perfect game.

According to Whitey Ford in his book *Slick*, Turner called to the bullpen and told Whitey to start loosening up as Larsen went out to pitch in the sixth.

The same call was made by Turner in the seventh, eighth, and ninth innings. Whitey complained in his book that he saw none of the perfect game. "I could see only the shortstop and third base from the bull pen."

In the fourth, Mickey Mantle put the Bronx Bombers ahead with a home run into the right field stands which barely stayed fair. Yankee announcer Mel Allen was able to give his battle cry: "Going-going-gone!"

Mantle then stole an extra base hit in deep center field from Gil Hodges. With one out in the fifth, Mantle raced back on Gil Hodges' long fly and made a magnificent over-the-shoulder catch on the run almost 450-feet from home plate. Mantle said it was the finest catch in his career.

The next batter, left handed hitting Sandy Amoros, crushed a ball into the right-field seats. Hank Bauer, the right fielder, said that the ball hooked foul by three inches at the last moment. Hank Bauer singled in a run in the sixth to make the score 2-0.

In the seventh, the Yankee Stadium shadows and smoky haze enveloped home plate. Larsen went into the runway to smoke a cigarette. When Mantle passed him near the water cooler

Larsen punched him on the arm and pointed to the scoreboard. "Hey, Mick, wouldn't it be funny if I pitched a no-hitter?"

Mickey just stared at him and said, "Get the hell out of here."

Soft-spoken Gil Hodges was victimized by another fielding play in the top of the eighth. Hodges banged a low liner to the left of third baseman Andy Carey. Carey dove for the ball and apparently caught it inches above the ground. But to be sure, Carey fired the ball to first base. Officially, the out was scored as a caught ball.

Big-boned Larsen with his long fingers and unorthodox delivery had retired 24 straight batters with remorseless efficiency with only 85 pitches by the beginning of the ninth inning.

The scoreboard showed 24 outs, no hits, no walks, and no errors. When Larsen came to bat in the bottom of the eighth, he received a standing ovation. Umpire Pinelli said that Larsen had the greatest pin-point pitching control that day, he had ever seen. Only Pee Wee Reese, the Dodger captain and shortstop, in the first inning, was able to get a 3-2 pitch. Pee Wee looked at a called third strike. Pee Wee received his nickname from his marble-shooting skills as a child.

Who did Larsen fear the most in the Dodgers line-up? Thirty-eight-year old Pee Wee Reese, playing on bad legs. Pee Wee had the ability to make things happen.

Yankee second baseman Billy Martin instructed his infielders, "Nothing gets through." According to the *New York Times*, one could hear a dollar bill drop in the huge stadium as Carl Furillo stepped into the batter's box in the ninth. Furillo already had five hits in the series. He fouled off four pitches, and then flied out to Bauer in right field. The crowd of 64,519 people roared. Roy Campanella stepped up to the plate and crushed a long foul off the second deck down the left field line. Campanella had hit 41 home runs in 1953. There was a second roar, however, when Roy Campanella bounced out to Gil McDougald.

Walter Alston was the manager of the Dodgers. Alston would manage the Dodgers for 23 years, winning seven pennants and four World Series. He was still managing when Dodger Sandy Koufax pitched his perfect game against the Cubs nine years later in 1965.

Walter Alston sent in Dale Mitchell as a pinch hitter. This would be his last time at bat. Dale Mitchell, who had a .312 lifetime batting average, took the first pitch, a wide called ball. Yogi called for a slider, and Babe Pinelli called the pitch a strike. Ten-year veteran Mitchell swung at and missed the next fast ball.

Yogi called for another fastball and left-handed Mitchell fouled it into the stands. The crowd was now screaming on each pitch. The count was 1-2, and Mitchell, who had struck out only 119 times in 4,000 at bats, was behind on the count. He had to protect the plate. Only he could stop the perfect game and the no-hitter. Larsen saw Yogi's fastball signal through the smoky haze. Larsen admitted after the game that his rubbery knees almost buckled during the ninth inning.

The agile, 220 pound hurler threw a high pitch, his 97th, across the outside corner of the plate.

All eyes were focused on the National League umpire Pinelli. He seemed to hesitate for a moment, but thrust his right arm into the air.

"Strike three," was the historic call.

"How about that!" announcer Mel Allen shouted.

Mitchell turned around to complain about the bad call. Pinelli was gone. He would retire after this World Series. Mickey Mantle was later quoted as saying he was too far away to see how far Yogi had to jump to catch the ball.

Yogi Berra was gone. Newspapers showed stubby Yogi leaping into the arms of Don Larsen. Other Yankees ran out of the dugout to hug, slap, and shake Larsen's hand. Fans poured out of the stands to try to touch their hero.

Plate umpire Pinelli later said, "It was a fat pitch. No hitter will see a much better strike."

Poor Dodger Bums—the pinstripers had won again. First base coach Jake Pitler was the only Dodger to reach first base that day. *The New York Times* front page headline on the next day was "Larsen Beats Dodgers in Perfect Game; Yanks Lead 3-2 on First Series No-Hitter."

The Yankees would go on to win the series. Mickey Mantle and Yogi Berra would each hit 3 home runs in the series, and Berra would have 10 RBIs. But Don Larsen, the tall pitcher with slouching shoulders and a no-wind-up delivery would be voted the MVP of the series.

Larsen was a regular at McAvoy's, a Manhattan bar. After the game, patrons at the bar polished his stool and put a sign on it saying "This seat reserved for Don Larsen." Later that evening, as if to demonstrate his footloose attitude, he showed up smiling at the bar, and according to *Sports Illustrated*, he closed the place down. "For Larsen, it was the perfect end to a perfect day."

Yogi Berra, in his book, *Yogi, It Ain't Over*, indicates that Don Larsen never shook off a signal from him during the game. Actually, he shook off two pitches, but eventually decided to pitch the original selection, anyway.

Yogi, of course, is noted for many quotes. His description of baseball itself is appropriate. "You gotta work hard at it; it's not an easy game, which is what I thought it was as a kid. But it beats working."

This current season had been a good year for the Yankees, finishing at the top of the East Division of the American

League. The Yankees were matched against the wild-card team, the Chicago White Sox. The West Division Texas Rangers were matched against the Central Division leader Cleveland Indians.

Douglass now had to be considered an expert in ballparks and bathrooms. Someone had left a note on his desk: "King of the Bathrooms." It was not a joking matter. Douglass and Walker were sitting in the stands in Yankee Stadium for the second game between the Soxs and Yankees. The Yankees had won the first game, 3-2, as Chuck Knoblauch singled home Paul O'Neill with the winning run in the eighth inning.

Called the "House that Babe built, and Mickey Mantle furnished," the stadium was opened in 1923 and baptized by a game-winning home run by Babe Ruth, the King of Swat. Yankee Stadium was torn down and rebuilt in 1974-1975, and the current stadium had survived the Ballpark Killer and Murderer's Row, possibly the best hitting team ever—the 1927 Yankees.

Although the stadium had been full yesterday, the stands were less than fifty percent full today. They could see a sea of blue empty seats and the blue outfield fence. Many in the stands were photographers hoping for valuable shots. Representatives of bloodsucking attorneys were handing out business cards outside the gates, hoping to obtain future business. People were scared to come to the game. Every bathroom had a police officer. There was a police officer at every concession stand. Everyone was videoed as they entered the park. There were posters of the person called Sandy, offering a $1 million reward, along with warnings not to pick up baseball cards.

Both Douglass and Walker were at the game early, so Walker took Douglass to see the center field monuments and plaques now no longer in the field of play. Before the 1974 and 1975 renovations, the monuments of Babe Ruth, Miller Huggins, and Lou Gehrig were in fair territory. Walker told Douglass that Casey Stengel once watched his center fielder having trouble picking up a long drive behind the monuments. Stengel shouted, "Ruth, Gehrig, or Huggins, someone throw that darned ball in here now!"

Since 1976, the monuments and plaques have been hidden by a succession of fences moved closer and closer to home plate. Now Yankee Stadium is an easy home-run field for left-handed hitters.

Douglass was in constant touch with Chicago. His cell phone rang and an agent reported that Milt Pappas did not appear to be making plans to come to New York City. On the day of the game Pappas went to his work in Burr Ridge, a suburb of Chicago. At about the time the Yankee game started, Pappas left his work and drove home. Douglass was confused. He relayed this information to Walker.

Walker said, "Maybe I was wrong, and he's not the perp. When he skipped Cone's game and hit the Montreal—San Diego game, I really thought he was playing games with us— giving us a slightly different signature."

"That's okay. Criminal profiler Richard Ressler has conducted many interviews with serial killers, and he discovered that serial killers are often the last people you would suspect," Douglass said.

"That's the exact approach that auditors must take. Everyone is a suspect. Anyone under the right conditions may commit fraud or cook the books. Often it is the most trusted employee that commits the dirty deed."

"You're right," Douglass agreed. "You know that FBI work is excellent training for forensic accountants."

"I was searching the Internet last night and found a story that the army spilled 140 gallons of the deadly nerve agent Sarin at their Utah chemical weapons incinerator in December 1998."

"Yep, I've read about that," Douglass replied. "Now where would the terrorist go? Certainly not the rest rooms."

Walker replied. "All of the food places are closed. Wait a minute! There's a memorabilia shop here in the stadium. There's where I would drop a card. It's open. We better go there."

Talking into his lapel phone, Douglass almost shouted, "I'm moving to the memorabilia shop. Everyone stay alert."

Douglass and Walker walked toward the memorabilia shop, passing a Café Ole Stand that normally serves eight types of international coffee. Several fans passed them.

Walker stops Douglass with his arm and said quietly, "I think we just passed him."

"What?"

"The chubby man with the beard who just passed us may be Sandy," Walker said carefully.

Douglass and Walker turned and began following the suspect. "Why do you think it's him?" Douglass asked.

"It looked like him, and he seemed to be avoiding us, as if he knew us. He was wearing a baseball glove and carrying a cooler."

Whispering into his lapel phone Douglass ordered "Clarke, Keith, Tom, and Davey, come to the north side of the Café Ole Stand, quickly. We may have spotted Sandy."

As Douglass and Walker got closer to the man, he began to speed up his walking. "Sandy, stop!" Douglass shouted.

The man continued to walk, but he reaches into his shirt pocket and pulls out a clear sandwich bag.

Douglass draws his gun. "I order you to stop, Sandy, or whatever your name might be. It's over."

Douglass shouts to the now curious onlookers. "Everyone get down. I'm a FBI agent." Douglass holds up his FBI identification.

People nearby see Douglass holding a gun, and many of them begin running. Some scream, and some fall on the floor.

The man stops and turns around to face Douglass. He is holding a clear sandwich bag in front of his chest. Douglass sees a capped test tube inside the sandwich bag.

"Hello, Douglass. Hello, Fleet. What can I do for you? You need to check for dead people inside the memorabilia shop. You don't have time for me."

Without a gun, Fleet begins walking slowly backwards. He takes a gas mask from his coat pocket. Before putting it on he says, "Be careful Douglass. We don't know what kind of deadly poison he could have in the test tube."

Douglass ignores Fleet and continues the stand-off with the man. "Sandy, I have at least a dozen sharp shooters stationed throughtout the stadium. There are at least 400 FBI agents and police here. Give it up. It's over."

Talking into his lapel phone Douglass says, "The suspect is a white male with a beard. He is wearing a blue Yankee shirt and blue jeans." Douglass turns his gun on the man.

The suspect looks at Douglass and says, "I have sarin in this tube, and I'm warning you Douglass to call your bloodhounds off. Let me leave peacefully, or you'll have the death of your good friend Fleet and many innocent people in the stadium on your hands."

The man slowly and carefully removes the tube from the sandwich bag with his gloved hand. He pulls back his arm as if he were going to throw the tube at Fleet.

"Fleet, get down," ordered Douglass.

"You wouldn't dare shoot me," the man called Sandy shouts. "This is deadly sarin."

Douglass fires three shots which hit the man fully in the chest. Although the man was wearing a bullet-proof vest, the force of the three bullets cause him to fall backwards. The tube falls to the floor next to his face, splashing the liquid onto his neck. The man begins to frantically wipe at his neck with the collar of his shirt. People nearby began to cover their mouths and noses with articles of clothing.

Both Doulgass and Fleet stare in horror and disgust as the man writhes momentarily on the stadium floor.

"Oops. You got me Douglass. Don't forget Milt Pappas." The man grabs his chest, gasps for air, vomits, and dies.

Douglass still walking backwards slowly shouts, "Everyone stay away from this area." Talking into his lapel phone he orders, "Get the chemical unit over here. We may have sarin on the floor. The suspect is down. People are dropping like flies. What have you found in the memorabilia shop, Tom?

People downwind of the sarin mist began to die. Both Fleet and Douglass continued to back up to a safe distance. When Fleet reached a safer distance he took off his gas mask and says, "The poison got him. We must have been upwind, or you would be on the floor with Sandy. There must be at least 50 people down."

After the game Douglass walked to the office of Joe Torre, the current manager of the Yankees. In the windowless office, Douglass thanked Joe and George Steinbrenner for their co-operation. On Torre's concrete-block wall were photos of Babe Ruth, Billy Martin, and Lou Gehrig. Torre had been fired as manager by the St. Louis Cardinals in 1995 and was hired in November 1995 by Steinbrenner for $1.05 million for a two year contract. Torre proceeded to lead The Yankees to a World Series Championship over the Atlanta Braves in the 1996 season.

Fleet Walker and the New York Yankees had not avoided the "Big R." Internal audit risk assessment and audit planning had not successfully addressed the areas of greatest risk to the Yankee organization. The lawyers had won. The FBI did catch one of the killers. Walker would have a long negative risk assessment audit report using a conventional style with graphics and footnotes. George was not happy. Fifty-one people died from the sarin, and many were hospitalized.

What else could happen to bring harm to the Yankee organization? The lease at Yankee stadium expires in 2002, and Steinbrenner has threatened to move the Bronx Bombers. What would be their new nickname?

Walker never knew what to expect from his boss. Some people called Steinbrenner a temperamental rascal who made 17 managerial changes in his first 17 seasons. He hired and fired Billy Martin five times. Could Walker survive?

★ ★ ★ ★ ★

The woman called Janice went to the Yankee playoff game and observed the many police officers throughout the stadium and outside the stadium. There were posters of "Sandy Kojak" throughout the stadium indicating that this person was suspected of being the "Ballpark Killer." A reward of $1 million was posted for information leading to the arrest and conviction of the killer.

Before the sixth inning was over, Janice boarded the subway at the 161st Street Station. She kept humming the Kenny Rogers' song, "The Gambler." "You gotta know when to hold 'em, know when to fold 'em, know when to walk away, know when to run." Janice knew when to run away. "You never count your money when you're sitting at the table. There'll be time enough to count when the game is over." She thought about leaving some poison ball cards on the subway, but the risk was too high.

The one other passenger in the subway car looked confused when Janice began to sing softly one of Sandy's songs:

Yeah now, I found her down at the pawn shop,
And she was looking kind of beat.
Yeah, but I put down the money honey,
Cause I don't need to eat.
And the man said you just bought that two tone Fender,
With a black strap 'cross my shoulder.
I played her day and night,
With the landlord banging perfect time on my door.
The rhythm rocked so right,
Raising off the roof with my two-tone Fender.

She wished she could sing as good as Sandy. "I hope he makes it out safely," she thought.

Chapter 15

Epilogue

To avoid serious problems, organizations must acknowledge their need for risk management reviews and act accordingly. The rationale for risk management reviews seems to be constantly escalating along with management mandates, changes in organizational structure, and insurance errors.

Robert L. Bernens

Two days after the Yankees' play-off game on October 8, the Chicago police arrested Milt Pappas for being a member of the ballpark killers. A telephone number was found in a pocket of the man called Sandy. The number was to Pappas' home phone. The *Chicago Tribune* headline read: "Former Cubs Pitcher Arrested, Alleged Ballpark Killer." The accompanying news story gave details:

Milt Pappas, a pitcher for the Chicago Cubs for four seasons, was arrested by the Chicago police as a suspect in the series of diabolical murders connected to the sixteen perfect games. According to informed sources, one of the murder victims was Moose Phommin, a former professional umpire.

On September 2, 1972, Milt Pappas faced and retired 26 San Diego Padre players. With only one more out for a perfect game, Pappas walked pinch-hitter Larry Stahl. Pappas missed a perfect game by one strike. The umpire behind the plate was Moose Phommin.

254 The Big "R"

Obviously, Pappas was upset, believing that the umpire had called at least two strikes, balls. After all, the score was 8-0—not a close game. According to informed sources, the authorities believe that Pappas plotted revenge for the umpire's bad calls. The series of killings was a smokescreen to kill Phommin. At each of the baseball-related killings, the killers left a baseball card of a San Diego player on the 1972 Padres roster. One killer died in Yankee stadium when the deadly poison sarin he was carrying in a test tube broke.

One hair and some skin cells have been found on the baseball cards left at the scenes of the crime. Also, hair samples were found in the hotel room where the alleged killer using the name Sandy Kojak stayed in the Dallas/Fort Worth area. Police have asked for hair samples and skin cells from Pappas in order to perform DNA studies. The entire case against Pappas may hinge on the DNA results—shades of O.J. Simpson.

Through his attorney Pappas released a two sentence statement. "I am innocent. Someone is framing me."

Pappas played 17 seasons in the majors, 9 seasons with the Baltimore Orioles. He played the 1968, 1969, and 1970 seasons with Cincinnati and Atlanta, before being traded to Chicago during the 1970 season. Over seventeen seasons he compiled a 209-164 won-loss record, with a 3.40 ERA.

Born Miltiades Stergios Papastegios in Detroit on May 11, 1939, the right hander's best season was 1972 with the Chicago Cubs, with a 17-7 record. The trade by Cincinnati of Frank Robinson to Baltimore for Pappas is remembered by many fans. Robinson played for 21 seasons, and became a manager. Robinson was inducted into the Hall of Fame in 1982, but Pappas is not in the Hall of Fame.

DNA or genetic fingerprinting allows authorities to positively identify or exclude criminal suspects. Except for identical twins, no one has the same DNA make-up. DNA samples can be obtained from blood, semen, hair, skin, or saliva. DNA refers to deoxyribonucleic acid. A human cell contains about a meter—39 inches—of coiled DNA strands. DNA strands are in the shape of a twisted ladder, called a double helix. In general, DNA does not indicate the age or race of a person, but DNA results will indicate the gender.

However, under microscopic tests of a hair, the race, body area, how removed from the body, bleaching, and dyeing can be determined. Under the microscope, sex may be determined, depending upon the condition of the hair root.

The structure of the DNA will be obtained from samples found at the crime scene and compared to the DNA structure of the suspect, Milt Pappas. Barry Wilkerson, a crime scene technician for Chicago Police Department, says the chances of someone's DNA matching another person is one in five billion, which provides better results than blood-type testing.

Wilkerson points out that fingerprinting is still the most accurate form of identification, almost 10 times more reliable. Also, Wilkerson says DNA samples are best when fresh at the time collected or frozen immediately. Once the DNA sample starts to break down, the resulting data is not as reliable.

Unlike the fierce battle to block DNA evidence by the O.J. Simpson's defense team in 1994, Pappas' attorney P. Lee Bailey wishes the DNA fragments to be processed immediately. The results will prove his client's innocence. However, DNA matching takes up to twelve weeks to complete, and the attorney says his client has been falsely accused and will pay a heavy price because of an aggressive and misguided prosecution.

DNA from the hairs and skin cells found on the baseball cards and DNA from Milt Pappas' hair and skin cells will be cut into short fragments by an enzyme. Once processed, the patterns derived from both DNA samples will be compared like fingerprints. These patterns resemble supermarket price codes. The forensic scientists line up the bar codes and compare.

★ ★ ★ ★ ★

Twelve weeks after his high profile arrest, Milt Pappas was quietly released from Chicago County jail in the early morning. The DNA results from the crime scenes and the hotel room did *not* match the DNA pattern from Milt Pappas' hair and skin cells.

Later that afternoon P. Lee Bailey, Pappas' attorney, filed a $20 million lawsuit against the City of Chicago, the FBI, and the Baseball Commissioner for false arrest, false imprisonment, slander, libel, and defamation of character. Likewise, internal auditors must be very careful when accusing someone of fraud for fear of a defamation lawsuit. Any investigation involving fraud should be handled with the utmost secrecy and discretion to ensure that the reputations of innocent employees are not harmed. There were no comments from the City of Chicago, the FBI, or the Baseball Commissioner about the lawsuit. Pappas' 1998 autobiography *Out at Home* has zoomed to the top of the *New York Times* best seller list.

★ ★ ★ ★ ★

Authorities indicated that they have now expanded their search for the killers to include players damaged by the 1994 strike and the twenty-two umpires "fired" in 1999. Another likely suspect is Jack Kralick, a former southpaw for the Minnesota Twins. On August 26, 1962, this frail-looking southpaw retired 27 of 28 Kansas City Athletics in a 1-to-0 no-hit victory. He lost a perfect game when he walked George Alusik, a pinch hitter, on a 3-2 count with one out.

The first pitch to Alusik in the ninth was called a strike by home plate umpire Jim Honochick. Honochick then called two inside pitches balls, and Alusik then hit a ground foul ball down the third base line. Then the next outside pitch was a called ball. Alusik fouled the next pitch back of the plate. The count was 3-2. Honochick called the fatal pitch high and outside. The next two batters fouled out to preserve Kralick's no-hitter. Kralick pitched for only 5 more seasons.

Home plate umpire Jim Honochick told the FBI that he had been sent two free tickets on several occasions during the season for games at the parks on the dates of some of the perfect games. "Luckily I was busy and did not use the tickets. I gave them away," Honochick said.

Kralick was unavailable for comment.

★ ★ ★ ★ ★

Three weeks after the DNA results proved that Milt Pappas was not the Ballpark Killer, Douglass received a typed message in a white envelope postmarked from New York City:

I know who did the ballpark killings. I hate the guy worst than you do. His name is Jack Kralick, and he is a super creep.

Signed: Anonymous

The FBI quickly arrested Jack Kralick, but he had an airtight alibi.

★ ★ ★ ★ ★

Several weeks after this occurred, Fleet Walker, Bill Douglass, and Fred Campbell were enjoying dinner and drinks courtesy of the FBI when the subject of the anonymous letter was raised.

Fred Campbell observed, "You know most fraudsters are caught that way. I bet this guy took a women into his confidence, perhaps because he needed her help, and then wronged her. She then turned him into the authorities. It is a classic scenario and fortunately for us one that we see over and over again. Another weakness of fraudsters is that they always spend the money. You would think those guys would wise up and just sit on the money until the coast is clear."

Bill Douglass added, "I know, but it is still frustrating that after all the resources and precautions that we took, the case was solved because Kralick wronged his accomplice. Finding fraud is much like finding a buried treasure. The fraudster does not give you a map; yet you have to dig it out."

Fleet Walker closed by saying, "We were lucky; perhaps the next time the perpetrator will have better people skills and not be reported. That is why we have to have good sound internal controls to prevent this from happening again. Besides how do we know Kralick did it? Who was the woman helping him? Maybe the bad guys wrote the letter."

★ ★ ★ ★ ★

Three weeks later Douglass received a typed message in a white envelope postmarked from New York City:

Thanks for the $300,000 seed money.
Wait until next year.
Think random games.
Baseball *will* pay us!

Sandy K

A baseball card of Don Zimmer was in the envelope. Zimmer was wearing a Brooklyn Dodger uniform. Referring to his copy of *The Baseball Encyclopedia*, Douglass noted that Zimmer never played for the San Diego Padres. Assuming the note was a copy-cat, Douglass filed the note and card away.

Three days later while talking to Fleet Walker on the phone, Walker told him that Don Zimmer was the manager of the Padres when Pappas pitched the almost perfect game.

"More trouble for baseball next season," Douglass predicted. "The baseball world will be traumatized again. Sandy's helper is still alive."

"What did you find in his apartment?" Walker asked.

"Nothing," Douglass said. "We found no poisons. Someone cleaned out his place. They wiped down his entire apartment, so we found no fingerprints. We have no ideas as to who he was working for or with. We cannot locate his girlfriend."

★ ★ ★ ★ ★

In a value-added audit, auditors not only search out the hard dollar recoveries but also recognize the soft dollar savings resulting from the audit. Suppose that, in reviewing documents in an accounts payable audit, an overpayment to a vendor is discovered by the internal auditor. The vendor is contracted, and a refund is received. Actual cash back would be a direct dollar or hard dollar savings.

Soft dollars, on the other hand, may accure when, as a result of implementing an audit recommendation, the risk of a loss is decreased.

James K. Seaman

Appendices

Panel 1

Competency Framework for Internal Auditors
Individual Attributes for an Internal Auditor

Cognitive Skills

Technical Skills

- Communication
- Numeracy
- Computer literacy
- Organizational understandings
- Accounting/financial literacy
- Legal literacy
- Internal auditing applications

Analytic/Design Skills

- Information literacy
- Research
- Problem structuring/resolution
- Commercial and financial analysis
- Organizational analysis
- Internal auditing applications
- Systems design
- Developing technologies/methodologies

Appreciative Skills

- Discrimination
- Precision
- Critique
- Responsiveness
- Value orientations
- Strategic thinking
- Internal auditing approaches
- Complexity management

Behavioral Skills

Personal Skills

- Morality
- Inquisitiveness
- Balance
- Flexibility
- Directed
- Coping
- Intelligence

Interpersonal Skills

- Communication
- People skills
- Team management

Organizational Skills

- Organizational awareness
- Value negotiation
- Task management
- Function management
- Function development

Source: Birkett, W.P., M.R. Barbera, B.S. Leithead, M. Lower, and P.J. Roebuck, *Competency: Best Practices and Competent Practitioners*, Altamonte Springs, Florida: The Institute of Internal Auditors Research Foundation, 1999, p. 21.

Panel 2

Competency Framework for Internal Auditors
Units and Elements of Competency

Unit 1. Develop understanding within an organization about the risks associated with its functioning and contexts.

Element 1.1 Understand an organization's objectives/ strategies, processes, capabilities, and the contextual dynamics affecting its functioning.

Element 1.2 Profile the organization's philosophy (attitude/stance) on risk.

Element 1.3 Understand the risk management strategies of the organization.

Element 1.4 Provide advice/recommendations relating to the organization's risk management philosophies, strategies, and their implementation.

Unit 2. Develop understanding within the organization about the adequacy and effectiveness of its control strategies, structures, and systems.

Element 2.1 Profile an organization's control philosophies.

Element 2.2 Determine the control strategies and structures of the organization.

Element 2.3 Assess the adequacy and effectiveness of existing or proposed control strategies, structures, and systems.

Element 2.4 Promote understanding within the organization about the adequacy and effectiveness of its control strategies/structures/systems.

Unit 3. Contribute to improvements in the functioning of the organization's risk management and control systems.

Element 3.1 Establish authority/credibility for involvement in improvement initiatives.

Element 3.2 Establish the purposes and types of involvement to be sustained with relevant parties within the organization.

Element 3.3 Conduct particular assignments.

Element 3.4 Provide follow-up advice/support.

Element 3.5 Establish the level of acceptability/satisfaction with, and the effectiveness of, the outcome.

Unit 4. Provide ongoing assurance to the organization that it is in control relative to its risks.

Element 4.1 Establish assurance strategies/plans.

Element 4.2 Establish the scope of assurance projects.

Element 4.3 Identify/develop the methodologies relevant to an assurance project.

Element 4.4 Establish a project plan.

Element 4.5 Conduct the assurance project.

Element 4.6 Communicate/negotiate the results of the assurance project with relevant parties (clients) within the organization.

Unit 5. Manage the internal auditing function.

Element 5.1 Establish the objectives/purpose of the function within the organization.

Element 5.2 Manage key relationships and networks.

Element 5.3 Establish/secure the capabilities required by the function.

Element 5.4 Structure the work of the function.

Element 5.5 Manage quality control/improvement.

Element 5.6 Contribute to the development of the profession.

Unit 6. Manage the dynamic contexts that affect the work of the function.

Element 6.1 Implement responses in internal auditing work to relevant forms of contextual imperative or change.

Element 6.2 Proactively negotiate and/or construct the contexts within which internal auditing work will be conducted.

Source: Birkett, W.P., M.R. Barbera, B.S. Leithead, M. Lower, and P.J. Roebuck, *Competency: Best Practices and Competent Practitioners*, Altamonte Springs, Florida: The Institute of Internal Auditors Research Foundation, 1999, pp. 51-56.

Panel 3

Other Books by Larry Crumbley
Aka Iris Weil Collett

Deadly Art Puzzle: Accounting for Murder (advanced accounting), Dame Publishing Co., 7800 Bissonnet, Suite 415, Houston, TX 77074.

Simon the Incredible (finance), Dame Publishing Company.

The Bottom Line is Betrayal (general business), Dame Publishing Company.

Costly Reflections in a Midas Mirror (cost/managerial accounting), Thomas Horton & Daughters, 26662 S. New Town Drive, Sun Lakes, AZ 85248

Trap Doors and Trojan Horses (auditing), Thomas Horton & Daughters.

Accosting the Golden Spire (basic accounting), Thomas Horton & Daughters.

The Ultimate Rip-off: A Taxing Tale (taxation), Thomas Horton & Daughters.

Computer Encryptions in Whispering Caves (accounting information systems), Dame Publishing Company.

Chemistry in Whispering Caves (chemistry), Dame Publishing Company.

Nonprofit Sleuths: Follow the Money (governmental accounting), Dame Publishing Company.

Greenspan, *Burmese Caper* (finance), Thomas Horton.